PRODUCING, FINANCING AND DISTRIBUTING FILM

PRODUCING, FINANCING AND DISTRIBUTING FILM

SECOND EDITION

Paul A. Baumgarten

Donald C. Farber

Mark Fleischer

LIMELIGHT EDITIONS
New York 1995

Third Limelight Edition, July 1995

Library of Congress Cataloging-in-Publication Data

Baumgarten, Paul A.
Producing, financing, and distributing film : a comprehensive legal and business guide / Paul A. Baumgarten, Donald C. Farber, Mark Fleischer.—Rev. ed.

   p.   cm.

"The original hardcover was published by Drama Book Specialists 1973 co-authored by Baumgarten and Farber"—

ISBN 0-87910-108-3. — ISBN 0-87910-107-5 (pbk.)

1. Motion picture industry—Law and legislation—United States. 2. Motion picture industry—Finance—Law and legislation—-United States. 3. Motion picture industry—United States. 4. Motion picture industry—United States—Finance.   I. Farber, Donald C.   II. Fleischer, Mark.   III. Title.

KF4302.B38 1992
384.8—dc20

91-43708
CIP

To Annie and Sue

with love

and to Mark's mentor, Joseph Horacek III.

Acknowledgments

Portions of this book were read by Wayne Alexander, Jody Graham-Dunitz, Sidney Kiwitt, Stephen R. Langenthal, John La Violette, Jeffrey Mandell, Michael Rudell, Rose Schwartz, and Laurie Soriano. We thank them for the time they spent, their criticisms, comments, and suggestions, all of which were very valuable, and much of which we incorporated. Of course, however, we take full responsibility for the contents of the book. We did not always share the same views, and to some extent the book is an amalgamation of different views and experiences, but we all agreed on the final result.

Mel Zerman, our publisher, proved to be not only a conscientious publisher but a terrific editor and with the help of Jan Lurie and Bonita Rothman served to improve the readability of the book. It was sometimes difficult for us to judge whether a particular thought had been expressed so that people outside the entertainment industry could fully and readily understand it. The questions and comments of Mel and his associates made us strive for clarity and accessibility, and the book benefits significantly from their editorial guidance.

Donna Mosera, Laurie Elliott, and Linda Major typed and retyped the manuscript and put up with the terrible handwriting of at least one of the authors. Paul particularly remembers with fondness the late Harold Berkowitz, who taught him the motion picture business and was both a mentor and friend, and is grateful to his partners at Rosenman & Colin for their support and encouragement.

CONTENTS

4

CONTINGENT COMPENSATION 47

5

THE PRODUCTION-FINANCING AND DISTRIBUTION AGREEMENT 75

7

8

INTRODUCTION

E veryone knows that film is big business, involving millions and millions of dollars. Although there are fabulous success stories surrounding a few low-budget films that have grossed tremendous sums, most films usually end up in limited distribution at a loss to the financier. However, great risks may bring huge potential profits, and therefore there will always be people ready, willing, and able to finance and make films.

If there is no business like show business, there is certainly no business like the motion picture business. The motion picture business is complicated and confusing. Many in the industry are ready to take advantage of the devoted but unknowledgeable persons who are willing to spend time, energy, and effort in making motion pictures. It is a business that is contract driven, and the ability to understand the contracts (and therefore, the business) requires extensive knowledge and constant attention.

When the original edition of this book went out of print, demand for it remained. There was apparently a desire to understand the business of motion pictures, by persons already in the business, those who knew they wanted to go into it, and those who needed help in deciding whether or not it was for them. So eventually we realized it was time for a rewrite, but this presented a very special kind of challenge: in the years since the first edition was published, the industry had changed tremendously and had become much more complicated. Forms of agreement had become much longer; new technologies created problems in delineating rights, and financing of films apart from the studios had become more prevalent.

A word about those agreements. To serve a useful purpose, this book had to reduce complicated contracts to their basic components as expressed in language simple enough for the unsophisticated layman to grasp. This was not an easy job.

We have been in this business for a long time and have negotiated and written many, many contracts, covering every facet of the film industry. Not a week goes by, however, that we aren't confronted with something new and different in a contract negotiation or contract provision—a different twist, a different angle, or a different way of defining something. For this reason, no book can answer all of your questions. That is an impossible task. We have striven for clarity, in hope of enlightening the reader. However, we expect that you will want to study certain parts of this book carefully; you may even find yourself rereading certain paragraphs more than once and sometimes more than twice.

All the contracts relative to a film constitute a totality, and each contract is dependent in some measure upon the others. For example, certain terms used in the production-distribution agreement must be related to the terms used in the star's contract. The way in which net profits are defined in the production-distribution agreement can determine net profits for other participants. In negotiating a particular contract, one may give up a position in one clause to gain something in another. Some of the industry contracts are written so as to gain advantages for the draftsperson that are not readily apparent. Bear in mind, also, that were we to write a book four times as long as this, we would still be unable to set forth all the exceptions that occur every day.

The most important thing one can learn about an industry is its vocabulary, and the terms used in the film business, as in most other businesses, sometimes have very peculiar meanings. Moreover, the same terms under different circumstances can have different meanings. As a result, some expressions must always be defined. For example, "gross receipts," "gross profits," "net receipts," and "net profits" have no intrinsic meaning. The words mean whatever the participants decide they mean. If their specific sense is not clearly spelled out in the agreement, a dispute about their intent may later end up with a judge announcing what he thinks they mean. Burdensome as it may be, it is far better for the parties to an agreement to define their terms in advance—even if it requires 30 or more single-spaced pages to explain "net profits" (as it does in some film contracts)—than to chance taking their problems afterwards to a judge who may know little or nothing about the film industry. In writing this book, we had the choice of attempting to define the terms completely or of being very flip in giving them quick definitions. We decided not to over-condense or over-simplify.

We soon discovered that some of the terms that are so common to those of us working in the business are used infrequently outside of a particular aspect of the film industry. We found that defining some of the terms in simple, non-legal language was somewhat of a problem, but we have attempted to do so. Understand, however, that no single definition of any of these terms is applicable in all contexts. As an example, to accurately use a term like "deferment," one must know until when the payment is deferred, and which payments takes precedence over the deferred payment.

We very seriously considered including some examples of typical forms as part of this book; however, we came to the conclusion that this would serve little purpose. A typical production-distribution agreement would add another sixty or more pages to the book, but would explain little about the variations used by different studios. Hopefully, the discussion of the terms of a production-distribution agreement and the negotiation of that agreement—which we have discussed in detail and in depth—will be of more value than a form.

No book can answer every question a reader may have about film production and distribution, and this book doesn't pretend to. But there is no substitute for doing, and our collective experience serves here to elucidate how a film deal is put together.

Finally, no book on this subject is a substitute for an attorney. You cannot hope to read this book and learn what one learns from years of experience in negotiating contracts. It can, however, help you to understand most of the components that go into the business of putting a theatrical film together, financing it, and getting it distributed and exhibited. It will be helpful for you to know what your attorney is doing; for you to know and understand some of the contracts which you may negotiate yourself if you are producing a film; and for you to have a knowledge of some of the terminology that is thrown around in the business, which some people think they understand but actually know very little about.

We said before that the book was not easy to write. It also may not be easy to understand. But if you work at reading it the way we worked at writing it, you should find the experience useful and rewarding. It was our goal to untangle knots and to illuminate clouded places, and we hope that at least to a significant measure we have accomplished what we tried to do. We also hope that you will one day find the satisfaction in filmmaking that we have had in writing this book.

1 ACQUISITION OF A LITERARY PROPERTY

Each motion picture is based on an underlying literary work. The underlying work is often referred to as a "property." The property can and does take many forms. It may be a novel, a play, or an original screenplay; it may first have taken form as a story outline, or merely a concept. Sometimes a literary property is purchased mainly for the title. In any event, a producer who wants to make a motion picture must first acquire motion picture rights to the property. From the property everything else flows; the writing is the starting point for the entire motion picture. The job of the producer is to acquire motion picture rights to a literary property and to develop it to a point at which an investor or a motion picture distributor is willing to finance its production.

As the terms are used in this book, a *producer* is the individual responsible for the production and completion of a film. A *distributor* is the entity that markets and exploits the film in a medium or media or in one or more territories.

For example, let us examine what happens when a producer becomes interested in a certain book, first published in the U.S., on which he wants to base a motion picture. The book that the producer believes will make a successful motion picture is usually a published work. The motion picture rights to the book usually have been retained by the author and have not been acquired by a publisher. But to make sure, the contract between the author and the publisher must be examined, and the producer should obtain a quitclaim of motion picture rights from the publisher.

Many producers are able to obtain manuscripts in galley or pre-published form. In this case, the approach is to contact the author or the author's agent to negotiate the terms of a deal.

Most producers do not have unlimited funds, so they usually attempt to acquire an option to purchase the motion picture rights to the book. An option is the exclusive right, for a specified period or time, to acquire the rights at a specified price. If a book is not too well known, it is not unusual for the producer to acquire an option for between one and two years. Options on books are often for longer periods of time than options on screenplays because the producer needs the additional time to have a screenplay written before being able to approach financiers. Some of the variables determining the length of an option include: the author's reputation, the number of copies of the book sold, the successful penetration in a particular country, and whether the author will write the script. If possible, the right to extend the option for additional periods should also be obtained. Generally, if the option is exercised, whatever has been paid for the option applies toward the purchase price of the motion picture rights of the book. If the option is extended for additional periods, subsequent option payments are sometimes retained by the author and not applied toward the purchase price. It should be noted that if the author of the book is also going to write the script, the producer will usually insist on having the right to extend the option period automatically for any amount of time by which the author is late in delivering the script.

CLEARANCE PROCEDURES

The first step should be to make sure that you are dealing with the actual owner of the rights. When the author is represented by a agent, who claims that the author owns the rights being sought, it is reasonably safe to assume that this is the case. To make certain, it is customary to search the records in the U.S. Copyright Office in Washington, D.C. to determine whether or not the book has been registered for copyright, and if so, who the copyright proprietor is. The prudent author usually sees to it that the copyright of the book is registered in his or her own name, and this is additional proof that the author owns the rights. However, on occasion a publisher may register the copyright of the book in the publisher's name and then reassign the copyright to the author, reserving only those specific publishing rights that the publisher requires. The copyright search will also disclose recorded assignments relating to the work. In addition, the producer usually engages one of several organizations that keep a copyright registration file, press clippings, and other records relating to specific titles. This additional information sometimes gives a clue to possible outstanding option agreements, uses of the work for radio or television performances, and whether other works have identical or similar titles.

If the copyright search reveals no copyright registration whatsoever, it does not necessarily mean that the work is in the public domain. It may merely mean that no registration was filed. If the work bears a proper "copyright notice," it is protected (barring special circumstances), even in the absence of registration. Present copyright law, under the adherence of the U.S. to the Berne Convention, protects a work published after the date of adherence, even when no copyright notice appears on the work. Lack of notice does, however, among other things, adversely affect the remedies of a proprietor and his right to statutory damages if there is an infringement. If the work bears a copyright notice, the film rights should be acquired from the party whose name appears on the notice, unless there is a clearly documented chain of title indicating some other proprietor. If the work is unpublished or bears no notice, the purchaser must rely upon the author's warranties of title.

If the book has been published outside the U.S., it is even more important to examine the book to see what copyright notice, if any, appears. If, prior to the U.S.' adherence to the Berne Union, the book contained a form of copyright notice required by the Universal Copyright Convention (which is a convention to which the U.S. adhered prior to its adherence to the Berne Union and to which it continues to adhere), then the book is protected in the U.S. as well as in all countries that are parties to the convention.

This includes most of the major entertainment markets of the world. The form of notice includes the name of the proprietor, the year of copyright, and the copyright symbol. Now that the U.S. is a signatory to the Berne Union, publication in the U.S. or a Berne Union country protects the work in all Berne Union countries, which include signatories to the Universal Copyright Convention.

If one of the principal reasons for acquiring rights to a book is to use a unique or interesting title, it is advisable to have a title search made to determine if there are conflicting titles of books, films, or other properties that might lead to claims of unfair competition. Since titles of books cannot be copyrighted, unless perhaps the title is extraordinarily long, the only way a title can be legally protected is under the law of unfair competition. It must be shown that the title is widely associated in the mind of the public with the claimant's work (for example, *Gone with the Wind)* and that someone else is passing off his work as the claimant's, thus creating confusion. Many financier-distributors are signatories to the title registration procedure of the Motion Picture Association of America. That procedure creates a contract among the signatories giving the first registrant of a title certain rights that may prohibit another member from dealing with the title even though, under the law of unfair competition, the other member might otherwise have the right to use the title.

The producer should also check to see how much time is remaining in the copyright to the work. Under the current 1976 Copyright Act that went into effect in 1978, the copyright to a work written by an author exists from the time it is first fixed in a tangible medium of expression until fifty years following the death of the author. Works of corporate authorship exist for seventy-five years. Prior to the 1976 Act, U.S. copyright law provided protection for an initial term of twenty-eight years, which could be renewed for an additional twenty-eight-year renewal term, for a total of fifty-six years. At the time the 1976 Act went into effect the twenty-eight-year renewal term was automatically extended for an additional nineteen years for a total renewal term of forty-seven years.

If the work was copyrighted prior to the 1976 Act, is in the original term of copyright, and the author dies prior to the vesting of the renewal of the copyright, the U.S. Supreme Court has recently held that the renewal proprietor can, absent agreement, prevent the owner of a derivative work (for example, a movie) from exploiting the derivative work (for example, a sequel or remake) in the U.S. Some courts have held that, once the renewal term has begun, for an author to vest renewal rights in his assignees, he must file a renewal application in the twenty-eighth year of the original term. One court recently has held that the author must survive the twenty-eighth year. Therefore, whether or not the commencement of the renewal period is near at hand, it seems imperative (absent new legislation) that at the same time the grant of rights is obtained from the author, the producer also acquire an assignment of the renewal copyright from the renewal term proprietors: i.e., the spouse and any children, and in the absence of a spouse or children, the executor of the estate, and if none, the administrator. In order to bind the estate, one should prepare a codicil to the author's will that would direct his executor to convey the renewal copyright if there is no spouse or children. In the event that the spouse and children of the author convey their copyright renewal rights expectancy, there should be a statement in the literary purchase agreement that the spouse and children are receiving a proportion of the purchase price paid to the author. If an inadequate consideration is paid to the spouse and the children for the renewal copyright, they can properly claim that the conveyance of the copyright renewal is void.

Under the 1976 Act, the author, or if he is dead, his widow, or if the widow is dead, the children, or if there is both a widow and children, a majority of the widow (who under the 1976 Act owns one half of the author's interest) and the surviving children (who own the other half) have the right, for a period of five years beginning at the end of the fifty-sixth year, to terminate any extension of rights for the nineteen year term on at least two years prior written notice. Such termination does not affect derivative works made during the fifty-six year period so that if a film were made during that period the film could continue to be distributed notwithstanding the termination. The termination does affect the right to make remakes, sequels, additional episodes of existing television series, and the like. Therefore, if the work is in its renewal term of copyright, it is important that the rights for the nineteen year extension period be acquired from the widow and children.

THE OPTION

Assuming that the rights are in order, the next step is to negotiate for an exclusive option. The producer should obtain an option that will extend for a long enough period to do development work on the property and to arrange financing and distribution for the proposed film. For this reason, the option agreement should always provide that as long as the option is in effect, the producer has the right to engage in certain preparatory work with respect to the property—such as the writing of the screenplay, the preparation of budgets, preliminary casting—and to announce that the property is being developed.

The option agreement between the author and the producer typically has annexed to it some form of "Literary Purchase Agreement" that will become effective if the option is exercised. Sometimes in lieu of an option agreement there is an initial outright grant of the rights, subject to reversion to the owner if the full purchase price is not paid, or an initial grant for the option period, subject to extension if the option is exercised. In this case the first installment can be considered the same as the option price, and the principal installment payment (the purchase price) would be the equivalent of the payment made to exercise the option. From the point of view of the author, an option is much preferable to an outright grant with provision for reversion if the purchase price is not paid. If the purchaser were to go bankrupt after an outright grant, before the full purchase price is paid, the bankruptcy complicates the author's getting the property back. This should be enough to convince the author or his representative that the proper thing to do is to not have an outright grant until the option has been exercised. Ordinarily, it is wise for the producer to have the author execute (the form of) the literary purchase agreement along with the option. The option agreement should provide that if the option is exercised, the producer or his assignee simply countersign and date the literary purchase agreement, which would then become effective. The option price for the initial option period often represents about 5 to 10 percent of the total purchase price payable if the option is exercised.

The option is always exclusive, incorporates the warranties and representations of the literary purchase agreement, and states that if there is a breach, the option period is extended for the period of the breach, not to exceed a time limit.

There are times when a desired literary property cannot be optioned. If there is unusual film interest in the property or if the author is an important writer or the property is a best-seller, the agent may insist upon an outright sale of the rights to the literary property rather than accepting a lesser sum of money for an option that may never be exercised. Since the option is exclusive to the purchaser and no other deals for the property can be entertained during an option period, the longer the property is optioned the longer the author's work is off the market.

There is no rule of thumb for determining how much should be paid for the acquisition (not just the option to acquire) of a particular literary property. The price may range anywhere from $500 to $15,000 for a short story, article, or unknown novel, and can be as much as $1 million or more for a well-known best-seller. In the following discussion of the form of agreement used to acquire film rights to a literary property, reference will be made to the different and varied types of payments, such as an escalation clause pegged to the number of copies of the book sold in paperback, hardcover, or both, and/or whether or not the book makes a best seller list. If the book is optioned, the purchase price will ordinarily be higher than if the book is purchased outright in the first place.

LITERARY PROPERTY AGREEMENT

Part of the negotiation of the Literary Property Agreement involves knowing the ultimate financier of the motion picture. If it is clear that the picture will be financed by a studio, then the producer must keep in mind the requirements of the studio's legal department in negotiating for rights which the studio might require. For example, an independent producer might be satisfied to acquire the right to make one motion picture. On the other hand, the studio would expect to obtain all television rights, all motion picture remake and sequel rights, and would object to provisions permitting the author to recapture rights not exercised within a stipulated period of time. If the project is a marginal one for the studio, any restrictions on rights acquired can jeopardize or completely eliminate the possibility of a studio deal. If the author's representative knows that the project will ultimately be developed at a studio, if at all, then the representative must be sensitive to the requirements of the studio's legal department because if its requirements are ignored the studio deal will not be available. However, if the project is to be independently financed or financed through an independent film company, there is generally more flexibility in the negotiations. Since we believe that it is useful to discuss all of the ramifications of the negotiation, the following discussion assumes that the film will be independently financed. Where appropriate, we have indicated those matters which a studio's legal department might find burdensome.

Description of Property

Every literary purchase agreement should include the title, the name of the author, the publisher, the date and place of publication (if previously published), and any copyright registration information. If the work is in manuscript form, it is a good idea to identify it by the number of pages and the date of its completion. If the author has entered into an agreement for the publication of his book, that fact should also be described. The date for the publication of the book set by the publishers should be referred to also since part of the purchase price may be based upon the anticipation of publication. Of course, if the book proves a financial success, it will be much easier to finance a motion picture based on it.

Rights Granted and Reserved

The agreement usually states that the purchase price of the book includes the exclusive and perpetual right throughout the universe to the plot, theme, title, characters, prior and future translations, adaptations, and versions. Sometimes the agreement will also provide (and the studio may require) that if any sequels to the book are written by the author, the purchaser acquires the same rights in the sequels that he acquired in the original property. In that event, a payment would be made if the sequel is made into a film. Quite frequently, the author's agent (with some justification) will take the position that only the rights to one particular book are being sold and the purchaser should acquire no rights to any sequels or characters in the original book. The resolution is frequently the retention of sequel or character rights by the author, subject to the author's agreeing not to transfer or utilize such rights for a given number of years. This subject will be discussed in greater detail later in this section.

If the book was originally written in a foreign language, or if it contains illustrations and the purchaser is acquiring rights to the illustrations as well, he must make sure that the author owns the rights to the illustrations or translation so that the author may assign these rights to the purchaser. If the author does not own such rights, the purchaser must negotiate separately for these rights as well if it wants to use them. Since the author may revise the book, may permit its translation into another language, or may write different versions of it, the purchaser must make sure that he acquires the same film rights to the revision, translation, or other versions that he acquires in the property. This ensures against the possibility of the motion picture rights to the book being sold twice in two different versions to two different purchasers.

From the point of view of a producer who is interested only in producing a motion picture, certain rights—other than the rights to make one motion picture—may not seem important. But from the point of view of a financier or a studio that may desire to turn a motion picture property into a remake, a sequel, or a television movie or series, these other rights are very important. For this reason, the producer will almost always insist on acquiring the right to make any number of motion pictures, whether produced initially for television or theatrical release. This would include a remake motion picture or a sequel motion picture.

A sequel motion picture utilizes a principal character or characters or a plot device of the original picture but puts them in new situations—such as a different plot. A remake of a picture is usually the same story retold and possibly brought up to date. The literary rights may be utilized in a musical, narrative, or any other kind of motion picture. The motion picture can be exhibited in any form, such as a wider or narrower negative width, or self-contained cassettes or cartridges; it can also be distributed in any manner, including theatrical exhibition, nontheatrical exhibition (auditoriums, colleges, clubs), home video, and free or pay, or basic cable television.

The recognized rights available in a literary property and the film upon which it is based are:

Theatrical: This is the right to exhibit the film in theaters before paying audiences.

Television: This is the right to exhibit the film on all forms of television. These include live television where the performance is broadcast at the time it occurs; taped (or filmed) television, where the performance is broadcast on a delayed basis; free (broadcast) television (for example, over networks such as NBC, CBS or ABC, or local independent television stations); and cable television, of which there are two types: (a) basic cable, where the broadcast signals of free television are received by an enhanced central unit which then delivers the signal to the subscribers' homes by means of a cable, and (b) pay cable, where the subscriber pays a separate fee for a particular service, such as HBO or Showtime, or in which a subscriber pays to view the film at a particular time (pay per view).

Videocassette: This includes the right to exhibit the film by means of videocassette (also known as home video).

Non-theatrical: This is the right to exhibit the film before audiences in contexts other than theaters, television, or videocassette, such as on university campuses, hospitals, airplanes, ships, oil rigs, armed forces installations and on 16mm film or cassettes.

Music: This includes the right to produce and release a sound-track album or single from the film and to publish the music from the film.

Merchandising: This is the right to manufacture and distribute (or license others to do so) items of merchandise, such as shirts, coffee mugs, toys and the like, bearing the name and/or likeness of characters, or physical items (such as a certain type of airplane) appearing in the literary property and/or film.

Print Publication: This is the right to publish the literary property and/or the screenplay of the film based on the literary property, in addition to the right to "novelize" the screenplay. A novelization of the screenplay would be a book based on the screenplay as opposed to the published book itself. Normally this right would not be available if the literary property had already been published. An additional print publication right is the right to publish a "photo-novel" of the film, which is a book containing still photographs from the film with various captions describing the action and/or dialogue.

Legitimate Stage: This is the right to adapt and present the literary property and/or film as a stage play or musical.

Retained Author Rights

Certain rights in the literary property are reserved to the author. Many author's representatives want the contract to state that all rights not specifically granted the producer are reserved to the author. The agent will argue, on the one hand, that the producer is acquiring only certain limited rights, that is up to the producer to spell out the rights he wants, and that if the producer does not identify those rights, they should be reserved to the author. On the other hand, the producer's representative (and certainly a studio) will argue that he cannot chance that some now unforeseen use (especially if a competitive use) may preclude him from doing the very thing for which he has bought the literary property. If broad language is used in the clause that gives the producer the right to any and all uses of the property regardless of when they are devised, it contradicts the clause stating that all rights not specifically granted to the producer are reserved to the author. This can result in the question of whether or not a new use was, in fact, granted to the producer or reserved to the owner.

One possible solution to this conflict is to provide that all rights analogous to the rights specifically granted to the producer are granted to the producer, and all rights analogous to the rights reserved to the author are, in fact, reserved to him.

Authors typically attempt to reserve publication, radio and audiocassette (non-dramatic straight reading in both cases), live television, and legitimate stage rights. When the underlying work is a book (whether or not published), the author is almost always successful in reserving publication rights, with the exception of the producer's limited publication rights discussed below. Even where the author is successful in reserving any or all of those other rights that are sometimes reserved (and the studio resists the reservation of any of those rights), the producer will usually require that the author not exploit those rights (except the print publication rights) for a certain period of time. This is called a "holdback." Once the holdback has expired, the producer will also require that the author first negotiate with him, should the author desire to dispose of the rights, and that the producer has a right to match any third-party offers. These are called the right of first negotiation and the right of first or last refusal.

With the right of first negotiation, the author is obligated to negotiate with the producer in good faith for a specified period of time (usually ten to thirty days). With a first refusal, if the negotiations do not result in an agreement, the author is then free to dispose of the rights to a third party on the terms last offered by the author to the producer and rejected by the producer during the negotiation or on terms more favorable to the author. If the author wishes to dispose of the rights on terms less favorable to himself, the producer's right of first refusal is triggered—the author must first offer the deal to the producer before concluding the agreement with the third party. Usually, the producer has a period of between three and twenty days to accept or reject the deal. To verify that the author has been offered terms more favorable to him than the one last offered by the producer, the author is usually required to disclose to the producer all the terms of the third party offer and the identity of the third party and to provide the producer with a copy of the executed agreement between the author and third party once that agreement is concluded. Since it is sometimes hard to judge which of two deals is the more favorable to the author, one solution is to isolate a number of the financial terms. If all the terms are the same with the exception of one or more terms that are more favorable to the author, the agreement is deemed overall to be more favorable to the author. A last refusal gives the producer the right to match any third-party offer.

The holdbacks and rights of first negotiation/last refusal usually last for the shorter of (1) five to seven years from the date of acquisition of the property, or (2) three to five years from the initial general theatrical release of the first picture based on the property. The use of alternative dates, from agreement and from release, gives the author assurance that on an ascertainable date the restrictive period will end, and the producer assurance that he has time to produce and release the picture. The theory is that five years from the first public exhibition takes the picture through theatrical release, video, pay television, and into network release on television (or through the license to a basic cable system or for the first licenses to television syndication, if there is no network license). The producer will argue that this period should be longer to protect the picture into network release and all the way through television syndication.

The film industry distinguishes between the right to make a feature-length motion picture and the right to make a television production. The former may be released on TV, while the latter may or may not be released theatrically. If the author is to be granted a profit participation from the first motion picture based upon his literary property or if his fixed compensation is calculated as a percentage of the budget of such a motion picture (usually 2.5 to 5 percent with a floor and a ceiling), then the fixed compensation payable to the author would be much higher if the film is a theatrical feature as distinguished from a television movie-of-the-week. Also, the financial structure of the typical television movie-of-the-week makes it even less likely to reach net profits than a theatrical feature. This happens because syndication revenues get absorbed by distribution fees, union residuals, the difference between the production cost of the movie-of-the-week (plus over-head and interest) and the amount paid by the network or pay cable company to reimburse the producer for production expenses, and by the fact that the budgets of movies-of-the-week are generally lower than those of theatrical features. So distribution other than by television is remote. Since fixed compensation and percentages of profits for a remake and sequel are less than for the original, one might want to provide that if in the unlikely event the feature film follows the television movie, the payments for the feature are not decreased. In addition, the right to make a film would include the right to use excerpts of a film in a featurette for advertising and promotional purposes.

Television Rights

The producer should also acquire the right to produce the property for television whether in lieu of, prior to, or after the release of a theatrical film. Television rights are generally categorized as film, tape, or live. Filmed or taped television rights are the rights to record the program; presently that means either on videotape or film. A filmed or taped television program is intended to be repeated a number of times in each market. On the other hand, live television does not usually mean that the program is transmitted as it takes place since almost every live television program is now recorded for delayed broadcasting in other markets. A live television program, if prerecorded, is usually shown once in each market unless the contract specifically provides for additional uses. Ordinarily, the producer acquires filmed television rights—that is, the right to produce and market an individual television program and television series. Live television rights are usually reserved to the author, but a studio will expect to acquire these rights as well as those for tape or film.

While the author will usually reserve live television rights and dramatic rights, there is no logical reason why it is customary for the author to grant television series rights or film television rights to the purchaser at the same time reserving live television rights for himself. Nor is there any logical reason for most motion picture distributors not to insist that the purchaser of movie rights acquire dramatic rights. The theory was that motion picture producers are interested in what goes on film—that is, the motion picture, the filmed television rights, the possibility of taped or recorded radio rights—and that the transitory uses of the property, such as a one-time television program or a stage play, are not the primary interest of most motion picture producers; nor, theoretically, do most producers of feature films have any expertise in utilizing rights for live television or the stage, which represent a completely different use of the property. Therefore, the author would reserve such rights for disposition to someone who could use them better, such disposition to be limited by the motion picture sale agreement. In fact, producers and film distributors frequently invest in stage presentations. The coordination of live and filmed presentations of a work is important in ensuring that there will be no competition in the exercise of the rights.

The purchaser should attempt to acquire at no additional cost all radio rights—that is, the rights to broadcast the property or excerpts of it by means of radio, either live or by records or transcriptions. If the author reserves such rights, the reservation usually relates to straight non-dramatic readings of the property. The author may want to reserve the right to authorize readings of the property by means of cassette—a form of publishing. If this right is reserved, it should be limited to audio-only rights. The purchaser, at the very least, must acquire the right to advertise and promote the motion picture by means of radio and television. The author may insist that these broadcasts be limited in time, usually to five minutes each, and that the producer receive no financial remuneration with respect to such broadcasts.

The author reserves all publishing rights, except for the rights usually granted to the purchaser to write synopses or fictionalizations for promotional purposes, usually not exceeding seventy-five hundred to ten thousand words each, that are utilized for advertising and promotional purposes, and the possibility that the purchaser may obtain the right to publish the script or to write a novelization of the script.

It is customary to provide that the author's reserved rights do not relate to anything done by the producer in connection with the literary property. For example, if in writing a screenplay a new character is added by the screenwriter, the author does not acquire any rights to that character.

Even if a literary property has been published, it is sometimes possible for the producer to acquire the rights to publish a script or a novelized version of the script or a photo-novel of the picture. This is usually done for promotional purposes in connection with the release of the motion picture. In addition, it may be possible to obtain the right to utilize excerpts of the property in publishing a book about the filming of the motion picture. Ordinarily the author of the original property would ask to share in any royalty or advance received by the producer for any publication rights.

Usually the author does not want to write the novelized version of the screenplay, which is frequently merely a routine rewrite of the script, and the author would therefore insist that he not be credited as author. If such publishing rights cannot be acquired from the author because the author reserves them or has previously conveyed them to a publisher, it may be possible to make a tie-in deal with the publisher of the paperback version. This permits the publisher to utilize the motion picture advertising artwork as part of its publishing promotion. The paperback version containing the artwork would be published near the release date of the motion picture and would become a promotional device for the film, as well as for sales of the book. When the producer grants the publisher the right to use the artwork from the picture in connection with the sales of a new release of the book, he bargains for a percentage of the income received by the publisher from the sales of that edition, usually in the range of 20 percent to 30 percent of that income, which might be expressed as a royalty per copy sold.

Generally, the purchaser of motion picture and allied rights to a literary property acquires the exclusive rights to use merchandise and to enter into commercial tie-ins in connection with the property, or any versions of the property. Merchandising rights now typically are thought to include video game rights. Additionally, the purchaser acquires the right to utilize the title of the property in connection with the picture, and sometimes, for such other use as a song or television series title.

The author also customarily tries to reserve the right to write a sequel to the property. The studio may require the producer to have the same rights in the sequel as in the property. If the studio makes a sequel film, it should then be willing to pay the author as much as, or more than, was paid for the original property. If the author reserves the author-written sequel rights, since he could write one sequel after another and thus force the producer to keep purchasing the sequels to protect the exclusivity of his rights in the original work, the producer should insist on a long holdback before the competitive rights can be sold or utilized. This protects the producer's rights in the first book published. In any event, the producer should limit the author's reservation of sequel rights to the right to author full-length published sequel books. In this way the purchaser can assure himself that the author must at least write a full-length bona fide work to preserve his rights, and not force the purchaser to buy, for example, a short story sequel to protect character rights in the original work.

As we discussed, however, the producer will usually try to acquire the motion picture and ancillary rights to make sequels utilizing the characters appearing in the original book. Otherwise, the producer's right to make a sequel to his motion picture could be interfered with because character development in the original and sequel films might differ from that in the book. Even if the reserved sequel book rights restrict the exercise of competitive film rights for a substantial period, a film based on such a book could conflict with the sequel film rights of the producer. This is particularly so if his film and a competing film are released within a short time period. The author may attempt to have sequel rights revert if such rights are not exercised within a particular period of time. If such rights are exercised (i.e. a sequel is produced), the rights may again revert after a particular period of time unless a second sequel is produced, and so on. The sequel may be a feature film, a movie for television, or a television series. The holdback periods would vary accordingly.

Adapting The Literary Property

It is perhaps surprising that the one part of the typical literary purchase agreement that is almost never questioned is the unlimited right of the producer to vary, change, modify, and rearrange the property and characters in any way he wishes. From the producer's point of view, he must have this exclusive right because if the author has any veto in the development or production of the property there can be an impasse and the producer's money will have been lost. The author of a legitimate stage play is in a completely different position in that the producer of a stage play cannot change a single word without the author's approval. There is good reason for this difference, which can be explained historically.

Through the years, the author of a stage play would emerge from his attic and humbly present his play to a potential producer who, if he wanted to produce it, would make a nominal "option" payment. Under the Dramatists Guild's Minimum Production Contract, the option payment was $2,000 for a one-year option. The Minimum Basic Production Contract has been replaced by the Approved Production Contract, but even under that, the option payment is only $18,000 for a one-year option on a musical play. If there are three individuals who comprise the "author"—that is the bookwriter, the composer, and the lyricist—they each end up with the munificent sum of $6,000.

If the play were produced pursuant to the option, the author of the play could make a great deal of money from the royalty payments. But, since he was paid so little for the option and there was great uncertainty as to whether there would ever be any royalty payments, the author retained control over the content of the play and the other uses of the play in all media. The producer might share in the subsidiary rights income if the play ran a certain period of time, but control of the play remained with the author.

Contrast this with the development of the film industry. In the 1920s and 1930s the large studios literally bought authors. They would pay them huge sums of money, $250,000 more or less per year (which in those days was a huge sum of money), and would put them in a room with a typewriter. In such an arrangement, for the $250,000 they wanted to own everything that came out of the typewriter—and they did. The screenwriter was an "Employee for

Hire" and as such the employer owned the copyright in the work and could change the dialogue, the plot, the characters and add to it, subtract from it, or make any changes desired.

The important point is that in any agreement involving rights, the person who makes the final decision regarding the exercise of those rights must be made clear. Most literary purchase agreements contain a clause in which the author waives any so-called *droit moral or* "moral rights," a doctrine that under the laws of France and some other foreign countries gives an author the right to prevent a third party from substantially altering his work, even if the author contractually agreed to let a third party alter the work, since any waiver of moral rights is invalld.

In the U.S., the validity of a clause waiving moral rights has not yet been upheld, although some recent court decisions have begun to recognize a moral right and such right may soon be granted in some states by statute. If a literary property were to be purchased from a French national, it is quite possible that a motion picture that materially changed that property could be held to violate the French author's moral rights in an action commenced in France and that the author might conceivably have the ability to enjoin the release of the film in France, whereas in the U.S., the claim would most likely be rejected as being contrary to U.S. law.

Payment for the Literary Property

The producer acquiring the broad spectrum of rights, as just enumerated, generally makes one of several types of payment. First, there is the payment for the film rights in the literary property itself. If the payment is in cash, it may be made at the execution of the agreement, or if the author agrees, it may be spread over a period of time. Spreading the payment may be a tax-saving device to defer the author's income over a number of years; a most important consideration here is the solvency and financial stability of the producer, for if the producer goes out of business, the author may not get the balance of his money.

Escalations may be built into the purchase price based on sales of the book after it has been published. One common formula is the payment to the author of $.50 per copy of the trade edition sold in the U.S. and Canada for a period of two (or three, four, or five) years after first publication in excess of thirty thousand, forty thousand, or fifty thousand copies. The trade edition is the original published version of the book and is usually defined as an edition for which the retail price is not less than a stated sum of money. The producer is usually willing to pay the additional amount if the book in fact sells large quantities because this huge success makes the film rights all the more valuable. Some producers do not like to make contingent payments based on the number of books sold after the release of the film on the theory that the film is then selling the book and not vice versa.

In addition, there may be escalations built into the purchase price based on the hardcover, trade paperback (high-quality), and paperback sales. For example, the producer may pay the author a set sum of money per copy for each paperback sale in excess of one million copies in the U.S. and Canada. The idea is the same here—the more sold copies in circulation, the more the book is known, and theoretically, the more people will go to see the movie.

Sometimes the purchase price escalates a certain amount for each week the book appears on *The New York Times* best-seller list. For example, a payment of $5,000 per week may be made for each week the book rates one through five on the list and $2,500 per week for numbers six through ten. Sometimes the purchase price escalates for each adoption of the book by a well-known book club, such as the Book-of-the-Month Club or the Literary Guild. Purchase price escalations generally apply only to works by well-known authors or to unpublished books that seem to have the potential of becoming best-sellers.

If a producer cannot afford to make a substantial initial payment to acquire motion picture rights to a literary property, he will sometimes give the author a "deferment." A deferment, as will be discussed in Chapter Four under "Deferments," is a contingent obligation to pay a fixed sum of money from the revenue stream derived from the exploitation of the picture, usually payable immediately prior to the payment of net profits. The producer may also, or instead, agree to make a payment upon commencement of principal photography of the film. In such a case he is assuming that by the time principal photography begins, he will have the money for the author's payment since it will then be a budget item.

An author should always insist that any fixed payment agreement relating to the start of principal photography also include an "outside date," a time that payment is due even if principal photography has not yet commenced. This is especially crucial if the payment due on principal photography is a substantial part of the total cost of acquiring the rights. If this is not done, the producer could make the nominal payment provided for and never make the much larger payment due at commencement of principal photography because it never occurs. The net effect here would be to take the author's book off the market forever since even though he would not have received the major part of the consideration he could not legally sell screen rights elsewhere. Even if there is an outside date by which the payment must be made and a provision that rights revert in the event of non-payment, the extended time for payment may be the equivalent of an additional option period.

If the purchaser of a literary property is making a payment to the author consisting of a percentage of the producer's net profits, he must be careful about how the agreement is worded. Typically a producer will receive a percentage of net profits in one of two ways: (1) the producer will receive a fixed percentage, or (2) the financier and the producer will split the net profits (often 50 percent to each). This second case occurs especially where the producer has developed the picture and brought it to the financier (such as a studio). The producer pays out of his 50 percent share all net profits to be granted to third parties other than parties financing the picture. For example, net profits may go to the director, book author, screenwriter, and actors. If the agreement calls for the author's percentage of net profits to be a percentage of the *producer's* net profits, this will be interpreted as entitling the author to receive a percentage only of either the producer's share, or (even worse for the author) a percentage of whatever share the producer is left with after being reduced by other third parties. For example, if the author is entitled to 5 percent of the producer's net profits and the producer is splitting net profits 50-50 with the financier and has given away 30 percent of the net profits to other third parties, the author will only be entitled to 5 percent of the 20 percent remaining to the producer—or a grand total of 1 percent of the net profits of the picture. To avoid this inequity, the net profits can be based on a fixed percentage of 100 percent of the net profits of the picture (that is, all of the net profits and not merely the producer's share). (See Chapter Nine under "Producer's Profits.")

In addition, a detailed formula for computing net profits can be annexed to the agreement as an exhibit. The trouble with this alternative is that every distribution company has its own formula, and that formula may vary from the one used by the producer. The distribution company may object to some provisions in the formula utilized by the producer. This problem is commonly avoided by providing that the net profits payable to the author will be defined, computed, accounted for, and paid in accordance with the standard definition utilized by the U.S. theatrical distributor of the film. Since these standard definitions are invariably drafted in a way that is highly unfavorable to the net profit participant, the author will attempt to protect himself by adding language that the distributor's standard definition be subject to good faith negotiation. This may place the producer in some jeopardy if the author becomes unreasonable with the distributor and interferes with the financing of the picture. To protect himself, the producer may agree to the language requested by the author, provided that the good faith negotiation will be within the customary business parameters of the distributor. In this way if the author becomes unreasonable, he will be in breach of his agreement with the producer. As the producer is sometimes granted a favorable definition of net profits, the author may request that the definition be the same as that applicable to the producer or that the author will have at least as favorable a definition as that applicable to anyone else. (The concept of one person being treated as favorably as all other persons is known as being on a "most-favored-nations" basis.)

It is generally a matter of industry custom to pay the author one-half of the original purchase price and one-half of the original percentage of net profits for every theatrical sequel motion picture photoplay and at least one-third of the original purchase price and one-third of the original percentage of net profits for any theatrical remake motion picture photoplay. The reason for the percentage difference is that the first picture may be a springboard to a whole chain of pictures—a springboard triggered by the literary property acquired by the producer. Consequently, a higher payment is justified for a sequel. On the other hand, it may be argued that the author should get more for the remake because it is directly based upon the author's work and not as much for the sequel, which represents more of the creative effort of the motion picture producer and subsequent screenplay writers.

With regard to television productions based on an original theatrical motion picture, the author will receive a set dollar amount per hour initially broadcast for television motion pictures (for example, sequels and remakes) and miniseries. For a television series based upon an original motion picture, the author will receive a fixed-dollar amount per thirty-minute, sixty-minute, or longer episode. In all such television production, payment is usually due on or shortly after commencement of principal photography of the production or episode, or no later than delivery to the network.

Payments are rarely less than $10,000 for each hour of a movie-of-the-week or miniseries, $1,250 for each episode of the series occupying a one-half-hour time slot, $1,500 for a one-hour episode, and $1,750 for an episode in excess of one hour. Payments for reruns of any episodes of a television series are usually made only for the first five reruns and are generally calculated by paying 20 percent of the initial royalty for each of the first, second, third, fourth, and fifth reruns of each episode. No payments would be made for any reruns after the fifth. If the series is to be a daytime serial, payments in a similar amount may be applicable for an entire week's episodes, rather than one episode, since the budgets for daytime serials are usually relatively low. Often the above-specified royalties pertain only to prime-time U.S. network television. The royalties pertaining to other forms of television (for example, non-prime-time network television or syndicated television) would be one half of the amounts pertaining to prime-time U.S. network television.

If the original motion picture is intended for initial television exhibition, an entirely different royalty structure will apply, since the economics of television production dictate that the payment be substantially less. Most agreements will provide, for example, that if the picture is initially exhibited theatrically (that is, in theaters) prior to its exhibition on television in the U.S. or Canada, the author will receive a bonus equal to 100 percent of the purchase price; if the picture is exhibited theatrically in the U.S. or Canada after its initial television exhibition in the U.S. or Canada, the author will receive a bonus equal to 50 percent of the purchase price; and if the picture is exhibited theatrically outside of the U.S. and Canada, whether prior or subsequent to its initial television exhibition in the U.S. or Canada, the author will receive a bonus equal to 50 percent of the purchase price. In no event, however, will the aggregate bonus payable exceed 100 percent of the purchase price.

Frequently an author will be concerned that the producer may exercise his option and acquire the motion picture rights in the book but then not actually make the film, resulting in the author's having lost the motion picture rights and any possibility of contingent compensation by way of payment on principal photography, or the possibility of payment of any net profits. To avoid this, an author will often insist that the rights he has granted revert to him if a motion picture has not started principal photography within a certain period of time (typically anywhere between eighteen months and ten years) after the producer has exercised his option. When a producer agrees to this (and a studio usually will not), he will often make reversion of rights subject to a lien; that is, if the author is successful in getting the film made elsewhere, then either at the time the author sets the film up with a third party or at the time the film commences principal photography, the producer will be repaid all the costs he incurred in connection with the project, plus interest (or, less often, the amount the author originally received from the producer for the literary property). Additionally, the producer may receive a percentage of net profits derived from the film.

Warranties and Indemnities

Authors are always required to warrant and represent certain facts about their literary work. A warranty is a promise that a fact is true when the promise is made. A representation is a statement of fact made to induce someone else to contract. The producer must require these warranties and representations for two reasons: (1) their existence will provide a surer basis for legal action against the author by the producer in the event the producer is sued by a third party as a result of an inaccuracy in the author's representations and warranties; and (2) without the author's representations and warranties, the producer will be unable to obtain the specialized insurance (known as errors and omissions insurance) that covers the producer against claims of copyright infringement, invasion of privacy, defamation, and similar claims.

The author is usually required to represent and warrant as follows: that he has the full right and power to enter into the agreement and grant the rights he is granting to the producer; that the literary work is original with the author (or in minor part in the public domain) and is not taken from or based on any other work (whether dramatic, musical, or otherwise); that the producer's exploitation of the rights granted to him does not constitute a violation of the rights of any party (including, without limitation, invasion of privacy, defamation, or copyright infringement); that no production has theretofore been produced based upon the property and that the property has not been exploited in any medium whatsoever (unless, of course, it has, in which case the known productions or exploitations, such as a publication, must be disclosed); that the work is validly registered for copyright in the U.S. and Canada and every other country offering similar protection (or at least that the work is susceptible to such copyright protection); that the rights granted are free and clear of any encumbrances; and that there are no claims threatened, outstanding, or pending that might in any way interfere with the producer's full and complete enjoyment of the rights granted to him. While the author will often attempt to limit these representations and warranties by making them only to the best of his knowledge, the producer must be very careful to ensure that he obtains sufficient representations and warranties to satisfy his errors and omissions insurance carrier and the studio. The author will covenant that the producer's exploitation of rights will not violate personal and property rights, and that the property will not be exploited by the author in the media covered by the agreement, and that the work will not enter the public domain.

The producer will also require the author to indemnify him for any liability (including attorneys' fees and costs) that he may incur as a result of the breach or alleged breach of the author's representations, warranties, and covenants. This can create a serious problem for the author because, unless the author is granted the right to control the defense of any claim against the producer for which the author is providing an indemnification, the producer would have the right to settle a frivolous claim with the author's money. On the other hand, if the claim is serious and represents a substantial liability to the producer, he will not want the author to be able to interfere with a reasonable settlement. This is true particularly if the author is financially unable to pay such a liability, thus making the producer's demand that the author indemnify him completely meaningless. Generally if the author is financially responsible, there should be no reason why he should not have the right to defend and settle, particularly if the settlement does not interfere with or diminish the rights of the producer. If the author is not financially responsible, then the producer may well insist upon the right to defend and settle. Sometimes the author will try to limit his liability for breach of warranty to the amount that he is paid for the rights. This is done on the theory that he does not want to be exposed to damages in excess of what he receives. Most producers and all studios will take the position that the liability should be unlimited since it is the author, and not the producer, who knows and should be responsible for the content and originality of what he has written.

It is usually very difficult for a purchaser to determine whether or not a particular work contains infringing material. Additionally, it may be argued that if the author must return only that which he has received, his potential liability is inadequate to ensure the reliability of his warranties, particularly in light of the sums involved in producing and distributing the film.

Usually if there is a claim against the author, and if the author is not considered able to pay a judgment of settlement, the producer will also want the right to withhold payment to the author sufficient to cover the claim and costs to defend such an action. If the claim takes place after the release of a film, the damages are multiplied. If the agreement provides that the author must consent to a settlement and he refuses to consent because he thinks he has committed no breach, then the whole production of the photoplay may be suspended. As a condition of not withholding, or permitting the author to defend and settle a claim, the producer may permit the author to bond the claim. In such a case, if the author can secure a surety bond, then he would be responsible for the defense of the claim, and the bonding company would make good any loss to the producer. As a practical matter, it is unlikely that an author could secure a bond for any serious claim, since the bonding company will want cash or cash equivalents as collateral for its bond in the amount of the claim. If the author can obtain the right to defend and settle, he will be considered creditworthy by the producer and therefore the rationale for withholding disappears.

Also, as a practical matter, if the literary property is a published work that has been in print for any length of time and reasonably widely circulated, any claims of infringement would normally have been made before production of a film commences. If the author has not received a notice of claim after the book has been in print, providing the book has had a general circulation, then it is unlikely that he will, and he probably does not have to worry too much about claims arising from the book (although he may have to worry about claims arising from a screenplay based upon the book). For this reason, the author will also require the producer to similarly indemnify him against any liability arising out of any material which the producer adds or causes to be added to the author's material.

Billing

The producer must also consider the question of the billing the author will be given. The author ordinarily will receive screen credit on all positive prints of the photoplay, either on a separate card or on a card with the screenwriter of the photoplay. Under the Writers Guild of America Basic Agreement, if a story credit and a screenplay credit appear on the same card, the screenplay credit must appear first, occupy at least 50 percent of the card, and be in a type size at least as large as that of the author's credit. Occasionally an author will receive credit in paid advertising promoting the motion picture. As the Writers' Guild provides size and placement protection for the screenwriter's credit, the author will often bargain for a credit adjacent and of size equal to the screenwriter's credit.

A producer will sometimes try to reduce the purchase price of the property by providing the author with prominent billing, both on the screen and in paid advertising. From the point of view of a financier-distributor, the fewer the credits the better; the distributor is trying to sell the picture, and there are only certain names that are meaningful to the public. The distributor wants the right but not the obligation to use the name of the author in advertising.

The form of the author's credit will usually be: (1) if the film has the same title as the book, "From the Book by _____"; (2) if the film has a title other than that of the book, "From the Book _____ by _____."

Generally, distributors are much more concerned about the credits that appear in advertising than about the credits that appear on the screen. It's the advertising that sells the film. Once the patron has paid the price of admission and walked into the theater, it presumably makes little difference how many credits appear on the screen, although the growing proliferation of screen credits sometimes makes it seem as though they run half as long as the picture itself. Subject to requirements of the Writers' Guild and other guilds and unions, most of the credits are usually run at the end of the picture. If the author wants his credit at the beginning, he had better contractually provide for this, and he is likely to be successful in his request only if the credits to screenwriter, director, producer, and principal actors are also at the beginning.

Assignments and Waiver of Equitable Relief

An important issue to be covered in a literary acquisition agreement (and an issue that arises in almost all other agreements relating to the production of the film) is that of the right of the producer to assign to a third party his rights in the literary material. This right is a material element of any literary acquisition agreement, as various rights will have to be assigned to other entities in order to get the film financed, produced, and distributed. An author may be reluctant to allow a producer to assign rights in the material since he may come to trust the producer but not want to have to deal with a third party unknown to him. However, the producer, is not likely to waive the right to make third-party assignments as that would make the literary acquisition agreement unmarketable. While it is true that the producer may take the underlying material and treat it in a manner displeasing to the author, it must be understood that the producer needs that creative control. Translating literary material into film carries the material into a new medium, and the expert in that medium is presumably the producer, not the author; thus, it is the producer who must have the necessary control.

While the producer's *right* to assign is rarely at issue, his continuing liability in the event of an assignment often is. A producer will want the unlimited right to assign, and once he assigns he will want to be relieved of any further obligation. The author, on the other hand, will not want the producer to assign the rights to some insolvent or disreputable third party whom he will have to sue to collect money due to him. The common compromise is that if the producer assigns his rights, the producer will remain liable to the author, unless the assignment is in writing and made to a major or "mini-major" motion picture distributor or television network or to some other financially responsible party.

An absolute, but at first glance strange, requirement imposed by any producer acquiring rights to a literary property is that if the producer breaches the agreement with the author, the author must nonetheless waive his rights to terminate or to obtain injunctive or other equitable relief. This particular provision is also found in all other agreements relating to the production of the film (such as agreements with the screenwriter, director, actors, etc.). The reason for this requirement is that no financier or distributor would invest the millions and millions of dollars required to produce and deliver a film if its production or distribution could be terminated, enjoined, or otherwise interfered with by anyone with a claim against the filmmakers. While this requirement may seem harsh, a studio simply would not be willing to make a $20 million-plus investment if its investment could be jeopardized by some payment that was not made or some credit that was inadvertently omitted. It must be remembered that the author, or other individual, waiving his rights to injunctive and other equitable relief is not waiving his right to sue the producer at law for damages (i.e., for money).

In addition to the literary purchase agreement discussed, there are other related agreements that deserve mention. If the agreement is an option agreement, there also should be a short-form option instrument of transfer setting forth the fact that the producer has an exclusive option on the literary property. This form should be recorded in the U.S. Copyright Office. If the agreement covers the acquisition of rights to a literary property, a short-form instrument of transfer of the agreement should also be recorded. Both short forms serve merely as notice, and the terms of each should be made subject to the full-length agreement. If the purchased work has been published, the producer should obtain a release from the publisher stating that the latter has not acquired any rights that the producer is acquiring and confirming that the producer has acquired limited advertising and publicity rights. This hardly ever presents a problem.

2 THE SCREENPLAY AGREEMENT

After the literary purchase agreement has been executed, the producer must find a screenwriter to write the screenplay. Of course, many films are not based on books; their producers either purchase a completed screenplay or retain a writer to develop an original story idea. In either case, the producer generally acquires all rights, including publishing rights of the screenplay, in the following fashion.

TREATMENTS AND DRAFTS

There are various stages in the writing of a screenplay and the screenplay agreement should provide for all of them. The customary way of having a script written is to proceed in steps.

1. The first stage is generally called a "treatment." This is usually a narrative statement of the plot, a description of the main characters and locations, and sometimes sample lines of dialogue—all of which is approximately 20 to 40 pages in length and will indicate the direction that the screenwriter expects to proceed in developing a final script.

2. The next stage is the "first-draft screenplay," which generally requires twelve to sixteen weeks to write and typically runs from 120 to 150 pages in length. At this point, the dialogue is written,

the scenes and the characters are fully defined, and each action sequence is fully described.

3. Next there is a "rewrite" of the screenplay, based on the first draft screenplay and the producer's suggestions. This is usually completed in about four to six weeks.

4. Finally, there is a script "polish" period, which may take anywhere from two to three weeks. The producer may expect a screenwriter to work on a screenplay for approximately four to six consecutive months, to come up with a final script about 120 pages long.

After each draft is completed, there is normally a reading and consultation period between the writer and the producer which takes from two to four weeks. During this period the producer reads the screenplay, consults with the screenwriter, and gives the screenwriter any comments or suggestions he may have.

WRITERS GUILD OF AMERICA MINIMUM BASIC AGREEMENT

The contractual relationship between the producer and the screenwriter is extensively governed by the terms of an industry-wide collective-bargaining agreement, the Writers Guild of America Basic Agreement (WGA Agreement), assuming the writer and producer are parties to the agreement. It establishes minimum payments for certain work, forbids certain kinds of writing on speculation, and contains detailed billing credit requirements. The WGA Agreement should be referred to for the basic payment schedules, which change each time the WGA Agreement is renegotiated.

The WGA Agreement is the result of the collective-bargaining efforts of producers on the one hand and writers on the other. Consequently, the WGA Agreement is binding only on those parties who agree to be bound by it. Producers who agree to be bound by the WGA Agreement become signatories to the agreement, and writers who agree to become bound by it become members of the WGA. While a member may not perform services for a producer who is not a signatory to the WGA, a signatory producer may hire a non-WGA member to perform services so long as the producer affords that person at least all of the minimum protection provided members under the WGA Agreement.

A WGA member can avoid WGA jurisdiction only if his services are performed for a nonsignatory outside of the U.S. and if the agreement for his services is negotiated and executed outside of the U.S. The WGA will assert jurisdiction if the member's agent or lawyer travels outside of the U.S. for the purpose of negotiating the member's agreement. The WGA Agreement also applies to a writer whose services are loaned to the producer by means of a personal services corporation.

PAYMENT FOR THE SCREENPLAY

Compensation for screenwriters varies widely depending upon prior screenplays and their success, awards won, experience, and the budget of the film. The screenplay and literary purchase price together should not, except in unusual cases, exceed 5 percent to 7.5 percent of the total budget. Actually, most screenwriters of feature-length motion picture photoplays receive more than the applicable guild minimum, and some screenwriters receive many multiples of that minimum. Occasionally, in addition to cash compensation, a writer will receive either a deferment or a percentage of net profits. The principles that apply to a deferment and profit participation for the author of a literary property or for talent would apply to the screenwriter as well.

Ordinarily the producer-screenwriter agreement should specify certain cutoff stages in the writing of the screenplay. For instance, the producer may pay the screenwriter for a first draft screenplay, but if he does not approve it, he should be in a position to terminate the writer's services and not have to pay for revised scripts. This protection can be achieved by having the screenwriter write a treatment, or a first draft, and then giving the producer the option to order subsequent drafts. If the treatment is approved, the producer exercises the option and a first draft is written. If the first draft is approved, the producer then exercises his option for a rewrite.

Experienced screenwriters who are in a superior bargaining position can sometimes insist that they write the entire script (including the first draft screenplay, a rewrite, and a polish) and that they get paid whether or not the producer approves the first draft or any subsequent draft of the screenplay. Most often the final screenplay will not be written until after the director has been selected and engaged, since the director is likely to have his own ideas about the script and will want to work with the writer during the rewriting. For this reason, the producer will want the agreement to provide for at least one rewrite to be done at a later date, after a director has been selected, subject of course to the writer's availability.

OTHER PROVISIONS

Some of the provisions of the typical screenwriter's contract merit further discussion. Ordinarily, the agreement will provide that the screenplay must be of such quality that a feature-length photoplay based on it can be exhibited in first-run theaters in the U.S.

Although such language is frequently used, it sets only a very general and nonobjective standard. A screenwriter is expected to use his best efforts in writing, and generally a producer must pay for a screenplay even if it is not exactly what he wanted. Under the WGA Agreement, he has no right to condition payment to the writer on being satisfied with the results of the writer's work. Arguably, if a screenplay were to prove utterly useless, the producer could refuse to pay for it on the grounds that the writer had delivered nothing of what was required under the screenplay agreement.

Quite often the agreement requires the writer to work exclusively for the producer while the various drafts of the screenplay are being written. If he pays enough, the producer will feel that he is entitled to the writer's exclusive efforts, for a writer working on two or three projects at the same time cannot give the producer proper assurance that his project is getting the attention it needs.

Usually, the delivery date for each draft or revision is spelled out in the contract. If the producer has made other commitments that require principal photography to start at a specified time, then, the precept that "time is of the essence" should apply to delivery of a script. In addition, if money has been borrowed to finance production, the producer cannot afford to forget that interest will be running on the loan.

Most screenplay agreements provide that the producer may revise the writer's work in progress and make suggestions that the writer is expected to incorporate into the script. Some writers object to this as a matter of principle and feel that they should be permitted to write a complete script to deliver to the producer. But producers may want to see how the work is progressing on a day-to-day basis and may indeed want to work closely with the writer during the writing period. The idea here is that if the writer is on the wrong track, it is better to find out about it early than to wait until the screenplay is delivered. The producer usually prevails on this point.

The method of payment in screenplay agreements varies. Sometimes the producer will pay half of the fixed cash compensation for the treatments or draft on execution of the agreement and half on delivery. Sometimes he will pay half when the writer starts working and half when the writer finishes. The agreement may even provide for partial payment after the writer writes and delivers a specified number of pages. Other agreements will provide for payment in weekly installments. If there are a number of drafts, roughly 50 to 60 percent of the cash compensation should be paid for the first draft, 25 to 30 percent for the rewrite, and the balance for the polish. In any event, the producer should always be sure to withhold enough money to motivate the writer to finish his work in a timely manner.

It is important to consider what happens if the writer dies or is disabled during the writing of the screenplay. How much is half a screenplay worth to a producer? If the producer has to hire another writer to finish the screenplay, the second writer may very well demand the same price he would have been paid if he were to have written the entire screenplay in the first place. Because of this, the payment of the bulk of the cash compensation may be conditioned upon the completion by the writer of the entire screenplay. In fact, some contracts provide that if the writer does not complete the final screenplay on time, he is obligated to return all money he has received. If the writer properly completes the first draft and becomes incapacitated during the writing of a later draft, it is not unreasonable that he keep what he was paid for the first draft. Bonuses, deferments, and net profits are usually conditioned upon the writer's receiving some form of screen credit, as more fully discussed in the following paragraphs. Accordingly, the additional compensation will be paid if in fact the writer completes sufficient work to earn the credit.

The agreement may provide for a contingent payment to be paid on the first day of actual filming of the script. This is a beneficial arrangement for a producer. If he gets the financing to make the picture, such a payment will be part of his budget; if he cannot get the financing for the picture, he has lost nothing.

A writer may be paid a bonus if he gets sole screenplay credit and a smaller payment (usually one-half the amount of a sole credit bonus) if he gets a shared screenplay credit. If a picture falls under WGA jurisdiction, the producer and the writer have no right to bargain for what writing credit the writer is to receive. This is decided solely by the WGA. The WGA Agreement has a complicated formula for determining screen credits. Often the matter of screen credits is the subject of a WGA arbitration.

Sometimes a producer will commit to hire a writer for a first-draft screenplay, a rewrite, and a polish, and then decide to postpone the project for some time. The screenwriting agreement covers this possibility by providing that if the producer does not ask the writer to start services on the next stage of writing by the expiration of the immediately preceding reading period, the writer will be paid in accordance with the schedule set forth in the contract, just as if the services had been timely requested and rendered. Within some time period thereafter (usually one year), the producer will have the right to require the writer to deliver the material the producer has already paid for but not previously requested, subject only to the writer's then-existing professional commitments.

Ordinarily a writer will be paid round-trip transportation and living expenses if he is required to work sufficiently far from his residence so that overnight accommodations are reasonably necessary. Sometimes he receives a weekly flat sum instead of a per diem for his living expenses. The amount and class of travel (first-class or business) is negotiable. (The WGA Agreement requires that its members travel first-class.) The more established writers also often require an office and a secretary at the producer's expense while they are rendering services to him.

In addition to the fixed compensation, the WGA requires the producer to make certain additional payments for union fringe benefits, the amount of which is a percentage of the base compensation paid. A WGA writer also receives residual payments for exhibition of a motion picture in "supplemental markets" such as: network television exhibition, pay television exhibition, videocassette exploitation. These payments are based upon a formula relating either to the gross receipts derived from the exploitation of the motion picture in the applicable medium, or the number of times the film is exhibited on television

Under the usual screenwriter's agreement, the producer acquires all rights to the screenplay from the writer as an employee for hire and the screenwriter retains no rights at all. However, if the screenwriter writes an original script, he may be entitled to what is called "separation of rights" under the present WGA Agreement. This means that the screenwriter reserves certain rights when he creates the underlying story and characters. If the screenplay is based on another underlying work (known as "assigned material"), separation of rights is not available to the screenwriter.

The publication rights in the script belong exclusively to the writer entitled to separation of rights, but he cannot exercise the publication rights prior to three years from the date of the employment contract, or six months following the general release of the picture, whichever is earlier. The producer holds the synopses and fictionalization rights. If the producer decides to publish a paperback novelization of the script for the purpose of publicizing the picture, he can do so—provided that publication does not take place earlier than six months prior to the initial scheduled release date of the film and the writer is given the first option to write the novelization. If the writer does not want to write the novelization, he receives a third of the sum paid to the person who does write it.

The producer loses the dramatic or stage rights and they revert to the writer if the former does not utilize them prior to two years following the general release of the motion picture, or if he does not commence principal photography of the motion picture within five years, plus up to six months for postponements outside of the producer's or writer's control. If the producer exercises the dramatic rights, he pays the writer sums equal to 50 percent of the minimum amounts payable to an author under the terms of the Dramatists Guild Inc. Minimum Basic Production Contract, which is the contract applicable to Broadway and other first-class stage productions.

When the producer makes a sequel theatrical motion picture, the writer gets 25 percent of the fixed compensation that he was paid for his first script. If the screenplay contains a character used as the basis for a television series, the writer receives payments in accordance with the WGA Agreement. Of course, the writer of an original script can also negotiate for rights as if the script were a published work.

The producer may contend that the screenwriter is not entitled to separation of rights if the screenplay is based on a story outline furnished by the producer, since the screenplay would then not be original. Ultimately, in such a case, the WGA will make the determination.

The agreement between the producer and the screenwriter will also apply to numerous other issues discussed in connection with the acquisition of the rights to a book. These issues include the writer's warranties, representations, and indemnifications of the producer; the writer's waiver of the moral rights of authors and of his injunctive and equitable relief; and the producer's right to suspend and/or terminate the agreement for events outside of the parties' control (known as events of *force maieure*) or the writer's death or disability.

3 THE AGENT

After the producer has acquired the film rights to a literary property and has had a screenplay written, he is then in a position to interest a motion picture distributor or financier in the project. There are, of course, exceptions to this rule since producers have successfully approached film distributors or financiers when they have only the literary property and no screenplay or, sometimes, when all the producer has is an idea. Sometimes a producer will suggest to a distributor that he acquire a particular property for the producer to produce, and the producer becomes attached to a project without risking any money at all. One common problem in producing a film is that the producer usually needs a certain minimal sum of money to develop a project to the point where someone becomes interested in it, and the producer usually loses his investment if no one does.

It is axiomatic that the more elements a producer can wrap up in a package before going to a distributor or financier the more definite and concrete the project will be. While the additional elements may make the project easier to sell, they may also increase the producer's risk: he may have to pay to have a screenplay developed or even make a financial pledge to secure the services of a desired actor or director. The fact remains that if the producer has a literary property and a script, a fairly detailed production budget, a proposed shooting schedule, and commitments from a known director and one or more principal actors, for all practical purposes the picture is ready to be made, and he will find it far easier to arrange an immediate financing deal.

A successful producer must combine creative ability, salesmanship, and production expertise. He must grasp the commercial potential of the property that he wants to film and be able to assemble the creative elements of writer, director, and cast. And he must then manage to sell his package to a financier or a distributor or a combination of the two.

For several reasons, when a producer is ready to make a presentation to a major motion picture company or to one of the smaller independents or even to a private group of investors, it may be wise for him to have a good agent. There are a number of talent agencies that specialize in motion picture production. If they represent major stars or directors, they enjoy easy access to the offices of the film executives who hold the power to decide which films will be produced and which will not. A good agent can also make worthwhile suggestions for creative elements and may even represent one or more of these elements. Some agents themselves have substantial creative ability and can advise a producer on how to improve a literary property or a screenplay and how to present a project most effectively.

The agent usually charges a flat 10 percent of all compensation the producer receives. This includes the producer's fee, his percentage of receipts, and any other income he derives from the picture but does not include his reimbursement for living expenses. The producer will usually exclude from the agent's percentage any sums paid to the producer as reimbursement for his development costs. The typical agency agreement entitles the agent to 10 percent of everything the producer receives in the entertainment field for the term of the agency, which is at least one year. Of course, the agent is entitled to a fee on any deal made during the stipulated period even if it continues after the stipulated period, as well as on any deal negotiated during the stipulated period and renewed afterward. In some cases, agents have been known to reduce their ten percent fee, and the basis for computation of the commission can be negotiated as well, depending upon the bargaining power of the producer.

A major difficulty in working with some agencies is that in their role as packagers they may represent three or four components of the same deal and thus have conflicts of interest. For instance, if they are the agent for the director, the principal actor, and the producer, each may wonder whether the agency is favoring any one of them as against the others with regard to compensation, credit, and ultimate control of the project. But it should also be borne in mind that sometimes without this multiple representation the picture would not get produced. The conflict of interest must be weighed against the services the agent can provide in negotiating the deal for the producer and getting the producer entrée to sources of financing or to a motion picture distributor.

While quite rare in theatrical motion pictures, an agent sometimes will attempt to charge a "package fee." This can occur when he assembles a number of the elements for a film. In such situations, the agent does not take his commission from the salaries and other compensation payable to his individual clients; instead, he bases his commission on the budget of the film. As 10 percent of the budget would usually result in an enormous commission, an agent asking a package fee will often reduce the percentage amount. Moreover, he may ask to have only half the fee paid at the time the film is financed, with the other half to be paid out of the film's net profits or perhaps some form of its gross receipts. The package fee is proposed mainly when an agent packages a movie or series for television (in which case the agent would be basing his commission on the license fee paid by the network or other buyer). More common at the present time is for an agent to sell the film (or various rights in the film) to distributors and to take a commission on the money paid by the distributors to acquire the applicable rights.

One of the more important functions of an agent is to act as a buffer between the producer and the distributor or the financiers. He is apt to appear to be the "bad guy" to protect the producer. If the producer wants something outrageous, he may tell the agent, who passes the word to the financier or distributor; then if the financier-distributor complains too loudly, the agent will say it was really his own idea and not the producer's. The "good guy-bad guy" game is a standard negotiating ploy in the film business and the only amazing thing about it is that so many people take it seriously. What it really amounts to is a face-saving device for both the distributor and the producer; each can blame the agent for whatever goes wrong. The agent takes the blame, becomes the butt of jokes—and earns 10 percent of everything.

4 CONTINGENT COMPENSATION

An important element of the compensation paid to the producer of a film (or any other major participant such as the writer, director, and star, for that matter) is the right to participate in the financial success of the film. This right of participation is usually structured in one or both of two ways: (1) as a sharing in the receipts of the film (whether in the net profits or in some form of gross receipts), (2) as a right to a particular lump sum when the receipts of the film reach a prenegotiated level or at a predetermined point in time (a deferment). A deferment is often paid out of the first net profits or out of the gross receipts of a film, rather than as a lump sum, when a specified level is reached. Compensation is *contingent upon the performance of the film* except in the case of the deferment payable at a specified point in time. By far the most common form of contingent compensation, however, is a participation in net profits.

NET PROFITS

While the term "net profits" (sometimes also called "net proceeds" or "net receipts") sounds very much as if it should be an accounting concept with an industry-wide understanding of what constitutes revenue and what constitutes expenses, it is far from that. Both the revenue that is included in the gross receipts of the film and the types of deductions that reduce that revenue are usually the subject of extended negotiation because the net profits are the sums remaining after all permitted deductions are made from these revenues.

As a starting point, "net profits" is usually defined as the gross receipts remaining after the distributor has recouped the following items in the following order of priority: (1) distribution fees, (2) distribution expenses, (3) interest on negative cost, (4) negative cost (the cost to produce the picture), and (5) deferments and gross participations. Under this formula, the aggregate of all expenses from all costs (both production and distribution) related to the film are deducted from the aggregate of all gross receipts of the film from all media.

Gross Receipts

Even before turning to the question of what revenue constitutes gross receipts, the first question to be answered is which company's gross receipts are being calculated? Generally speaking, gross receipts means that revenue received by the distributor of the film from its licensees; namely, those who exhibit the film or otherwise exploit it directly to the public. For example, gross receipts always means the revenue received by the distributor from theater exhibitors and not the revenue received by those exhibitors at the box office. (Typically, the distributor will see on the average between 45 percent and 55 percent of the box office gross.)

The issue of how to treat subdistributors is more difficult. As there are some variations among the practices of distribution companies, depending upon the geographical territory in which they themselves distribute and the territories in which they use subdistributors, there is always a question as to whether gross receipts will mean the revenue received by the distributor from its subdistributors or whether gross receipts will mean revenue received by the subdistributors from their exhibitors and other licensees. In the case of a major motion picture company that itself distributes pictures in the major territories of the world, gross receipts would be the aggregate amount received by the distributor from each local branch or subsidiary.

In the type of distribution engaged in by most of the major studios there are some small territories in which the majors do not themselves distribute films: distribution is carried on instead by subdistributors under license from the distributor. In other cases, independent distribution companies distribute in only a few major territories and primarily through subdistributors elsewhere. Sometimes the subdistributor's total receipts are deemed gross receipts for purposes of accounting to the producer, but only if the subdistributor actually pays the distributor's share to the distributor. If the subdistributor does not remit the distributor's share for any reason, the distributor does not treat the subdistributor's receipts as gross receipts for purposes of accounting to the producer.

Obviously, if a producer is receiving a percentage of net receipts from a distributor, one very basic question is whether a distributor will itself be distributing all over the world or will be using subdistributors. In either case, one of two methods of accounting will apply: (1) the distributor includes the subdistributor's gross receipts as its receipts, subject to the distributor's receiving its share of remittances from the subdistributor as indicated in the preceding paragraph. In this event the subdistributor's distribution fee will be aggregated along with the distributor's distribution fee, subject usually to a cap, and the subdistributor's expenses will be aggregated with those of the distributor; or (2) the distributor reports only the receipts actually paid to it by the subdistributor as gross receipts. In this case only those receipts will be treated as gross receipts, and the distributor will be permitted to deduct only its own expenses—not the subdistributor's expenses as well. If the participant is to share in net profits, a distributor utilizing subdistributors usually has the right to decide which method of reporting subdistributor gross receipts to follow and may switch from one to the other from time to time.

If, let's say, major talent has negotiated for a participation and, like the producer, is to receive a percentage of gross receipts; that makes the distributor's choice of accounting methods much more significant, for obvious reasons. A distributor that utilizes subdistributors and pays only on the revenue it receives from them will pay less than if the subdistributors' total revenues were to be included in its own gross receipts.

If a participant is to receive 10 percent of gross receipts, and the distributor receives $100 from a sub-distributor, representing the sum due to the distributor after the sub-distributor deducts and retains its fees and expenses along with any advance, the participant receives $10 (10 percent of $100). If a distributor reports a subdistributor's gross as its gross and must pay a percentage of that money to a participant, and if no money is due the distributor from the subdistributor (based upon the subdistributor's accounting to the distributor because the subdistributor has retained from its gross, for example, its distribution fees and expenses), the distributor would be obligated to make a payment to the participant even though it had received no money from the subdistributor.

To avoid this result, a distributor will try never to be required to pay out to the participants more than it actually collects from a subdistributor, despite the fact that it may very well consider a subdistributor's gross receipts as its gross receipts. For example, assuming a participant is to receive 10 percent of the distributor's gross receipts, if a subdistributor has revenues of $100, distribution fees equal to $30, and expenses of $100, the subdistributor does not owe the distributor any money. The distributor shows $100 as gross receipts in its reports to the participant, but since it received nothing from its licensees, it does not (at that point) have to pay any part of that sum to the participant even though the latter was to receive 10 percent of the gross receipts. If, however, the subdistributor earns another $300, has distribution fees equal to $90 and expenses of $150 and remits $60, then the cumulative figures indicate that the subdistributor's gross is $400, and the distributor has received $60. The participant is then entitled to his $40, because the distributor received $60, which is a larger sum than the distributor was required to pay the participant. If the subdistributor's expenses had been $200 instead of $150, so that only $10 instead of $60 had been remitted to the distributor, the participant would receive only $10 instead of 10 percent of $400 or $40 since the distributor received only $10. One thing to keep in mind in this discussion is that it is to a distributor's advantage to maximize gross receipts in order to increase distribution fees (a percentage of gross receipts) to a net profit participant, and minimize gross receipts to a gross receipts participant.

Outright Sales

In some cases, a picture is licensed to a territory on an "outright" basis; in other words, the distributing company receives a flat sum from the subdistributor in the territory and whatever the subdistributor earns from all licensed rights in the film in that territory the subdistributor keeps. This form of distribution is common in the minor territories (i.e., countries in Africa, Latin or South America), or in territories where it is difficult to remit money. Gross receipts are then deemed to be the flat sum or sale price received by the distributor from the subdistributor, regardless of the rentals earned by the subdistributor from its distribution in the territory. For this reason, most producers attempt to provide that outright sales cannot be made in major territories (e.g., United Kingdom, Japan, Canada, Germany, France, Italy, Spain).

Gross Receipt Sources by Media

Gross receipts are derived from the following major areas of exploitation of the film: theatrical rights; television rights including network, syndication (i.e., licensing to individual stations); cable, both basic and pay (e.g., HBO, Showtime) as well as pay-per-view, home video rights; non-theatrical rights (e.g., on airplanes, ships at sea, military bases, hospitals, and other closed-circuit systems, 16mm film, oil rigs, and college campuses); merchandising rights; publishing rights (such as novelizations and photo-novels); and music rights (sound track and music publishing). Other minor sources of gross receipts include government subsidies, copyright royalty tribunal income (revenue derived from noncommercial broadcasting licenses and compulsory cable television secondary transmissions), income derived from the exploitation of trailers of the film, and net recoveries from lawsuits (such as copyright infringement).

Motion Picture Theaters: Theatrical gross receipts are revenues payable to distributors by motion picture theater owners for exhibition of a film in motion picture theaters. These revenues are usually a percentage of box office receipts. Until recently, in the U.S., as a result of a settlement of a government antitrust action against the studios known as the Paramount Consent Decree, film distribution companies that were parties to the decree were not allowed to own theaters. Now, however, some of these studios have succeeded to an extent in modifying the consent decree so that they may own theaters. Additionally, from time to time, film companies have been leasing theaters on a so-called "four-wall" basis in which the distributor rents the theater from the theater owner, tells the theater owner which pictures to book and on what terms, and keeps all revenue derived from their exhibition. In such situations, what then are gross receipts? To prevent a participant from claiming that all sums received by the theater as box office receipts comprise gross receipts, the distributor sometimes agrees to account to the participant for those gross receipts that the distributor would have received from the theater pursuant to an arm's-length deal with the theater for the film. Alternatively, a distributor can provide that all box office receipts less the cost of running the theater are the distributor's gross receipts, or that all box office receipts are gross receipts and all theater rental costs are distribution expenses.

Paradoxically, some theater chains have started motion picture production and distribution enterprises, and some of the major distribution companies own their own theaters in foreign countries. For the producer, this is both an advantage and a disadvantage. On the one hand, the motion picture distributor owning the theaters has an assured outlet for its product, and if such theaters are well located and operated, the distributor's pictures will be favored over those of some third party subject to anti-trust laws prohibiting such discrimination. On the other hand, the distributor can make self-serving agreements with its own theaters at the producer's expense. For example, the distributor can enter into an exhibition agreement with its own theater that gives an artificially low percentage of the theater's revenues to the distributor. The distributor then receives only a portion of the receipts from that theater's showing of the film for which it must account but it actually retains 100 percent of the profits of its wholly-owned theater operation.

Some producers insist that any agreements entered into by a

distributor with a theater owned by the distributor must be made in good faith. To resolve any question of what is or is not good faith, a distributor could (and some do) annex to its agreement an exhibit indicating the terms and conditions pursuant to which it licenses films to its own theaters.

Television: No special problems here. Gross receipts are what the distributor receives from the network, cable, pay-per-view, or syndication. See, however, the section on allocations, below.

Videocassettes and Discs: The most hotly contested issue relating to the revenue to be included in gross receipts concerns videocassettes. When the motion picture industry first began dealing with home video, it analogized its treatment more to the royalty participation concept common in the record industry than to the net profits concept common in the motion picture industry.

As with records, on each videocassette sold the participant is entitled to a royalty that is equal to a percentage of the cassette's wholesale price. The standard royalty is 20 percent, although some participants with extraordinary leverage have managed to negotiate a 25 percent or even 30 percent royalty. The result is that the studio includes only 20 percent of videocassette revenue in gross receipts and puts most of the remaining 80 percent in its pocket. The financial significance of this becomes apparent when one realizes that films will often sell two hundred thousand or more cassettes at a wholesale price of $50 to $56 each. Out of the $10,000,000 generated, the studio includes $2,000,000 in gross receipts and keeps the remaining $8,000,000. Then, returning to film industry practices, the $2,000,000 included in gross receipts is subject to the distributor's distribution fee on home video gross. While the studio bears the costs, except residuals, relating to the cassette (manufacture, duplication, fulfillments, and advertising) out of its share and does not deduct such costs as a distribution expense, the totality of such costs (excluding advertising) is usually less than $6 per unit and most of the advertising is a function of the theatrical release (and to the extent characterized as such is deducted as a distribution expense). The $2,000,000 then becomes part of the "pot" of revenues from which *all* the expenses relating to the film are deducted.

If this practice were carried to its logical extremes, where home video rights are granted to a subdistributor, the subdistributor would remit 20 percent of its wholesale selling price to the distributor, which, in turn, would include 20 percent of what it has received from the subdistributor in gross receipts. The producer would then receive only 20 percent of 20 percent, or 4 percent of 100 percent of the wholesale selling price. As a result, distributors occasionally agree to include 100% of video revenues in gross receipts when they are licensing video rights to an unaffiliated third party or, at the very least, to include in gross a royalty equal to 20 percent of the wholesale price without reference to the actual video revenues received by the distributor.

Music Publishing: Music publishing is another source of revenue. If the distributor administers the music publishing, it typically includes 50 percent of music publishing receipts in gross receipts after deducting an administration fee (usually around 15 percent) and all its costs and expenses, including royalties payable to any composer. If the distributor does not administer the music publishing, it will not charge the administration fee. If there is a third party publisher, the distributor usually includes in gross receipts all revenue received from that publisher after deducting adistribution of around 15 percent fee and all costs and songwriter royalties.

Records: Music-recording revenue (CDs, cassettes, black vinyl) is treated in much the same way as music-publishing revenue. If the distributor directly engages in the business of releasing the sound track album (or single), then it includes 50 percent of the revenue derived from that source as part of gross receipts after deducting a "packager's fee" (usually between 25 percent and 30 percent) and all costs, expenses, and royalties. If the distributor does not directly engage in that business and licenses that right to a third party, it will usually include in gross receipts all income received from that third party after deducting an administration fee of around 15 percent and all costs and royalties.

Merchandising: The merchandising rights to some films can be very valuable. These rights include the right to license, manufacture, distribute, and sell articles of merchandise, such as T-shirts, coffee mugs, and the like, utilizing the names and likenesses of characters, actors, and other physical items appearing in the film. If the distributor simply hires an unaffiliated merchandising agent to enter into licenses with merchandisers, it will normally include as gross receipts all revenue received from that agent after deducting an administration fee (usually between 15 percent to 20 percent) and all royalties and costs. On the other hand, if the distributor acts as its own merchandiser, it will usually deduct a larger administration fee (between 40 percent to 50 percent).

Advances From Third-Party Licensees

Also included in gross receipts are advances the distributor receives from third-party licensees for the right to exploit the film in some manner. The licensee can recoup his advance from the distributor's share of revenues derived from the exploitation of the film. For example, a foreign subdistributor may give the distributor $2,000,000 as an advance for the right to subdistribute the film in a particular territory. Usually the subdistributor is entitled to a distribution fee on all the money it collects and a deduction for expenses; the remainder of the money goes to the distributor. However, the subdistributor can keep the distributor's share of the revenues until it has recouped its $2,000,000 advance.

Typically, the distributor will not want to include advances in the gross receipts reported to the net profit participant until the subdistributor has "earned" the advance or forfeited it. That is, it will not include these advances until such time as the subdistributor has either recouped the advance it paid the distributor or forfeits its right to do so, because, for example, the term of the subdistribution agreement has expired. Thus the distributor may keep the money without having to account for it for a substantial period of time. Advances are often included in gross receipts when they are nonreturnable—for instance, upon delivery of the film to the subdistributor. The distributor will not want to include advances in gross receipts if, as sometimes happens, it is required to return the unearned portion or all of an advance to the subdistributor.

Remakes and Sequels

Distributors rarely include in gross receipts any revenue derived from remakes, sequels, and television productions based on a film. A participant may ask that a rights payment for these other productions be included in gross receipts, but that request is hardly ever granted. Participants who sell literary rights or who perform writing services, however, usually do receive royalties relating to subsequent productions as described in Chapters One and Two. Producers and directors, while rarely receiving royalties, often are granted a right of first negotiation or some right to produce or direct those subsequent productions. For theatrical sequels and remakes, the right of first negotiation is usually on financial terms no less favorable than those applying to the original film.

Blocked Funds

Distributors usually insist that gross receipts include only revenue that they receive in U.S. dollars. This allows the distributor to withhold from gross receipts money earned in countries that prohibit or restrict its removal. These are referred to as "blocked funds." However, the distributor will usually agree to deposit in a bank in the foreign country involved the profit participant's share of blocked funds if the participant so requests; or, if the distributor uses the blocked funds in that country for any purpose, it may agree to credit gross receipts with an amount equal to the blocked funds used. It should be noted that a distributor may choose to keep money overseas, even if it is not blocked, and may time remittances to take advantage of exchange rates—which may not be to the participant's advantage.

Allocations

A frequent dispute between producers and distributors involves the question of allocations. The problem arises when, for example, a distributor licenses a picture as part of a double feature with another picture from the same distributor. In such a situation, the distributor will usually receive revenue from the two films without any breakdown of how much money was generated by one film and how much by the other. Therefore, the distributor will have to make some sort of allocation vis-a-vis the profit participant. If the distributor owns one picture outright but has the other picture on a net profits arrangement, or has one picture for which costs have been recouped and for which there are net profits payable to third parties and one picture that is in deficit, the temptation may be to allocate a larger portion of receipts to the picture that is owned outright or unprofitable and thus to discriminate against the picture in which a portion of the net profits must be paid to third parties. The same is true with television packages. It is not uncommon for several pictures to be sold at the same time to a television station. To avoid antitrust claims of "block booking" in the U.S., the distributor will allow a station to license all or a portion of the pictures in the package. Distributors are supposed to insist that the purchase price of each picture in the package be negotiated separately, but participants may be skeptical.

Many television stations want to make allocations themselves, for their own accounting purposes, because they feel that the cost of a film should bear some relationship to the advertising dollars it can earn in selling time. That allocation, if permitted by a distributor, would seemingly be fair. However, to simplify the negotiation with individual stations, distributors to television sometimes assign letter values to each picture in a package so that, for instance, an AA picture may be worth twice as much as an A, and an A may be worth 50 percent more than a B, and so on. These allocations are at best rough estimates, and sometimes a participant will feel rightly that the allocation to his picture is less than it should be. However, in allocating among films, a distributor must take into consideration more than just the picture's theatrical gross receipts. The market for pictures on television differs from the market for pictures theatrically. Some pictures are too sexually explicit to play on free television at all; others cannot be shown on prime time. Foreign language films, because they must be dubbed or subtitled into English, and black-and-white films are difficult to sell to television.

Under the usual television deal, pictures are sold to television well in advance of the time that they will be aired, and the money due is usually payable to the distributor in installments. Even with the assumption that the total license fee has been properly apportioned to each film in a package, the question still remains as to how to allocate a portion of each installment payment to each individual photoplay. One method is to allocate the money as it is paid to the distributor in the order that each picture is used or made available for release on television. Another method would be to allocate each payment when received pro rata among all of the pictures. This allocation is generally not regulated by contract but rather by practice, and producers and distributors can and do differ on what is a proper allocation.

The same sort of allocation problem will arise when a number of pictures are licensed to a foreign market either on an outright sale basis or for a minimum guarantee against a percentage of the gross receipts.

Allocation in the advertising of several films at the same time can also create disputes. Sometimes a company will run single ads which include a number of films. Should the cost of such ads be prorated to the amount of space devoted to each picture, to the theatrical gross receipts derived from each picture, or to some other standard? If one promotional trailer is make for several of the distributor's motion pictures, the same allocation questions occur. There is no problem to the extent that the costs involved can be directly attributed to each of the films, but some of the expense of producing the trailer would be common to all of the pictures it included.

Distribution Fees

The first step in calculating net profits is for a distributor to deduct and retain from gross receipts what is known as a "distribution fee." Theoretically, the distribution fee represents those operational/overhead costs incurred by the distributor that cannot be directly allocated to specific films. It is generally assumed that a substantial portion of the distribution fee simply constitutes profit to the studio—depending on the total gross receipts received by the studio from all films in a fiscal year.

The distribution fee is calculated as a percentage of gross receipts. Typically, studios will charge a 30 percent distribution fee on gross receipts derived from all sources in the U.S. and Canada, 35 percent to 37.5 percent of gross receipts derived from all sources in the United Kingdom, and 40 percent of gross receipts derived from all sources in any other territory in the world. The studios' exceptions to this are: a 15 percent distribution fee on gross receipts derived from theatrical outright sales, a 25 percent fee on gross receipts derived from U.S. network prime-time television sales and pay cable revenues, and no distribution fee on governmental subsidies, aid, and prizes. Sometimes the distribution fee on videocassettes may be reduced or even waived altogether, depending upon the royalty rate at which videocassette revenue is included in gross receipts (the lower the royalty rate, the lower the fee, and vice versa).

An even more complex problem arises when the distributor utilizes a subdistributor that also charges a distribution fee. Depending upon the leverage of the parties, this issue may be resolved in any number of ways, from the distributor charging its full fees on the net amount received from the subdistributor after the subdistributor has also charged its full fees, to the distributor charging no fee at all even if the subdistributor charges a distribution fee. There are three frequent compromises: (1) the distributor charges its full fees but absorbs any distribution fee charged by the subdistributor; (2) the distributor agrees that the combined distributor's fees and subdistributor's fees will not exceed a prenegotiated percentage of gross receipts (usually 50 percent); or (3) the distributor charges an override (for example, 20 percent) on the net sums remitted to the distributor by the subdistributor. Under the last formulation, the override would be charged on any advance and on any revenues in excess of the advance received from a subdistributor.

Distribution Expenses

From the gross receipts remaining after the distribution fee has been deducted, the distributor then deducts its distribution expenses.

By far the most significant of these expenses relate to the costs of manufacturing prints of the film and those relating to advertising. Most distributors make a further deduction in the form of an "advertising overhead" charge, usually equal to 10 percent of the actual advertising costs.

Other distribution expenses usually include the cost of converting and transmitting money from foreign currency to U.S. dollars; taxes other than income and corporate taxes; costs incurred in checking attendance and box office receipts of theaters; costs of collecting gross receipts; trade association fees; residuals (residuals are payments to the applicable guild based on a percentage of the gross receipts derived from the exploitation of the film in the applicable supplemental market), reuse and other guild-required payments; costs of making foreign-language versions; costs of reediting the film for television, videocassette, and other such exhibition; costs of shipping and delivery; royalties; insurance; copyrighting costs and costs incurred in protecting against copyright infringement; litigation costs; and industry assessments. Most profit definitions include an additional catch-all clause that permits deduction of all other costs customarily incurred by distributors but not specifically mentioned above.

Distributors and participants may disagree on whether certain taxes are deductible from gross receipts. Some taxes are clearly based upon a film's gross receipts or the remittance of money it has earned and must be regarded as legitimate distribution expenses. But other taxes are not so clearly categorized—they may, for example, be based on a foreign subsidiary's earnings—and there may be disagreement as to whether such taxes are deductible as distributor's expenses.

The greatest advertising expense is "cooperative advertising," in which the distributor and the theatrical exhibitor share the cost of ads and other materials used to promote the picture in a locality and in the theater itself. How the cost is divided is a matter of negotiation, but the advertising expense is usually shared in the same ratio that the exhibitor and distributor share in the box office receipts. If the split of box office receipts is 90 percent to the distributor and 10 percent to the exhibitor over a "house floor" (which is a rough approximation of the exhibitor's overhead and may vary depending upon the bargaining power of the parties), the distributor will usually bear the entire cooperative advertising charge. It is difficult to predict what the cooperative advertising will amount to as a percentage of theatrical film rental. A very rough estimate is around 40 percent. If a film is very successful, the cooperative advertising costs for the first weeks will be relatively high but for later weeks will be substantially less because once the film is well launched, people simply want to know only where it is playing and when. At that point, the percentage will usually be lower than 40 percent. On the other hand, if the film is a failure, obviously the cooperative advertising costs must still be paid, and may indeed prove greater than the distributor's theatrical gross receipts.

Interest

Once distribution expenses have been deducted, the distributor deducts the interest on negative cost (the cost to produce the film). This interest is usually calculated at 2 percent over the current prime rate or 125 percent of prime rate. The justification given by the studios for this mark-up is that it is necessary to help recoup the cost of their compensating balances (funds that are not subject to interest but which the banks require the studio to maintain in the account) and some studios borrow at above the prime rate of interest.

An important concern in calculating interest is the point from which the interest runs. The studio will typically take the position that interest runs from the time a financial obligation is incurred (the date money is owing, as opposed to the date it is paid). From the participant's view, that interest should run from the time the money is actually spent. (Some studios have been known to claim that an expense is incurred when they merely plan to spend the money!) Since it is virtually impossible to calculate the exact moment when interest is to run on each item, some definitions of profits provide that all obligations will be deemed to have been spent (or incurred) on the first day of the accounting period in which the obligation was actually spent (or incurred). Such a provision is more favorable to the studio than to the participant. Accordingly, the participant will usually endeavor to have the calculation refer to the last day of the accounting period. Sometimes a compromise is reached where the obligations are deemed spent (or incurred) at the midpoint of an accounting period.

The reason interest on negative cost is recouped before negative cost itself, of course, is that the longer negative cost is unrecouped the longer interest will run on that unrecouped cost.

Negative Cost and Overbudget Penalty

Negative cost is the next item that the distributor recoups. This expense usually includes not only the direct cost of production, but also an overhead charge calculated as a percentage of that cost, usually between 12.5 and 15 percent. A frequently negotiated point is whether interest is to be charged on overhead. Distributors sometimes try to designate items as negative costs that producers think should be distribution expenses, since negative costs bear overhead and interest and the penalty discussed in the following paragraphs.

For participants who have some control over the production of the film, distributors typically impose what is known as an overbudget add-back penalty. The purpose of this penalty is to provide an incentive to those who control the production to be fiscally responsible and to keep the film within its budget. Typically, an overbudget add-back penalty provides that for the purposes of calculating the participant's net profits, negative cost will be artificially increased by an amount equal to the amount by which the film goes overbudget (that is, the amount by which the actual cost of production exceeds the final approved budget).

Since a film may go overbudget for many reasons that are not the fault of the participant, studios will usually agree to two areas of compromise. First, they will permit a "cushion" before the film is considered to be overbudget. Usually the cushion is 7.5 to 10 percent, i.e., only those costs in excess of 107.5 percent or 110 percent of the budget will be included in the overbudget penalty. Second, the studio will usually agree to exclude certain costs from the calculation entirely—costs such as those due to acts of God, industry-wide increases (e.g., raises in guild minimums), and changes in the film (e.g., additional scenes) approved or requested by the studio, as well as expenses for which insurance has provided a recovery, and sometimes expenses resulting from third-party breaches.

An illustration of an overbudget add-back would be as follows: The budget of a film is $10 million while its actual production cost comes to $12 million (none of the excess being subject to the above-referenced exclusions). The overbudget add-back cushion is 10 percent (i.e., only those costs in excess of 110 percent of the budget will be included in the penalty). Thus, only costs in excess of $11 million (110 percent of the $10 million budget) would be included in the penalty. Accordingly, for the purposes of calculating negative cost for the profit participant in question, negative cost will be deemed to equal $13 million (the $12 million actual cost of production plus a $1 million penalty, the amount by which the actual cost of production exceeded 110 percent of the budget).

Often at issue in the negotiation of an overbudget add-back penalty is whether the penalty portion bears interest and/or overhead.

A relatively small proportion of all pictures ever achieve net profits. When one does, the distributor is usually so pleased that it often will not want to jeopardize its relationship with the producer by penalizing him because the picture has gone over budget. As a result, the penalty provisions will not be invoked. On the other hand, if the producer has been wasteful or sloppy, the distributor may feel that even though the picture shows a net profit, the producer should be penalized, as allowed by the contract.

Deferments and Gross Participations

Distributors will usually attempt to include as a negative-cost item deferments and gross participations paid in connection with the film. It is most advantageous for the distributor to charge these items as negative-cost items, because they will then bear both interest and overhead.

The effect on net profits of computing gross receipt participations as negative cost can be devastating, as the example at the end of this chapter will show. If possible, a net profit participant should get the right to approve any gross participations, since the adverse accounting effect of a gross participant needs to be balanced against the value of that participant to the film. More typically, the studio will agree to deduct gross participations after negative cost is recouped, thus structuring it so that the gross participation does not bear interest or overhead.

THE NATURE OF THE PARTICIPATION

The net profit of a picture is the amount remaining from which the participant will receive his agreed-upon percentage. It is very important to establish whether a percentage of profits is based on 100 percent of the net profits or on another method of calculation, such as "producer's" net profits. Otherwise, the participant may end up with a percentage of no more than the net profits left after the producer has deducted profits to other participants. (See Chapter Nine under "Producer's Profits.")

In a recent case, Art Buchwald sued Paramount Pictures in connection with the hit movie starring Eddie Murphy called *Coming to America*. Buchwald as a net receipt participant was compelled, he claimed, to accept the Paramount standard form definition of net receipts, and under that definition Paramount claimed the picture was substantially unrecouped even though it was one of the studio's biggest hits. Buchwald's legal theory was simply that the agreement was unconscionable. The trial court agreed that the following provisions of the agreement were indeed unconscionable:

1. A percentage overhead charged on gross receipt participations.
2. A percentage overhead charged on advertising costs.

3. A percentage overhead charged on the cost of production.
4. Accounting for revenue on a cash basis while accounting for costs on an accrual basis.
5. Charging interest on overhead.
6. Charging interest on gross receipt participations.
7. An interest rate on the cost of production substantially in excess of producer's cost of borrowing.

As this book goes to press, no damages have been awarded. Whatever the result, it is clear that the decision will ultimately be appealed. It is unclear what the results of that appeal will be. If Buchwald prevails it is conceivable that the studios may even attempt to eliminate all net profit participations.

PARTICIPATIONS IN GROSS RECEIPTS

While sounding very simple, negotiating and calculating a participation in gross receipts is often more complex than negotiating and calculating a participation in net profits because there are many types of participations in gross receipts. The simplest is known as a first-dollar gross participation. Here the participant receives a percentage of gross receipts without deductions of any kind being made from them. This form of participation, however, is extremely rare, and can be achieved only by a handful of extremely powerful participants. Even then, the salary of most first-dollar gross participants is considered an advance against their participation, so that they do not actually start to receive money until their participation equals their salary.

Far more common is a participation in gross receipts after "break-even." Under this formula, once net profits has been reached, the participant is entitled to a percentage of the "adjusted gross receipts." These are gross receipts on which deductions are limited to a small number known as "off the tops." Typically, off the tops include checking costs (checking the accuracy of theater box office receipts), collection costs, residuals, currency conversion and transmission costs, taxes, and trade association assessments and fees. Studios may also attempt to deduct cooperative advertising expenses as an off the top, but this can usually be successfully resisted.

Sometimes a powerful participant can negotiate a "prebreak" gross participation. Under this arrangement, the participant is entitled to a percentage of the adjusted gross receipts once the film reaches net profits. However, net profits are calculated with a reduced distribution fee (usually from 12.5 percent to 25 percent), which means that net profit is reached sooner than would otherwise be the case.

A gross participation triggered when the film reaches net profits including full distribution fees is known as a participation in the gross receipts after actual break-even. A gross participation triggered when the picture reaches net profits with reduced distribution fees is often referred to as a participation in gross receipts after cash break-even.

It is interesting to note that for the purposes of reaching net profits, gross receipts will usually be defined in a manner that provides for as few deductions as possible (because the larger the gross receipts, the larger the distribution fee), while for the purposes of calculating the gross receipts from which the participant takes his percentage, gross receipts is magically transformed into "adjusted gross receipts," a significantly smaller sum.

An important concern in any gross after break-even or prebreak gross formula is how and whether the distribution expenses incurred after the time the film reaches break-even (with reduced distribution fee if prebreak) will affect the gross participation. Under one arrangement (a gross after initial, or fixed break-even), once the film initially reaches break-even, the participant begins sharing in the adjusted gross receipts and continues to do so even if there are subsequent distribution costs. Under another arrangement (a gross after rolling, or moving break-even), the participant begins sharing in the adjusted gross receipts once the film reaches break-even, but if the distributor later incurs additional distribution costs, it will be entitled to recoup those costs and a distribution fee, before the participant receives any more of the gross receipts. Under this rolling break-even arrangement, the distributor is entitled to take its distribution fee, but, once the breakeven point is reached, the distribution fee is calculated not on gross receipts but on the amount of its expenses. The distributor's total deduction, then, is that amount necessary to recoup first its fee and then its expenses. For example, if the distributor were entitled to a 30 percent fee and incurred $2,000,000 in expenses, the distributor would recoup an amount equal to the amount that would leave $2,000,000 after the original amount was reduced by 30 percent. The way this is done is to take the amount of expenses ($2,000,000), invert the distribution fee (subtract from 1 the distribution fee expressed as a decimal—an inverted .3 distribution fee is .7), and divide the expenses by that inverted fee. $2,000,000 divided by .7 equals $2,857,142.80. In other words, once the distributor took its 30 percent distribution fee on $2,857,142.80 (i.e., $857,142.80), the $2,000,000 in expenses would remain. This process is known as "grossing up" for the distribution fee.

A percentage point of gross after rolling actual break-even is commonly considered to be worth between 1.4 and 1.5 times a percentage point of net profits, and a percentage point of gross after initial actual break-even is considered to be worth 1.8 to 2 times a percentage point of net profits.

Problems of break-even accounting involve when that magical moment occurs, and how it can be manipulated. Clearly the time when break-even occurs can be manipulated by not remitting gross receipts to the U.S. or by delaying or advancing the incurrence (or payment) of distribution expenses.

DEFERMENTS

As discussed earlier, a deferment is a sum payable in a lump at a particular time or when a certain amount of gross receipts or net profits is reached, or a sum payable out of such gross receipts or net profits.

While some deferments are payable after an agreed upon period of time—let us say, three months after the initial U.S. theatrical release of the film—and are thus vested interests that will be payable no matter what, most deferments are contingent upon and triggered by some level of the film's receipts and are paid out of the continuing receipts, if any, after the trigger has been reached. By far the most common is a deferment payable out of the first sums that would otherwise constitute net profits of the film. Typically, these deferments are paid "pro rata" and "pari passu" with other similar deferments. Pro rata means that the participant will receive a share of the gross receipts or net profits on a basis proportional to all other deferments payable at that time. For example, if from the first net profits the participant is to receive a $1,000,000 deferment and the aggregate of all deferments is $5,000,000, then from each dollar of net profits the participant will be paid one fifth (or $.20) until he has received his $1,000,000 deferment. Pari passu means that all portions of the deferments will be paid at the same time, rather than any being paid in a superior or inferior position. Of course, some deferments could be made payable before others.

ACCOUNTING PROCEDURES AND AUDIT RIGHTS

The accounting provisions of the agreement relating to net profits should be examined with great care. Some agreements provide for monthly accountings but most require accountings to be quarterly for a stated number of years and thereafter semi-annually for a few more years, and then annually. Accountings are usually rendered either forty-five or sixty days after the end of each accounting period. The fewer accountings there are, and the longer the distributor has to render the accounting after the close of an accounting period, the more the producer loses, as he cannot earn interest on money he has not received and interest will be charged by the distributor on the unrecouped cost of production during that period. It is to the participant's advantage to receive accountings as frequently as possible during the period when the film is being continuously distributed, just as it is advisable for him to try to provide that once a substantial, stated amount of film rental is received, it must be reported promptly (within a stated period).

For example, let's say that the agreement covering a theatrically released film specifies that accounting statements be rendered yearly after the first five years of release. If this film is sold to television six years after release, the distributor could receive the television income, which might be substantial, and be under no obligation to report any of it to the producer for a year. Often, an agreement will provide that if there is a theatrical reissue of the film, the monthly or quarterly (as the case may be) accounting periods will be resumed for the life of that reissue.

Some agreements provide that the distributor does not have to render an accounting to the participant if the amount due for any accounting period does not reach or exceed a stated sum, such as $5,000. The participant may argue that he should get any money due him, but the distributor will object to rendering accounting statements if the picture is for all practical purposes out of release and its cost remains totally unrecouped. A compromise can provide that so long as the cost of the picture is unrecouped, the distributor does not have to render accounting statements unless the amount of gross receipts reported in any particular period exceeds $5,000.

The distributor ordinarily uses reasonable efforts to convert receipts into U.S. dollars at whatever rate of exchange it can obtain. To protect itself, the distributor provides contractually that if it makes a bona fide effort to convert to dollars it is not liable for any errors of judgment. As discussed earlier, usually the distributor will attempt to provide that no revenue is to be included in gross receipts unless and until received in the U.S. in U.S. dollars.

Most agreements impose artificial time limitations on the right to audit. For instance, they provide that a statement is incontestable unless objected to within a stated period of time and unless a lawsuit is started within a stated period from the date of the objection. As a practical matter, most major distributors will agree to extend the incontestability periods for an additional reasonable time simply for the asking. The agreement will probably also provide that audits be limited in number during a stated time period, can continue for only a limited period of time, and can cover only a stipulated number of accounting statements rendered prior to the audit. For example, the agreement may provide that the participant can make only one audit a year, that he can audit only a period beginning no more than two years prior to the date of the inspection, and that his audit cannot continue for more than thirty consecutive days. The reason for these restrictions, the distributor argues, is to avoid overburdening its accounting department. The distributor will not want to maintain its records for a long and indefinite period of time, nor will it want the participant's accountants disrupting routine and turning its records inside out.

On the other hand, a participant will try to secure unlimited audit rights. Usually the time periods are negotiable. The contractual provision for time limitations may put the participant in the position of having to enforce his rights by formally objecting to every statement and routinely sending accountants in to audit.

Accounting firms experienced in motion picture auditing can often assert claims for substantial sums as a result of an audit. A participant, however, must weigh the possible benefits from an audit against its cost, which may be substantial. To protect himself he can try to have the contract provide that if an audit reveals the distributor underreported the amount due him by more than a specified percentage or dollar amount, the distributor will pay the cost of the participant's audit. This hardly meets with favor among distributors, obviously, and can rarely be negotiated; nevertheless, a strong argument can be made that a distributor has an obligation to reimburse the participant for errors in accounting, whether deliberate or inadvertent.

One key concern of most distributors is that the participant have a right to audit only the books of the participant's film, not of other films. This, of course, makes it more difficult for a participant to check allocations or how his film was distributed. It is useful for a participant to know that while a certain picture that grossed X dollars had five thousand play dates, his film, which grossed Y dollars, had only three thousand play dates. It would also be enlightening for a participant to compare the relative sums spent on advertising and the number of prints ordered for different movies. Of course, the distributor's answer to all of this is that other movies it distributed are none of the participant's business, and disclosure of facts about them would violate the confidential relationship between the distributor and its other producers. This argument prevails as a general rule where an allocation question is involved.

However, if a particular distribution or exhibition agreement makes reference to more than one film, most distributors will allow the participant to inspect all relevant agreements, which will of course reveal the allocations made. However, the distributor will not ordinarily have to disclose underlying information with respect to the agreements.

At the end of an audit, the participant's accountants and the distributor's accounting department meet to resolve their differences. Generally they are able to do so; when they cannot—litigation results. By and large, this kind of litigation hinges not on contractual language but on accounting concepts and procedures. There is very little a distributor can do to cover all the situations that may arise and thus protect itself against this kind of litigation.

The auditor's job is to establish that the amount of money received was correctly reported as gross receipts and that any deductions from those gross receipts were proper. It is not an auditor's role to ask whether or not more gross receipts should have been obtained, for then he would be acting not as an accountant but as a critic of the sales policies of the distributor.

The distributor will ordinarily allow the auditors to examine only home office records and not the records of subdistributors in other territories or even those of the distributor's exchanges (regional offices where the films are licensed to exhibitors). Since most of the exchange office records are duplicated in the home office anyway, an examining accountant can get a pretty good idea of what is going on.

As a rule of thumb, any picture reaching net profits (or break-even) should be audited, just on general principles. Most of the time an auditing accountant will find enough discrepancies, which the distribution company will acknowledge, to justify whatever fee is charged.

HOW TO CALCULATE
WHEN A FILM WILL BREAK EVEN

It is useful to have a rough method of calculating when a film will reach net profits under a standard studio definition of net profits.

Let us assume a normal studio deal and a direct film production cost of $12,000,000. Add 15 percent overhead on production cost, which brings us to $13,800,000, and then interest at 10 percent on both production cost and overhead running for a projected two years until recoupment ($2,760,000). This equals $16,560,000. Also add print and advertising expenses, which will depend largely on the distributor. It is difficult for a studio to open a film for less than $8,000,000. If the film has any measure of success at all, a studio will often spend approximately 40 percent of gross receipts on prints and advertising; thus, on a film that has gross receipts of $40,000,000, it is fair to assume an expenditure of roughly $16,000,000 for prints and advertising. Added to the foregoing, this equals $32,560,000. It is then necessary to calculate the total amount that would be required for the studio to recoup the $32,560,000 after that total amount is reduced by the studio's distribution fees. To do this, gross up for the distribution fee. The average worldwide weighted distribution fee is typically 32.5 percent. Therefore, divide $32,560,000 by .675. This equals roughly $48,237,037. Thus, a ballpark estimate of where a film costing $12,000,000 will break even is at $48,237,037 of gross receipts or somewhere between 3.5 and 4 times the negative cost. (Remember, this is not box office receipts; rather, it is the gross receipts received by the distributor.) Where the negative cost is proportionately larger, so are the interest and overhead charges and the advertising costs as well. The studio of course will want to protect its investment—therefore, the multiple will be higher. If the negative cost is lower, then the studio may well spend less for prints and advertising, resulting in a multiple which is somewhat lower. If there are gross receipt participants, the multiple will again increase substantially.

Now take the above example and assume that the studio was permitted to include a 5 percent dollar gross participation as a negative cost item. As seen above, without including gross participations in negative cost, the film would have had to generate gross receipts of $48,237,037 to break even. Assuming the 5 percent gross participation, at what was the breakeven point, the gross participant has received 5 percent of that amount, or approximately $2,441,851. The studio, of course, will be entitled to recoup this amount before the film is considered to be at breakeven. If this participation is considered a negative cost item, however, it will also bear interest (10 percent over two years, or approximately $482,370) and overhead (15 percent, or approximately $361,771). This equals $3,255,998 which the studio will additionally recoup *after it recoups its distribution fee.* The weighted worldwide distribution fee being 32-1/2 percent, the studio would then have to recoup a total of approximately $4,823,700 ($3,255,998 divided by .675). Of course, this additional revenue will also be subject to the 5 percent gross participation. The gross participant, then, will receive an additional $241,185, which will also bear interest and overhead vis-a-vis the net participant and which the studio will recoup after, once again, recouping its distribution fee. This process will go on, *ad infinitum* and *ad nauseam.*

PRODUCER'S GROSS RECEIPTS

This discussion of gross receipts and net profits has assumed a studio distributing the picture in the U.S. and in other major territories. Of course, there are situations in which a producer must grant a participation to talent, a financier, or some other third party before the picture has commenced production and before he knows how it is to be distributed. Later he might find himself fractionalizing rights—that is, licensing to one distributor some rights in a territory and to another distributor the remaining rights in that territory. In that circumstance, many different licensees will be accounting to the producer, who in turn will, like a studio, have to account to the participants. A simple approach to satisfy a participant is for the producer to follow a formula in which gross receipts are simply the moneys actually received by him from all licensees in the picture. Such sums include net profits and advances from theatrical distributors, pay cable licensee fees, home video advances, and the like. The producer does not normally take a distribution fee on those gross receipts (although producers often attempt to take an override between 10 to 20 percent) but first deducts any distribution expenses he has incurred: preparation of duplicate negatives and advertising materials for licensees, possibly exhibition at film festivals, and other costs that were not covered in his budget. He then deducts interest on the cost of production (if he has borrowed money to produce the picture) and then deducts the actual cost of production. The balance remaining would be net profits. Accountings would be rendered by the producer and audits would be made of the producer's books and records. Some participants request a provision that if the film is distributed by a worldwide distributor, their profit participation be computed in the same fashion as was the producer's. They may request that the producer have the studio pay them directly, that they receive an independent accounting, and that they can, at their expense, compel the producer to audit.

5 THE PRODUCTION– FINANCING AND DISTRIBUTION AGREEMENT

Having examined the concept of gross receipts and considered how the elusive matter of net profits is arrived at, we must turn to the most traditional form of financing and distribution— one in which a major studio, "mini-major" studio, or independent production entity fully finances a film and controls distribution rights worldwide. This production-financing-distribution agreement is for convenience called the "P-D." The factors contained in the P-D crop up in many other parts of this book because many other types of agreements are patterned after it.

In the P-D, a motion picture distributor agrees to finance the production of a motion picture and to distribute it when it is completed. Most P-Ds are many pages long, and most of them contain substantial amounts of "boilerplate" (provisions which through the years have developed to the point where they have become standard) and the method of determining net receipts discussed in the prior chapter. There are, however, a great many items in the boilerplate that deserve greater attention than they normally receive, particularly when considered from the producer's point of view.

PRODUCER'S COMPENSATION

The producer comes to the distributor with a package. Assuming that the package consists of an option paid by the producer to acquire motion picture rights to a literary property and a screenplay, the first thing that the producer will bargain for and usually receive is repayment for whatever costs he has incurred in the project to date. These include not only the costs of optioning the literary property and having the screenplay written, but such other preproduction expenses as drafting the option agreement and writer's agreement, location scouting, legal fees, and other incidental expenses. Sometimes, however, such reimbursement is made only upon the commencement of principal photography. The producer will also want the distributor to assume all of his executory obligations pursuant to his contracts with the elements brought to the distributor (for example, rights payments).

Because the P-D ordinarily contemplates the development of a literary property or screenplay, most distributors want to make all or the biggest part of the producer's compensation contingent upon the successful development of the picture. In other words, only if the film is completed, will the producer receive all the money owed to him; if the film is not made, the producer would receive a limited sum, if any, for his services during the development period. Provisions for the producer's fee vary greatly in the amount of cash compensation, profit participation, and method of payment. Typically, the producer is paid a modest fee (rarely more than $25,000) to cover the period extending from when he enters into an agreement with the distributor to when the distributor either sets the picture for production or abandons it (to be discussed in this chapter under "Abandonment"). If the picture does go forward, the remainder of the fee is paid according to a variety of schedules, the most common of which allows for: 20 percent in equal weekly installments over the scheduled period of preproduction (usually about eight weeks), 60 percent in equal weekly installments over the scheduled period of principal photography, 10 percent upon delivery by the director of his first cut of the picture, and 10 percent upon delivery of the picture to the distributor. The producer may either get a fixed percent of the receipts of the picture (on a net profits or some gross formula basis), or such a percentage reducible by all non-financier third parties. This concept will be discussed more fully in Chapter Nine relating to the Producer's Profits.

THE CONTRACTING ENTITY AND ARTISTIC CONTROL

Under the format of the P-D, the producer ordinarily forms a new corporation as the contracting entity and engages all of the talent and other personnel. From the distributor's point of view, there are advantages and disadvantages to this arrangement.

The distributor may wish to avoid the necessity of entering into union agreements and the problems of doing business in different states, particularly if the picture is going to be filmed outside of the major domestic production locales of New York or California. With this arrangement, it is also easier for the distributor to walk away from a deal assuming it wants to do that: since the producer has signed all the contracts with third parties, he is solely responsible for those contracts unless the distributor has been obligated to guarantee some of them.

If, however, the distributor wants day-to-day control over the course of the film's production, it makes more sense for it to utilize its own production subsidiary and directly engage the talent. Then, if there are disputes between the producer and the distributor, the rights are vested in the distributor, and the producer will have a much more difficult time enforcing his desires. If the producer's production company is the contracting entity, all of the distributor's rights are derivative and thus harder for the distributor to enforce. Cognizant of that fact, distributors take either an assignment of each contract or a power of attorney from the producer in the P-D to enforce the producer's rights under his contracts. The producer will of course want to use his own production company, since this gives him more autonomy and creative control over the project.

If the producer has a number of different film projects in development at the same time, when a P-D is entered into he should attempt, if possible, to set up a timetable establishing the point at which the production will proceed past the preproduction stage and into principal photography. In that way he can ensure that he will have only one picture in the principal photography stage at a time. Ordinarily the distributor will insist that the producer render exclusive services to the film for six or eight weeks prior to the commencement of principal photography and at least until principal photography is completed, and thereafter on a first-priority basis.

There are various formulas for the control of creative elements in the film that range from the distributor having the sole and uncontrolled right to approve each element at its sole discretion to the producer retaining some right of cast selection and approval that is binding upon the distributor. Rarely, the producer may have the right to designate all the elements. Because it is financing the project, the distributor will ordinarily have all cast and director approvals.

A related question is which of the parties has the right to select the personnel—whatever the approval rights. Under most P-Ds, the producer proposes and the distributor disposes. In other words, the producer makes the selections and the distributor approves or disapproves them.

A producer may propose a number of alternative individuals for a function from whom the distributor must select one. Sometimes a distributor will insist that an actor or director under prior contract to the distributor be used. If the package already includes talent and a director, the removal of one element by the distributor may jeopardize the package. The distributor sometimes allows the producer to designate minor cast and production personnel under certain conditions: salaries must be within the budget and not in excess of any individual's normal rate, no work permits are required, the personnel are guild members and are experienced in their professions, and the distributor has not experienced difficulties with any individual before. Generally, if a distributor does not like the producer's selection, the producer may choose others in order to secure approval, but the P-D must provide that one party or the other has the final right to designate.

One sensible way of setting up the P-D is to provide that the producer shall, within a certain number of weeks after delivery of a first draft screenplay, give the distributor a rough budget breakdown. Provided no location scouting that involves travel is required, the producer can generally hire a production manager for a fairly modest cost, someone who can assess the first draft of the screenplay and give a rough idea of what it will cost to produce the film, leaving aside, of course, the cost of the principal stars and the director, which varies, depending upon the personnel selected.

The producer must also consider any timetable conflicts inherent in the script. For instance, if the picture can be made only in the winter because of the nature of the story, the package must be arranged with that particular season in mind. Should the project require a particular locale, this can create another problem. No matter what the P-D provides, the more organized the producer and the more carefully the production is planned, the more likely the distributor will be to give the producer's effort favorable consideration.

Once the distributor approves the producer's budget breakdown, the producer must sign the director and the principal members of the cast. The problem is then to coordinate these elements so that they are all available at the time principal photography is to begin. In addition, while the search for a cast and a director is going on, the producer must prepare, and the distributor should finance the cost of preparing, a detailed budget and a shooting schedule based on the script. Again, there are difficulties. When a director or particular actor is hired, each sometimes wants the privilege of supervising a revision of the script or at least a polish of it. Scene changes will increase script costs, they may increase or decrease production costs and may affect the shooting schedule and locations. Ordinarily the producer comes to the distributor with a proposed film at an estimated price. If the producer has a script, the distributor can make a more sensible evaluation of how much the picture should cost. This evaluation will change if there are script revisions and will necessitate a further review of other production details.

When the distributor approves the major items of the production—the principal cast, the director, budget, script, shooting schedule, locations, and laboratory—and has set a firm start date for principal photography, the P-D ordinarily provides that the distributor "set the picture for production." At this time the producer usually becomes "pay or play" for his full producing fee. This means that subject only to events outside the control of the parties and the producer's breach of contract, death, or disability, the distributor must pay the producer his full fee, even if the picture is never made or if the distributor fires the producer and replaces him.

PRODUCER'S RIGHT
TO CONTINGENT COMPENSATION

But what happens to the producer's right to contingent compensation (such as deferments and net profits) when the distributor sets the picture for production and completes it, but sometime between those two events fires the producer for reasons other than the producer's breach, death, or disability? The strong producer attempts to have 100 percent of his contingent compensation fully vested upon the distributor's electing to proceed with the production of the picture. The distributor, of course, will attempt to provide that no contingent compensation will be payable to the producer unless the picture is completed under his direct supervision. The usual compromise is that the contingent compensation will be prorated on some formula related to the amount of time he has worked. This is often calculated by giving the producer a fraction of his contingent compensation, the numerator of which is the amount of salary paid to him up to the time he is replaced, and the denominator of which is the total salary owed to him. For example, suppose the producer is to receive 15 percent of 100 percent of the net profits and a salary of $600,000. The picture is set for production, and the producer is replaced after having been paid $400,000. The producer would then be entitled to two-thirds of his original profit participation (or 10 percent of 100 percent of the net profits). Alternatively, the numerator may be based on the amount of footage photographed under the supervision of the producer and used in the final cut of the film, and the denominator is the amount of footage in the total running time of the film. The latter concept, however, is more typically applied to directors.

ABANDONMENT

If the distributor at any point prior to principal photography disapproves of any of the major elements of a production, the P-D ordinarily provides that the distributor may abandon the project. Indeed, most P-Ds afford the distributor the right to abandon the film at any time for any reason, and some P-Ds give the producer a right to force an abandonment under certain circumstances. For example, if a P-D is signed before the distributor is willing to set the project for production, the agreement usually specifies the steps the distributor must take toward getting the picture made within certain periods of time; not taking these steps, the distributor will be deemed to have abandoned the project. Usually, if the project has been inactive for a period of four to nine months (for example, no further writing has been ordered, no budgeting or casting is in progress, and no pay-or-play agreements have been entered into or negotiations underway for any major elements), the picture will be deemed abandoned.

Sometimes the producer in such a case will be entitled to a reversion of those rights (subject to a lien on those rights in favor of the distributor that is equal to the development costs it incurred up to that point of abandonment, plus interest). More commonly, the producer will have a "turnaround" right in the project. This gives him an option (usually of one year) to purchase all rights in the property from the distributor at an agreed upon purchase price (usually an amount equal to the direct costs incurred by the distributor until that time, interest on that cost, sometimes an overhead charge of between 10 percent and 15 percent, and a net profit participation of between 2.5 percent and 5 percent in the picture if it is produced elsewhere). If the producer does not exercise this option within the applicable period, he loses all his rights in the project. The distributor will also usually require the producer to resubmit the project if the producer decides to change any major element. The producer must be careful that he not be required to resubmit the project to the distributor for any reason once the distributor has been paid its costs, interest, and overhead. As a practical matter, however, when a producer is successful in setting a project up with another distributor, the turnaround provisions with the original distributor are frequently renegotiated, as the original distributor is of course quite happy to see the return of any of its investment at all.

The P-D may enumerate a number of reasons for which the distributor may abandon the project, some of which have nothing to do with the artistic merit of the project. For example, if the distributor has paid for the writing of a number of scripts or extensive revisions, and the production costs have materially escalated, the producer may be directed not to proceed. Sometimes the studio executive backing the project leaves and the project follows the executive to his new studio.

OVERHEAD AND PROFESSIONAL FEES

The producer must consider his own overhead when assessing his deal. Many producers employ a full-time secretary and development and production staff. While the picture is in the process of being produced, the salaries of secretary and staff, the office rental, the telephone, and all other overhead items must still be paid. The producer will ordinarily ask the distributor to pay or to reimburse him for all or a part of that overhead. Obviously if the producer has a number of projects going at one time, there will be an allocation of such expenditures.

Another item considered part of the producer's cost is attorneys' fees. Sometimes the producer's attorneys will do the legal work on the production, and the producer negotiates to include the attorneys' fees as an item in the budget to be paid for by the distributor. Sometimes a distributor retains an attorney to do the legal work on a reduced fee or flat fee basis, and may also add to the budget the cost of services of its own legal department. In negotiating the P-D, the producer and distributor will determine whether the distributor's in-house attorneys will perform the production legal work, or whether the producer will hire his own attorneys. Of course, the distributor is an adverse party to the producer in the negotiation of the P-D so the producer will need his own attorneys for this negotiation and will be solely responsible for their fees.

Some of the other basic negotiating points of a P-D relate to matters that also occur in the talent and director's agreements and are often contained in a separate agreement between the producer and the distributor's production company.

BILLING CREDIT TO PRODUCER

It is customary for the individual producer of a film to receive screen credit on a separate card from the other credits and credit in paid advertising in the form: "Produced by John Doe." A separate card means that the producer's name is displayed on the screen without any other names for a period long enough to be read. The producer's credit customarily immediately precedes the credit to the director (which is usually the last credit in front-end credits, or "main titles") and is of equal size. This is also true in advertising. The various types of "excluded advertising," in which the distributor does not have to give the producer credit, will be discussed in Chapter Seven, *Production Agreements with Talent*.

In addition to the credit just mentioned, some producers (or their production company) receive a production credit—"A John Doe Production"—both on the screen and in advertising. Whether the producer gets this credit, the size of the credit in relation to other credits and the title of the film, and the position of the credit are all negotiable points. While the production credit is usually more prominent and is above the title of the film, only the person receiving the "produced by" credit will be entitled to accept an Academy Award for best picture. In any event, distributors are becoming increasingly resistant to the proliferation of credits, both on-screen and in paid advertising.

A distribution company usually takes a releasing or presentation credit. Occasionally, one of the chief production executives of the distributor's company will want an executive producer or production executive credit. This is all negotiable and depends on the custom and practice of the distribution company involved. Some distribution companies insist on one thing, others on something else.

FINANCIAL CONTROL AND TAKEOVER OF PRODUCTION

Most important from the producer's point of view is a contractual commitment by the distributor that it will finance the total cost of the film's production (if it is an all-rights deal), that it will advance all of the moneys for the film's distribution (sometimes the producer will negotiate for the minimum amount the distributor will be required to spend on prints and advertising), and that the producer will not be liable for any production or distribution costs, whether or not the picture exceeds the budget. A distributor will sometimes agree to finance the cost of production of a film only up to a budgetary limit that it has previously approved. On these occasions, the producer will be required to secure a "completion bond"—a guarantee that the distributor can call upon if the cost of production exceeds the approved budget (see Chapter Six under "Completion Bond"). This is required, however, only where the distributor does not have day-to-day control over the production and is not using borrowed funds to finance the film. If the distributor agrees to finance over-budget costs, it may insist that it receive a fee payable to itself as guarantor as part of the budget—recoupable by the distributor as part of the production costs with overhead and interest.

Ordinarily the distributor, to ensure and oversee financial control, will require that a production account be opened in a bank approved by the distributor and will insist that all checks from the production account be cosigned by a representative of the producer and a representative of the distributor (the production auditor).

A procedure is usually established whereby the producer advises the distributor how much money is needed for the week's shooting, and the distributor then deposits that amount in the production account. A distributor will usually require a detailed weekly statement of costs and expenses, a schedule of the estimated amount of money needed to complete production of the photoplay, and a daily report showing which scenes of the script have been photographed that day. These breakdowns are prepared on standard production forms by the production manager or the associate producer.

Some distribution companies will insist on having a representative present throughout shooting to countersign checks and generally keep the distributor informed, particularly as to whether the production is exceeding budget or running behind schedule. Such a representative usually starts work a few weeks prior to principal photography and continues until one or two weeks after its completion or until the film is ready to be delivered to the distributor. The cost of the representative is not considered an artificial charge in that the distributor normally pays the representative a sum set forth in the budget. It is, nevertheless, a charge that the producer may feel is unnecessary because it is his responsibility to bring the picture in on time and on budget.

Usually, the individual producer of the film is primarily responsible for its packaging, for making the necessary staff and budgetary decisions, for making major production decisions during production and postproduction, and for keeping everybody happy. All of this is done under the supervision of one or more of the distributor's creative/production executives. The producer hires a line producer, an associate producer, or a production manager to do the actual detail work and to prepare the financial information and production reports mentioned above. The production manager also takes care of compliance with the various guild agreements and the other day-to-day matters that affect the production of the photoplay.

Given the possibility that the cost of production may exceed the budget, a distributor will ordinarily try to limit his exposure. For example, he will retain the right, under certain circumstances, to assume extensive control of the production. Usually, the P-D will provide that the distributor can take over production if it appears that costs are exceeding the budget by a stated amount (such as 10 percent), or if, for any reason at all, production is falling a specified number of days behind the shooting schedule. The number of days will vary from a minimum of five upward. (The take-over right is similar to that of a completion guarantor, as discussed in Chapter Six under "Completion Bond.")

Sometimes days lost as a result of events of force majeure (which include not only acts of God such as a fire or a flood, but strikes, war, and other factors outside the distributor's control) are excluded from the computation. Frequently the number of days the production is behind is directly proportionate to the amount by which the production is exceeding the budget. From a distributor's point of view, it should not matter greatly if the production is only a few days behind, as long as the production winds up on budget. Unfortunately, however, each day of shooting costs a fixed number of dollars, and if the production is running behind, unless unanticipated savings can be made, the cost of production will undoubtedly exceed the final budget.

It is questionable whether or not the right to take over production is meaningful; this may often depend on whether the distributor has personnel capable of actually assuming the production of the film. If the distributor does take over production, it has the right to remove any and all personnel connected with the film, including the producer and the director. Such a removal is usually effected under the pay-or-play clause, which provides that the person removed is still entitled to his or her full fees (and perhaps some percentage of contingent compensation, as discussed earlier under "Producer's Right to Contingent Compensation"). If the distributor, however, believed that any particular person behaved in a particularly irresponsible or egregious manner, the distributor might remove that person under the default provisions, claiming that the person breached his or her agreement with the distributor (or production company) and that no further compensation is due. Under these circumstances, the distributor might even bring suit against that person for damages, although that is extremely rare. Of course, any money in excess of the budget that is spent by the distributor to complete the film increases the negative cost of the film for the purpose of the net profits calculation (and would bear interest and overhead), and also triggers the overbudget add-back penalties for those who are entitled to contingent compensation as well as being subject to those penalties. (See Chapter 4, *Contingent Compensation*, under "Negative Cost and Overbudget Penalty.") Note that some participants such as writers and actors are not usually subject to those penalties, but a director and producer may be more subject to the penalties than an actor.

In actuality, a distributor's takeover of production is a very rare occurrence. Ordinarily, the producer has developed a relationship with the principal members of the cast, the director, and the crew, and also has the day-to-day knowledge of what is happening that a wise distributor will not want to lose. It is not unusual for the producer to be the only person who knows what is going on and, consequently, to become virtually indispensable. Moreover, distribution companies do not necessarily employ the personnel to take over a production. Therefore, a distributor is more likely to use the threat of a takeover as a club over the producer's head in order to effect economies in production or to modify the shooting schedule if it appears that filming is getting out of hand. The threat becomes a reality only as a last resort, as this usually requires shutting down production of the picture for a period of time—a delay that would be very expensive.

To avoid a distributor's takeover of production triggered by the film's going over budget, in negotiating a P-D, an experienced attorney for the producer will, for the purpose of determining when the film goes overbudget, ask for the same cushion and exclusions he would try to get in an overbudget add-back penalty or takeover provisions.

MULTI-PICTURE AGREEMENTS

In the event that a distributor signs with a producer or a production company for a multiple-picture deal, the distributor may be required to cover for a stated period all or part of the producer's overhead and to give him enough capital to commence and develop the projects. The overhead normally includes an office, a secretary, miscellaneous office and entertainment costs, and, sometimes, a limited development staff such as one or two script readers. The distributor treats this overhead as a cost of production of the first film to be reallocated among subsequent films, almost always charges interest on this cost, and usually attempts to impose its own percentage overhead charge as well. It should also be noted that the distributor will usually attempt to include this charge in the definition of negative cost for all profit participants. But those who have nothing to do with the producer's deal and do not benefit from it will usually object to this since it seems unfair to burden their efforts with the producer's overhead on completely separate projects.

Today, studios rarely cross-collateralize the net profits and losses among the various films produced under a multi-picture deal. But when net profits are cross-collateralized, the producer should provide for the periodic release of some net profits or face the certainty that he will not be paid anything for as long as even one of the pictures remains unrecouped. A common problem with multi-picture deals is that if the first picture is financially successful, the producer often attempts to renegotiate the contract terms, while if the first picture is not successful, the distributor may not want to have anything further to do with the producer.

OVERHEAD CHARGES

The attorney negotiating for the producer in a P-D must carefully consider certain additional charges the distributor may want to include in the agreement. One such charge might be the distributor's general overhead, which it will wish to include as a percentage of negative cost in the cost of production of the photoplay. Some of these charges have already been considered in dealing with the computation of contingent compensation. Other charges may be partially artificial, such as the cost of studio facilities, which is a percentage of the budget overhead charge. It may be difficult to determine how much of the charge represents costs that would have to be paid in any event, depending on the availability and price of the studio facilities. Most studios insist on a direct charge for the use of their facilities in addition to the overhead fee recouped as part of the definition of net profits. Note, however, that the overhead fee is rarely included in the budget itself. As we have seen, the studio may impose a fee equivalent to a completion bond fee for the risk of having to furnish over-budget costs.

STRUCTURE OF P-D

Some distribution companies provide in their contracts that ownership of all rights and the copyright in a photoplay are held by the distributor and that the producer has an interest only in sums equal to net profits derived from the film. The distributor's position is that its ownership of these rights place it in a better negotiating position in the event of a disagreement with the producer. Moreover, while at present there is no investment tax credit, if the law should change, such a credit might be payable only to the holder of legal title to the film.

Some distributors permit the copyright in the photoplay to be solely in the name of the producer until the film is delivered to the distributor, subject to the distributor's rights under the P-D. Where there is no guarantee, this insulates the distributor from claims made by those under contract to the production company. The P-D usually provides that a takeover by the distributor results in an immediate and automatic assignment to the distributor of all rights in the film.

In order to secure the money advanced to the production company, the distributor, in lieu of copyright ownership, may take a security interest in the picture, including the copyright in the literary property as well as the preprint film material. The distributor would then consider the monies advanced to the producer as non-recourse production loans and receive interest on them. Each time a sum of money is advanced to the producer under this arrangement, the distributor receives a promissory note for that loan from the producer. Usually such an arrangement provides that in the event the distributor has not recouped the cost of production by a specified date, the loan becomes due, and the distributor could acquire the producer's interest in the film in satisfaction of his debt. However, the producer is not personally liable to repay the loan. The producer could, in theory, prevent the acquisition by paying the distributor the unrecouped balance of the loan and interest. This possibility is usually eliminated by the requirement that the producer assign all of its rights in the film when the producer delivers the film to the distributor.

This kind of arrangement makes the P-D a loan transaction and holds certain inherent dangers for both the producer and the distributor. The producer naturally would want to retain copyright ownership but he would also want to be protected against a foreclosure that might eliminate his interest in net profits, particularly if the film is barely recouped or if after the foreclosure a new form of distribution emerges that promises to generate large sums of money for the picture.

On the other hand, the difficulty from the distributor's point of view is that if the producer retains ownership and copyright interest in the picture and there is a dispute between him and the distributor, the latter may find it both expensive and time-consuming to foreclose its lien in order to enforce its rights under the security documentation, particularly if the producer files for bankruptcy.

Another possibility, though unusual, is for the copyright to be held by the producer and distributor jointly. Under this arrangement, the producer grants the distributor a security interest in the producer's right, title, and interest in the film; as a joint ownerof the copyright and the underlying rights, the distributor would have more protection in the event of a dispute with the producer.

The contractual responsibilities of the production company, and how these responsibilities are affected by breaches by third parties, should also be considered. Bear in mind that in most cases the distributor will have final control with respect to all personnel, although it is still the production company's responsibility to select the principal members of the cast and production elements. If a person other than an employee of the production company violates his or her contract with the production company, this should not be considered a P-D breach on the part of the production company. In other words, if a screenwriter agrees to deliver a script by July 1, and does not deliver until August 1, the screenwriter may be in breach, but the production company would not be in breach of its P-D with the distributor. The more control the distributor has over the selection of production elements, the less responsibility the producer has if any element breaches.

INSURANCE

During the principal photography of the film, the producer must discharge various responsibilities, all of which are spelled out in the P-D. One such is to get the necessary insurance. Initially, the producer must obtain production liability insurance and, if the distributor does not already carry it, a form of insurance known as an "errors-and-omissions" policy that protects the distributor, the producer, and their employees against claims by third parties for copyright infringement, libel and slander, unfair competition, invasion of privacy, and other potential causes of legal action. Such claims might arise from defamatory or infringing material contained in the underlying literary property, the screenplay, the film itself, or, for example, from photographing a person without his or her consent or a place without a location release. (A production manager will generally know when and from whom releases are required.)

To protect itself against such claims, the insurance company usually requires that counsel for the production be reasonably experienced in film matters and take reasonable care in clearing rights. The fact is that most distributors carry errors-and-omissions insurance under blanket policies (which include coverage for a number of its pictures), and pay a lower premium rate than the producer would if he tried to buy insurance for only one picture. Generally, the distributor pays a fixed premium for each picture endorsed under the policy. If a lump sum is paid no matter how many pictures are endorsed, an allocation of this amount would have to be made for each particular production. Most distributors, while taking advantage of the blanket rate, charge the production company with the higher per-picture premium.

An insurance problem that occasionally surfaces is that the errors-and-omissions policy will cover only those claims against employees of the insured that are committed during the time of employment. Therefore, if a producer has a script written prior to obtaining errors-and-omissions insurance (or prior to making a deal with a distributor who already carries such insurance), and a claim is subsequently brought against the film, the insurance carrier may attempt to deny coverage to the producer on this ground. One solution, then, is for the producer to obtain preproduction errors-and-omissions insurance. It is particularly important that the producer be included as a named insured under the errors-and-omissions policy. If he is, then the insurance company waives any rights of subrogation it may have against the production company for any claim covered by insurance that might be deemed a breach by the producer of the P-D (such as his erroneous representations and warranties as to the originality of the literary material on which the film is based). In other words, even if the production company violated the personal or property rights of a third party, the insurance company waives its right to sue the production company. Some distributors agree to this inclusion, and ordinarily there is no extra charge for it. Even if there is an additional premium, the distributor may assume it; if the distributor will not, then the producer may wish to pay for the protection. Sometimes an insurance company will refuse to include the production company as a "named" insured but may agree to add the production company as an additional insured. This means that although the insurance company will not waive its right of subrogation, it will furnish the production company a defense reserving the right to sue the production company if it settles or loses. Since defense costs are high, the furnishing of a defense is a meaningful benefit to the production company. The insurance company will cover loss to the insured arising from any claim up to the stated policy limits, which are usually at least $1,000,000 for one claim and $3,000,000 for all claims, and are now commonly $10,000,000 for one or all. Of course, higher limits can be obtained. There is usually a deductible per claim of $10,000. The term of the errors-and-omissions insurance is usually three to five years.

The insurance company often will not cover losses incurred as a result of an injunction against the distribution of the film. In that event, both production and distribution costs could be lost. Even if the insurance company reimburses the cost of prints and advertising, there is a considerable gap in coverage.

The insurance company ordinarily requires a copy of the title report with respect to the underlying literary property. The producer's responsibility under the insurance policy includes checking fictional names and locations to make sure there are no real-life similarities, getting permission to photograph people and locations appearing in the script, and getting permission to use real names of people, places, or products mentioned in the script and any stock footage used in the movie. These are generally handled by the production manager or specialized companies hired by the production manager.

Cast Insurance

Another important form of insurance is "cast insurance." If any member of the cast covered by cast insurance should die or become disabled, the insurance company will pay the amount of the loss above a stated deductible. Again, many of the distributors have their own blanket cast insurance policy under which each of their pictures is included. The cost of this insurance is generally based on a percentage of the cost of film production, though it will also depend upon the number of weeks of principal photography. Cast insurance ordinarily begins four weeks prior to and continues to the end of principal photography. Under the cast insurance policy, the basic premium covers a minimum of six persons, usually the director and five of the principal members of the cast. When more people must be insured, the premium increases. Two conditions of cast insurance are that all members of the cast covered by the policy receive a medical examination by a doctor of the insurance company's choice and that they not engage in any especially hazardous activities or other activities specified in the policy. If a member of the cast does not pass the insurance examination, he may be excluded from the policy, a higher deductible amount may be fixed, an increased premium may be charged, or a particular ailment may not be covered.

It is possible to buy cast insurance covering a period longer than the time of principal photography—that is, for a stated number of weeks prior to principal photography—on payment of an additional premium. Under certain circumstances, the cost is worthwhile, particularly if expenses are being incurred well in advance of principal photography and the film is a showcase for an actor or director. In lieu of cast insurance, life insurance (which is much cheaper) is sometimes obtained for the period of film production to cover part of the risk.

Cast insurance policies can raise some very complicated questions. For instance, for a person with a recurring injury, was there, in fact, one injury with one deductible amount to be taken into consideration, or two separate injuries with two deductibles? This question can also apply in the case of an illness. Another difficulty involves actually proving the amount of a loss; and success in maintaining a claim will depend upon the ability of the production supervisor and the production accountants to itemize the elements of loss flowing from the inability to perform. For example, if the shooting of the photoplay must be rescheduled or shot in a different sequence because one of the members of the cast is ill, a determination must be made as to how much time has actually been lost, how much additional cost has been incurred, whether payments to other cast members who are on standby because of the illness should be included, and whether a scene must be reshot or a double used.

Cast insurance policies will contain a clause providing that losses must be due "directly" to an injury: if there is some intervening factor that could arguably have caused the loss, the insurance company need not pay. For example, if, on the day that a member of the cast became ill, a fire broke out and all the sets were destroyed, there would be no coverage and no payment under the cast insurance policy. The fire would be the intervening factor that caused the loss, and there presumably would be no claim.

To take another example, suppose a member of the cast became disabled for twenty days during which time snow was on the ground and snow sequences were scheduled to be shot for thirty days. If at the end of the twenty-day period, the snow was gone and the sequences had to be shot elsewhere at substantially greater costs, it must be determined whether the insurance company is liable for the greater cost of shooting the snow sequences in another location, or is liable only for the losses that occurred because of the inability to shoot the snow sequences for twenty days in the original location. Obviously, the insurance company will take the latter view. Disputes inevitably arise because no form of insurance policy can cover all of the potential contingencies.

If an actor who has completed half of his role suddenly dies, the cost of reshooting the entire film with another actor might well exceed the cost of terminating the production in the middle. The insurance company would prefer to terminate in this case, but the producer and the distributor might want to proceed—and reshoot many scenes—with a new actor. In such a case, the insurance company may argue that it was liable only for the costs incurred had the production in fact been terminated. This is not an unreasonable position and characterizes the uncertainty of the insurance protection afforded. Of course, no one will insure a producer against an actor quitting before completion of the film or other third-party breaches.

Miscellaneous Insurance

Other types of insurance obtained usually include "faulty stock insurance" and "negative insurance." All suppliers of raw film stock will limit their liability for defective stock to the cost of replacement. Faulty stock insurance will cover the cost to the producer (after the imposition of a deductible) of having to reshoot scenes because they were originally photographed on defective film. Negative insurance protects the negative of the photoplay, usually allowing for a deductible, against damage or destruction. All laboratories limit their liability for damage to a negative to the replacement cost of the raw stock; they are not liable for the production cost of the film itself. Negative insurance coverage usually is effective at the commencement of principal photography and is maintained until a duplicate negative is manufactured. After that, coverage is usually discontinued because it is very expensive. Ordinarily, the original picture negative and the duplicate negative are kept in separate places, so if one is damaged by fire or other accident, the other will not be harmed. The producer and distributor take the chance that there will not be simultaneous disasters at both places of storage.

Still other insurance normally purchased for a motion picture includes worker's compensation insurance; aviation insurance, if applicable; fire, theft, and property insurance; third-party liability insurance; and insurance that may be required for any special risks involved in the production. While insurance against events such as fire, flood, earthquake, etc., is sometimes available, it is usually so expensive that most producers forgo it. A number of insurance brokers specialize in entertainment insurance and are ready to furnish information about the types of insurance appropriate for a particular production.

UNION CONTRACTS

Most P-Ds provide that the independent production company will be responsible for entering into any collective bargaining agreements required or advisable to produce the picture. Some unions, typically the Screen Actors Guild, require a bond from the production company or a lien on the picture to secure payment of salaries and residuals but will accept, instead of the lien, the distribution company's guarantee to ensure payment of their members' salaries and the residual payments that go directly to the guild, assuming the distribution company has acquired global rights and is a studio.

It is occasionally possible to get some form of concession from the various guilds involved in production, either through separate negotiation or because they have announced concessions for low-budget films. The separate negotiations are often verbal and subject to agreement between the production manager and the union officials, and they vary from film to film. Ordinarily, the various union agreements are signed "as is" by the production company. Which concessions to "bargain for" depends upon the special problems involved in a film's production. For instance, if a lot of night shooting is required, one might negotiate a later starting time in order to reduce the overtime cost. Which guild agreements, if any, have to be signed depends upon which guilds have jurisdiction, and that, in turn, depends in part upon the place in which the picture is being made. If a film is being shot at more than one location and more than one guild claims jurisdiction, the conflicting claims may cause the producer serious problems.

Most unions will provide for a lower rate of minimum payments to their members if the production is a low-budget film. The definition of a low-budget film will depend upon the particular union's collective-bargaining agreement. A guild member may be hired at a time when the photoplay has not been fully developed (this is especially true of writers) and the budget of the film is not known. The producer is allowed to predict in good faith whether this will be high-budget or low-budget. But if the producer enjoys a low-budget rate and the film's budget subsequently exceeds a union's definition of "low-budget," the producer will be required to pay additional compensation as soon as the budget goes over that amount.

The major unions that affect theatrical motion pictures are the International Association of Theater and Stage Employees (IATSE) which through its locals has jurisdiction over such technical functions as those of cinematographer and camera crew, production designer, grips, and transportation workers; the Directors Guild of America, Inc. (DGA) which has jurisdiction over directors, assistant directors (including the first and second assistant directors), and unit production managers; the Screen Actors Guild (SAG) which has jurisdiction over the actors; the Screen Extras Guild (SEG) which has jurisdiction over the extras; the Writers Guild of America, Inc. (WGA) which has jurisdiction over writers (including jurisdiction over the option and purchase of motion picture/television material written by WGA members); and the American Federation of Musicians (AFM) which has jurisdiction over instrumentalists, arrangers, and copyists (but not composers).

A guild has jurisdiction only when a producer agrees to sign the guild's collective-bargaining agreement and thus becomes a signatory. Conversely, a guild will have no jurisdiction over a person's services unless he or she is a member of that guild or works for a producer who is a signatory. While no guild will permit its members to work for a non-signatory producer, most guilds will permit signatory producers to hire nonmembers so long as either they are treated as guild members (as is the case with the WGA) or they agree to become members of the applicable guild (as is the case with SAG).

An interesting feature of motion picture unions is that there is currently no reciprocity among them as to jurisdiction. In other words, a producer may choose to become a signatory to all, none, or any number of the unions without incurring any obligations to any other unions. Consequently, a producer may become signatory only to the DGA and SAG, which would allow him to use a DGA director and SAG actors but to have the film written by a non-WGA writer and to use a non-IATSE crew to produce the film.

The advantage to a producer in using union members lies principally in the fact that the most prominent and experienced talent and technical members of the motion picture community are invariably members of their respective unions. If a producer, therefore, wants to hire a star or a major director, he will have no choice but to become a signatory to SAG or the DGA. Of course, the disadvantage to the producer of becoming a union signatory is not only that this will result in greater expenses because minimum salaries will be higher and bear fringe benefit payments, but also because more restrictive working and related conditions will apply to the production of the film and residual and reuse payments will have to be made to most of the union members for release of the film in such other markets as network television, pay TV, and videocassette (known as the "supplemental markets").

If a producer is averse to becoming a union signatory, he may sometimes find that a major element (such as a star or director) will not agree to sign with him unless he changes his mind. This will happen particularly often with a major director, who will want to be assured that the writers, actors, and crew are all experienced professionals.

CUTTING, EDITING, AND DELIVERY OF COMPLETED FILM

Most P-Ds control the content of the film by requiring that before release it obtain a rating other than NC-17 by the Motion Picture Association of America (MPAA). Currently, the MPAA's ratings are: NC-17 (persons under age 17 not admitted), R (persons under 17 require accompanying parent or adult guardian), PG-13 (parents strongly cautioned: some material may be inappropriate for children under 13), PG (parental guidance suggested: some material may not be suitable for children), and G (suitable for everyone). Additionally, in the P-D the distributor may require the producer to deliver either a completed television version of the film (one that will comply with television censorship practices) or television "cover shots" (alternate scenes that would replace objectionable ones so as to bring the film into conformity with television standards).

Most P-Ds usually give the distributor the right to cut and edit the photoplay. However, under the DGA Minimum Basic Agreement, the director has the right to at least one cut of the photoplay, and the producer, depending on his bargaining position, may have additional cutting rights after the director has delivered his last cut and has had his last preview. Sometimes the director is entitled to two or three cuts, with previews after each one. In the discussion of the Director's Agreement in Chapter Eight, some of the specific issues relating to cutting and preview rights are more fully explored.

Some directors obtain the right of "final cut," which requires the distributor to release the photoplay exactly as delivered to the producer by the director. The director's final cut, however, is extremely rare and, when granted, usually applies only to domestic (U.S. and Canadian) theatrical release. Thus, even when the director has the right of final cut, the distributor will ordinarily have the right to cut the photoplay for reasons of censorship, for foreign exhibition, and for the requirements of television or home video viewing, which may also involve "framing the film." Since a television screen is squarer than a theater screen, part of the picture may not fit — so that if two characters are facing each other at each edge of the theatrical screen, the television screen will only accommodate one face, either talking or reacting. In addition, the film speed may be altered slightly for time continuity. The distributor also has the right to insert or to authorize the insertion of commercials for television and even for theatrical release in some foreign countries.

With delivery of the completed film, another responsibility of the producer is to make sure that the billing credits, both on-screen and in paid advertising, conform to the contractual and guild requirements with regard to talent and production personnel. Usually, the producer prepares a summary of the screen and advertising-credit obligations that must be reviewed and approved by the distributor.

MATERIALS TO BE DELIVERED

The P-D requires the producer to deliver to the distributor the negative of the completed film and other picture materials: certain preprint materials (such as the independent music and effects tracks, dialogue tracks, additional footage not used), a textless background of the main and end titles, and such other materials as all contracts entered into by the producer relating to the film, music cue sheets, editorial notes, and the like. Deliveries of all of these items are conditions that must be met before a distributor will accept a completed film. From the producer's point of view the extent of the list is relatively unimportant because the distributor ultimately bears the cost of the materials. If they are considered production costs, they bear interest and overhead. If they are regarded as distribution expenses, they carry no interest charge and usually no overhead, which is usually charged only on advertising costs.

LABORATORY

Ordinarily, the distributor will also want to choose the laboratory that does the processing of the negative materials and the laboratory that manufactures the positive (release) prints of the film. Most distributors have blanket agreements with—and a few own—a particular laboratory and will ordinarily pay lower prices than a producer for processing one photoplay. However, a producer, director, or cinematographer may have a strong opinion about the quality of the work of a particular laboratory, and most agreements between a distributor and a laboratory will give the former the right to have the printing done at another laboratory if the producer or director insists upon it. Whether or not the producer can insist upon selecting the laboratory depends upon his bargaining position and the reputation of the particular laboratory that he wishes to use.

The distributor must secure its interests in the picture materials that are in the laboratory's possession in the event it takes over the film (whether for the producer's breach, bankruptcy, or other reason). This is accomplished either by specifying that legal title to the materials from inception be in the name of the distributor at the laboratory, or by means of a "laboratory access letter" (or a "laboratory pledgeholder's agreement"), which will be discussed in more detail in Chapter Six under "Using Production Loans to Finance Feature Films."

DEFAULT AND TERMINATION RIGHTS

The more elements of production over which the distributor grants the producer sole discretion, the more likely it is the distributor can claim that the producer is in default under the terms of the P-D. It's questionable whether a producer should insist upon having the contract specify all his rights to control production when, regardless of the contract, those same rights would be granted to him as a matter of the distributor's customary business practice. Should the producer succeed in enumerating specific rights in the agreement and then not exercise those rights properly, the distributor can easily claim a breach of contract. Conversely, if the distributor has all rights and all approvals and has in fact approved everything, it would be hard to argue successfully that the producer has breached the contract. Still, the fact remains that a producer who does not insist on enumeration of rights, relying on the distributor's usual business practices, may lose all meaningful control of the production if the distributor enforces the contract as written.

Whatever the contract may say, it is always prudent for the producer to clear in writing all important decisions with the distribution company. For once the distributor approves a decision, it is virtually impossible for it later to claim a breach based on that decision.

Leaving aside the questions of security documentation (documents securing the distributor's interest in the film) and enforceability, all P-Ds will provide for rights of termination and rights in the event of default. Most P-Ds provide that the distributor can terminate the production of a film at any time and for any reason. The producer may insist that termination be justified only by an event outside the control of the parties, such as an act of God, the death or disability of the director or a principal member of the cast, a cost overrun, or some other specific occurrence, but the distributor fights for the right to terminate for any reason whatsoever, at its own discretion—and usually wins.

Most P-Ds will provide that if there is a termination, the distributor will own the photoplay (unless there are abandonment and turnaround rights that allow the producer to buy back the picture), but the distributior pays when due any costs expended or incurred by the producer prior to the date of termination. These costs will usually include the pay-or-play commitments made to the director, the stars, and the individual producers, and payments of any terms of employment guaranteed to the crew and other cast members. This assumes that there is no breach of contract by any of the foregoing. Should there be a termination, the P-D must provide answers to the following questions: Is the producer entitled to the full producer's fee if the film is terminated in mid-production or only to that portion of the fee that has accrued or become payable prior to the date of termination? (In the normal course of production, a portion of the fee will become payable only upon delivery of the completed film to the distributor.) Is the producer entitled to net profits if the distribution company later completes and then releases the film? If the distribution company later decides to resume production of the film, does the producer have the option to be the producer again? If so, on what terms?

There are no cut-and-dried answers to these questions. Ordinarily, the distributor will have incurred so much cost if there is a termination, that it is most unlikely that the production will ever be resumed. Furthermore, the distributor will argue that it has suffered so great a financial loss that the producer should share part of that loss by accepting only the accrued portion of the production fee. On the other hand, if the termination is not the result of a breach or other wrongdoing by the producer, he will argue that the distributor assumed all risks in return for the substantial rewards that even a moderately successful film is likely to earn.

In the event of a default by the producer, most P-Ds provide that the distributor, in addition to remedies at law or equity, has any or all of the following rights: to terminate the production and the P-D; to take over production of the film from the producer (giving the distributor the right to fire the producer or to retain the producer while requiring him to follow all of the distributor's instructions); to offset any damages against income (including salary and contingent compensation) otherwise due the producer under the P-D or other agreements between the parties; and not to pay the balance of the producer's fee. Note that where the distributor does not have to finance the balance of the cost of production, the production company may still be responsible for payment of all obligations under its agreements with directors, actors, and technical personnel, as well as for studio facilities and the like. In addition, should the production company have an ownership interest in the film and the distributor have been granted a lien on this interest, then the distributor may exercise its contractual right to foreclose the lien.

To what extent can a producer whittle away at these rights of the distributor? Many distribution companies will agree that their rights in the event of a default will be exercised only if the default is material. Producers request a grace period to cure a breach or default. From the point of view of the distributor, it is senseless to permit a grace period with respect to certain defaults. For instance, if a producer becomes disorderly on the set every day, what point is there in giving him a five-day period to cure each separate default? Often this is resolved by giving the producer the right to cure only the first default. On the other hand, there are certain breaches of warranty or breaches of agreement that could conceivably be corrected within a grace period without prejudicing the distributor.

Even if it has substantial assets, the producer must not allow his production company to be potentially responsible for all or a portion of the cost of producing the photoplay if there is a default, for this is the very thing for which the distributor was supposed to assume responsibility. Similarly, no individual producer should sign a personal guarantee of the obligations undertaken by the production company.

On the other hand, the distributor can argue that because of the producer's breach it has incurred production costs it otherwise would have avoided, and these costs, at least, should be paid by the producer. For this reason, many production companies are set up as "no-asset" (other than the film) or single purpose corporations. In this way, if the distributor exercises its rights under the default provision of the contract or attempts to enforce repayment of production loans by calling due its promissory notes, the production company has no assets other than the film and thus acts as a shield for the individual producer who should have no personal liability. In that event, like it or not, the distributor will probably have to pay the production costs itself or risk the anger of unpaid talent and their lawyers and agents. The use of the no-asset corporation has become such a common practice that any agent or attorney who is even marginally sophisticated in negotiating on behalf of a significant production element will require a guarantee by the distributor (or some other known and solvent entity) of the obligations of the production entity. And the distributor is likely to agree to this for all the reasons indicated above.

Using a no-asset corporation may limit a producer's opportunities to effect tax planning. But, unless his production company has a strong enough bargaining position to eliminate from the P-D its liability for production costs in the event of a breach, the producer should definitely use a corporation without assets other than the film. Many P-Ds as initially drafted contain so many ways of putting the production technically in breach that the producer, if he did not request substantial changes, would be in breach of the agreement as soon as he finished signing it. However, if the producer has a weak bargaining position, few or none of these changes can be negotiated, particularly with a studio.

In other P-Ds, the obligations of the individual producer are clearly enumerated and he is asked to sign, in effect, a ratification of the agreement. More commonly, the individual producer will enter into a formal producer's agreement (the form of which is discussed in Chapter Nine) with his own production company. In those instances, the distributor may try to provide that a breach of one agreement is, at the distributor's election, a breach of both, arguing that the production company is but a tool of the producer, and anything it does must be considered his responsibility. Such a provision would make the producer individually liable even though the concept of damages under an individual producer's agreement may differ from the concept of damages under a P-D. Ordinarily, in the producer's agreement damages are not spelled out but must be proved in a lawsuit, whereas in the P-D, liability may be fixed in terms of repayment of production costs (in addition to the distributor's other rights and remedies at law). Producers are usually able to argue successfully against the imposition of this liability.

Note that there may be certain breaches by third parties during the course of the production that are not the responsibility of the production company. For instance, if an actor defaults under the terms of his contract with a production company, that certainly is not the production company's responsibility. If there is an event of force majeure, that also is not the production company's responsibility.

Ordinarily, during the course of production there is so much at stake for the distributor and the consequences of a dispute between the producer and distributor are so potentially disruptive to the shooting of a film that, even if the producer is in breach, the distributor will either nominally retain him but actually rely on other production personnel to complete production of the film, or wait until production is completed before exercising its rights and making a default claim against the producer.

PRODUCERS WARRANTIES AND REMEDIES OF PARTIES FOR BREACH

The usual P-D calls for the producer to make numerous warranties. As we have already noted, the distribution company will acquire from producer his rights in the literary property. In the course of that acquisition, as part of the P-D, the distribution company will ask the producer to offer the same warranties that the author gave him when he first acquired the literary property. The producer will argue that he can make such a warranty not outright but only to the best of his knowledge, information, and belief, or that only the author should make the warranty. The distributor will argue that the producer must warrant that which he is conveying. The contractual issue of warranties and representations regarding the underlying material (the novel and screenplay), though troublesome, usually has little or no practical significance. The reason for this is twofold. First, the distributor would never agree to finance the production if it had not already examined and approved the contents of all literary materials underlying the film and all agreements pursuant to which such materials were acquired (known as "chain of title documents"). Second, a distributor will always insist that errors-and-omissions insurance (which covers third party claims , such as libel, infringement, idea piracy, etc.) be in place. Thus, the literary material and chain-of-title documents will have been subject to three levels of review (the producer's, the distributor's, and the insurance carriers).

A producer must make other warranties: that he will acquire the usual rights from the cast, crew, and other personnel; that he will obtain proper releases; that he will not create liens, and so on. If the producer follows the customary clearance techniques during filming, if his agreements with cast and (where necessary) crew have all been approved by the distributor, and if the distributor's attorneys have approved all the contractual forms to be used for the production of the film, the producer does not have to worry too much about his warranties.

The distributor will want the producer to indemnify it against any claims in the case of a breach of warranty and will want the right to settle or dispose of the claims. The same principles with respect to indemnification, rights to settle and defend, and so on apply here that were discussed in the context of acquisition of rights in a literary property from an author.

The producer's remedies against the distributor, should the distributor breach the contract, are severely limited in the P-D. Almost all P-Ds provide that in the event the distributor breaches or is in default, the producer can sue only for money damages; he does not have the right to rescind the agreement nor the rights which the P-D grants to the distributor to enjoin or restrain the distribution or the advertising or exploitation of the photoplay. To the distributor, this clause is an absolute necessity because of the risk resulting from its absence—namely, that if the producer were to claim a breach and the distributor were to dispute the claim but lose in court, the producer could then prevent the film from being completed or distributed. In fact, the mere assertion of such a claim or the threat of an injunction would be a powerful weapon in the producer's hand. Since the distributor invests substantial sums of money in financing production of the film, the distributor must do everything possible to protect that investment. Moreover, if the distributor had to mortgage all or part of its interest in the film in order to obtain financing, the financier will insist that the distributor have the unrestricted right to distribute the film free from any threat of termination or injunction. Obviously, the financier is prejudiced if the distributor's rights to a film, and hence, the financier's security interest in the film as collateral, can be terminated because the financier's rights depend upon the distributor's title to the film.

Actually, the basic defaults a distributor can commit prior to the distribution of the film are either the failure to furnish money or the failure to accord proper billing credits in advertising the film. If the distributor fails to furnish money, either in financing the film or in paying producer's fees, there is nothing to prevent the producer from ceasing to render services. Of course, unless the production company has adequately protected itself, it may incur substantial liability to third parties. As stated, however, it is very rare for a distributor to discontinue financing production of a film. Once principal photography has started it has already committed so much money to the project that, unless some freakish catastrophe occurs that is not covered by insurance or the production becomes a runaway or the distributor runs out of funds, it is almost inconceivable that it would walk away from a film at that point. If a producer feels forced to sue for money damages, he should, at the very least, be certain that the distributor has the financial resources to pay a judgment. Even then, despite the fact that the producer has spent time in developing a project, is accepting a relatively small fixed fee (considering the amount of time most producers spend developing a project), and is hoping that net profits from the distribution of the film will be a major source of compensation, the court may well decide that it is too speculative to award damages based on potential net profits that might never be earned. To the extent that an award in money damages probably cannot compensate a producer fully, should he not have some rights of termination or injunction if a distributor stops financing or becomes bankrupt? The producer's argument is well taken, but almost no producers have the bargaining power to impose this view on distributors.

Most disagreements about billing credit are due to the inadvertent mistakes of the distributor. If the producer's credit is omitted or not given proper size or prominence on the screen or in advertising, what should the producer's remedies be? The distributor argues that it should not be in a position in which the advertising can be enjoined or recalled if it is incorrect. The logic here is that if a distributor is commencing distribution of the film and advertising is enjoined or recalled, it would be impossible to prepare new ads in time for them to be effective in promoting specific engagements of the film. And, in the meantime, advertising space already committed would have to be paid for.

There may be an even bigger problem in connection with on-screen credits. Once the negative has been prepared, the preprint materials have been manufactured from the negative, the picture has been cut, edited and scored, and release prints have been manufactured, if there is a mistake in the credit on the release prints correcting it is time-consuming and fantastically costly. It is necessary to splice corrected film containing the proper credit to the negative, to manufacture new pre-print materials from that negative, and to ship each release print to the laboratory in order to have the new material spliced onto the existing print. In addition, if a new credit has to be added, it may disrupt the continuity of the action under the titles or the scoring geared to the existing credits. In short, no distributor wishes to face this possibility.

From the producer's point of view, it is very difficult, if not impossible, to prove money damages resulting from a failure to accord proper credits either on-screen or in advertising. Fortunately, for all concerned, unless the relationship between the two parties is so bad that the distributor becomes completely vindictive, it is most unlikely that a distributor would deliberately fail to accord the producer the correct billing credit. Furthermore, the producer usually has direct control over the credits that go on-screen, and therefore is in a position to ensure that his own credit is correct. Additionally, the producer prepares a statement for the distributor's advertising department that very precisely sets forth all the paid advertising credit requirements. Billing credits are or should be spelled out with such exactitude that no argument can arise, particularly since subjective words like "prominence" are conducive to dispute. The problem of billing credits is complicated by the fact that although the distributor may put in the press book (material furnished to exhibitors from which newspaper ads can be made) suggested ads that show billing as officially contracted, theatrical exhibitors may and do ignore these billing obligations and prepare their own advertising omitting certain credits. This, however, occurs on a theater-by-theater basis and usually is not a cause of great concern to either the distributor or the individual whose credit provision is not entirely honored. Even though the distributor has a contractual right to insist that the exhibitor honor the credits appearing in the sample ads and use the requested form of advertising, the distributor may be unwilling to enforce those provisions. After all, the distributor's main interest is in having exhibitors show the film, and it does not wish to alienate its customers. In addition, if the film's engagement is near its end, as a practical matter the distributor might decide that a suit against an exhibitor for improper advertising would accomplish nothing.

Most P-Ds (as well as other agreements in which credit is accorded) contain a provision stating that neither any casual or inadvertent failure by the distributor, nor any failure by a third party, to comply with the credit provisions constitutes a breach of the agreement, that even in the event of a credit breach, the producer would be limited in his right, if any, to recover money damages at law, and that in no event would the producer be entitled to obtain injunctive or other equitable relief. (Note that some guilds do have injunctive power to force the correction of improper credits to their members.) This waiver of injunctive or other equitable relief includes the waiver of the producer's right to interfere with or restrain the production, distribution, advertising, and other exploitation of the film. The producer, however, is usually able to negotiate an additional provision stating that in the event of failure or omission relating to the producer's credit clause, the distributor will be required to use good faith reasonable efforts to cure such failure or omission on a prospective basis. If the producer is successful in obtaining such a clause (and he usually is), then the distributor will usually add language to the effect that in no event will the distributor be required to recall any prints and/or advertising materials in existence or to which the distributor is irrevocably committed.

If the distributor fails to pay the producer any net profits due after commencing distribution, the same principles and arguments relating to the producer's right to injunctive relief for that breach apply. If the producer can terminate a P-D or restrain distribution, the distributor, besides jeopardizing its investment in the film, will breach its own agreements with licensees and subdistributors. A possible resolution is to make termination by one party subject to the assumption of existing agreements by the other party. But can the producer be expected to fulfill the distributor's obligations under such agreements? The answer is almost invariably no. Therefore, virtually all distributors (especially those who finance production) will refuse to enter into any agreement that contains provisions that might terminate distribution rights.

SECURITY DOCUMENTS AND CONSEQUENCES OF EXCEEDING BUDGET

The distributor, under a P-D agreement, generally agrees to fund not only the budget but also the over-budget costs. The distributor's rights if the film goes over-budget are equivalent to the rights of a completion guarantor and are discussed in Chapter Six under "Completion Bond. Of course, in other provisions of the P-D agreement the distributor has obtained production controls, check-signing privileges on the production account, and rights to take over production. Any security documentation referred to in the P-D agreement to secure any rights under copyright retained by the producer would be similar to the security documentation referred to in Chapter Six under "Bank Financing."

DOMESTIC DISTRIBUTION

In almost every type of P-D discussed in this chapter, the distributor retains sole and exclusive rights to distribute the photoplay by any and all media worldwide (or these days, throughout the universe) in perpetuity. Generally, there is no question but that the distributor will hold these rights if it has fully financed the production of the photoplay.

In the past some well-known talent had sufficient bargaining power to be granted ownership of all rights in a film and to lease the rights to a financier-distributor for a specified period. At the end of the period, all rights in the film reverted to the talent. At the present time, virtually no talent has that kind of bargaining position, although some well-known artists may be able to secure the right to distribute the film in certain territories or media. Most financier-distributors will refuse to put up the money for a film if it is to be licensed for only a limited term.

The distributor's rights to distribute by any method or media means not only the right to distribute in theaters, on all forms of television, for home video, or in non-theatrical locations, but also by media yet to be invented. Although a distributor may be experienced in distributing theatrically and non-theatrically and may have a television sales department experienced in making network and syndication sales, a producer may well ask whether or not a particular distributor has the expertise to distribute in some new media in which no distribution standards have been established. However, the distributor will insist upon the right to distribute in new media as well as old.

The advent of the newer media (such as videocassettes) and the explosion of the so-called supplemental markets (such as pay television) has to some extent reduced the distributor's risk in advancing funds for the production and distribution of a film. This is not only because there are many more sources of revenues for the exploitation of the film, but also because the distributor can hedge its risk when sublicensing a distribution right by requiring the sublicensee to pay an advance or a guarantee against the revenues to be derived from the exploitation of the applicable distribution right. Typically, a major studio will also have an "output deal" for certain rights which it does not itself exploit. For example, a studio may enter into an agreement with a pay television network pursuant to which the studio agrees to license the pay television rights to that network on all films made by that studio during the term of the agreement. In return, the pay television network will give the studio an advance, often calculated as a percentage of the budget of the applicable picture or a percentage of box office receipts, usually, in either case, with a ceiling. Thus a distributor is often able to protect a substantial portion of its risk even before the film is made. On the other hand, the distributor's risk has dramatically increased as talent costs escalate production costs and as distribution expenses similarly increase.

As will be discussed in Chapter Six, a producer is sometimes able to finance all or substantially all of the entire cost of a film's production by putting together the advances and guarantees made by various different distributors. So, the producer does have other options when he cannot get a studio to finance his film and distribute it in all media.

The difficulty with the movie business is that the greatest opportunity to make money is in distribution, but in order to acquire films the distributors must finance their production or acquisition. Even though there has always been public acceptance of low-budget films, particularly action-oriented movies, and many smaller distribution companies have entered the field (although many of them fall by the wayside), it is still a fact that most motion pictures cost many millions of dollars to produce and raising that money without turning to a major distributor is not easy. Some of the ways this can be done are enumerated in Chapter Six of this book.

Smaller distributors have difficulty in finding films of public appeal unless they are prepared to finance the production or pay advances for completed films. Can a small independent distributor successfully distribute pictures? On a small scale, and sometimes on a large scale, yes, but as of this date, there is no doubt that if one seeks a big, commercial theatrical release, a major distributor is usually a must. Only such a distributor has the sales force, the sales offices in major cities, the personal contacts with the theaters, the know-how to release a large-scale motion picture successfully all over the country, and the funds available to finance the appropriate level of advertising (which often is greater than the cost to produce the film itself).

With a small art house or low-budget, exploitation-type picture, an independent distributor may be able to achieve very satisfactory results primarily by using a regional release pattern as opposed to a national one, during the times of the year—February to June and late August to Thanksgiving—when the studios are not releasing their "blockbusters." This pattern of distribution seeks to skim the cream off the top of the market. Releasing a film in a relatively small number of marketing areas requires fewer prints and eliminates the need for expensive national television advertising. Small distributors say that a large sales force and large amounts of advertising are unnecessary for their purposes. They say that, more than ever before, successful films depend upon a combination of good critical reviews and word-of-mouth. Indeed, some pictures are so pitched to a defined, limited audience that word-of-mouth can assure their success whether or not they are liked by the critics. Note, however, that one of the challenges facing small distributors is expanding a big-city, small art-house release pattern into general commercial distribution.

It has been said that if a picture is bad, it doesn't matter how many salesmen try to sell it, and if it is good, no salesmen are needed because the film sells itself. Of course, this is an oversimplification. In fact, most pictures must be sold, and a good picture sold properly will do better than one sold poorly. Moreover, a bad picture, if it is effectively sold, will at least do some business. Then, too, the ancillary marketplace (e.g., videocassettes and pay television) has grown so significantly that it sometimes permits a distributor to recoup on a well-promoted picture even when it has performed poorly at the box office.

A distributor asked to put up all the money for a film's production will insist on having complete distribution rights. One could argue that while a particular distributor has great expertise in theatrical release, perhaps someone else would do better with the other media. In principle this argument may have some validity, but in the reality of present-day negotiations with major motion picture distributors it is worthless. The suggestion that a distributor not have certain rights simply means that it would have to bid for the right to distribute a picture it has financed. Additionally, many of the ancillary markets (especially home video) benefit greatly from the advertising dollars spent in the theatrical advertising of the film.

Most P-Ds have pages devoted to the proposition that the distributor can distribute the picture any way it wishes, free from any complaint by the producer, with the broadest possible discretion and latitude, and with its judgment valid and binding. In this type of P-D a distributor does not even agree to be obligated to release the picture, no less guarantee the type or pattern of release.

What can a producer do to modify the broad language of a P-D that gives the distributor such complete freedom? Some attorneys for producers will insist upon adding language to the effect that the distributor will exercise "good faith" in distributing the photoplay. The efficacy of this language is questionable, since it is most difficult to prove that a distributor acted in bad faith, and contracting parties are always deemed to act in good faith.

Some producers will try to add a clause to the effect that the distributor exercise "reasonable business judgment" in the distribution. From a business point of view a distributor can usually justify any decision it makes, even the decision not to release the film at all. Even so, the distributor's attorneys will probably resist more strongly an attempt to insert language like "reasonable business judgment" than they will "good faith." There are times when distribution is governed by factors other than what is best for a particular film. For example, from time to time a distribution company may run into financial problems, and these problems may cause the distributor to release a film sooner than expected in order to generate money quickly. To effect the quick return of income, the distributor may also make unwarranted sacrifices, such as an early television sale when a later one would probably prove more generous, or distribution of the film on a release pattern other than it would have followed had it the financial stability to sustain itself at that time. While it is possible that a producer would be treated unfairly by such arrangements, do they represent the distributor's failure to exercise reasonable business judgment? Perhaps so, but in any case, the distributor will not permit having its books and records examined to determine whether each engagement was the best one obtainable or whether a television sale might have been better had it been made at some future time.

There are, of course, well-known instances of films that were ineffectively distributed. Some errant distributors will even admit incorrect business judgment. For example, a film may have been given a general release when it would have fared better as a high-quality art house picture. That is, it might have grossed more by playing first in a few selected theaters for a long period of time—to build up the word-of-mouth. Instead, the picture was exhibited simultaneously in a large number of theaters for a limited period of time and, as a result, had completed its distribution before potential audiences could learn how good it was. Sometimes a distributor will not know the quality of the picture it has and will toss a film on the market with scant ceremony, only to receive glowing critical reviews.

In negotiating the P-D producers will also try to obligate the distributor to use its "best efforts" in distributing the photoplay. Here again, there is a question as to what constitutes best efforts and how to determine whether or not a distributor is in fact using them. In any case, this language is virtually impossible to obtain since it does in fact mandate a standard of conduct and has been construed by the courts to obligate a distributor to market a film so as to maximize its gross revenue, even if the distribution is not cost-effective for the distributor. Best efforts then might mean distributing a film to the detriment of another film of the distributor. Best efforts to maximize gross receipts might mean spending advertising or print dollars that, after recoupment, might prove to have reduced net profits.

All these attempts to insert in the P-D a generalized standard of conduct for distribution are calculated to give the producer a better litigating position in the event of a lawsuit. For in actuality, there is really no way to set up a specific *objective* standard for judging distribution. From the point of view of the distributor, the producer may know something about producing a film but will know very little about distributing it, and the distributor's good faith should be evidenced by the fact that it has paid all of the costs of financing the film and, therefore, at the very least, has a powerful inducement to recoup its investment.

Another effort (also usually doomed to failure) that a producer may make to exercise some control over the distributor is to seek agreement on a minimal prenegotiated dollar amount in advertising. But again, since expenditures for prints and for advertising together may often equal or exceed the film's production cost, the distributor will insist on retaining complete and absolute control over how much money it will invest in these elements.

Sometimes in a P-D all a distributor will agree to do is give a photoplay a theatrical release without defining the kind of theatrical release involved. The producer wants a theatrical release clause to be sure that the distributor does not merely license the photoplay to home video and then to television. So, what does the term "theatrical release" mean? Does it mean merely a release in one theater, or does it mean a general release in many theaters? While a producer may insist that the film be released in first-run theaters in certain key cities within a stated period of time, the distributor who agrees to a theatrical release (obviously for a film not created specifically for television) will usually specify no more than in movie theaters in the U.S.—and not details of the type of release the film will be given.

Additionally, the producer may request that the P-D provide for the distributor itself to distribute the photoplay theatrically in the U.S. But certain non-major distributors are not set up to distribute in all areas of the U.S. and must utilize licensees to handle subdistribution for them in those places they do not cover. Under these circumstances, the producer will argue in vain that having picked a certain distributor to distribute for him, he expects that distributor to do so. Furthermore, the distributor will insist on the power to assign certain distribution rights to a subdistributor or to assign the entire agreement to a corporation into which the distributor may be merged.

The best a producer can usually hope for is a limited right of consultation on distribution matters, with the distributor's decision being final, and agreement that the first general theatrical release of the picture will be handled by the distributor.

FOREIGN DISTRIBUTION

Certain distributors are organized to handle their own foreign distribution, while others have entered into output arrangements. With organizations that own theaters, the films they distribute will typically play in those theaters. All the contractual safeguards designed to ensure that distributors deal at arm's length with their own theaters should apply overseas as well as in the U.S. The distributor should receive from its overseas theaters the same terms that a third party would get if that party licensed a picture for exhibition in those theaters.

Aside from making sure that his picture is distributed in all parts of the world, the producer should request that it not be licensed on an outright sale basis, for a fixed sum, in such major territories as Canada, France, the United Kingdom, Germany, Australia, Japan, Spain, and Italy. A distributor will ordinarily agree to this without question. If it has its own subsidiaries or affiliates in such areas, it usually specifies that these companies will handle the distribution.

It is customary, however, for a film to be sold on an outright basis in many of the minor territories. This makes sense because it is usually difficult to remit money from these smaller countries or, even if remittances can be made on a regular basis, it is difficult to ensure proper accountings. Thus, even the major distributors will make outright film sales in those minor territories where it is not worth their while to keep sales offices.

A producer may try (usually without success) contractually to provide that if his film is not licensed in certain stated major territories within a given period of time that he can make his own deal with a subdistributor in any of these territories. Under such a provision, the original distributor could then either match the distribution deal in the territory or lose the territory; though in the latter case, the producer's subdistributors would have to account to the distributor. For instance, the agreement might provide that, if after a three-year period the film were not sold in the territory of France, the producer could find a subdistributor for France and present the proposed deal to the distributor. The latter would then have to go along with the subdistributor deal or lose the territory.

The distributor who accepts in such a situation would not usually be obligated to advance any sums to pay for prints or advertising and would take a reduced distribution fee for having only to administer the deal.

Although on paper this kind of proposition sounds good from a producer's point of view, in actuality, if the picture can be distributed in a territory on a sound economic basis, you can be sure the original distributor will do so or will arrange for subdistribution. Should the distributor choose not to distribute or be unable to license the film to a subdistributor in a territory there is small hope that the producer will be able to come up with a suitable subdistribution arrangement.

Opinions vary as to the kind of an agreement a distributor ought to make with subdistributors for a particular territory. Under most subdistribution arrangements, the subdistributor deducts a fee from its gross receipts, deducts its costs and expenses from the remaining gross receipts, and pays what's left of the gross receipts to the distributor; or, the costs will be deducted first, and the balance of the gross receipts divided between the subdistributor and the distributor in some predetermined ratio. If the subdistributor has paid an advance against the distributor's share of gross receipts for the right to subdistribute the picture, the subdistributor will keep all the gross receipts that would otherwise accrue to the distributor until the subdistributor has recouped the amount of the advance. The money that the distributor receives from the subdistributor after the advance has been recouped is known as "overages." If a distributor gets a large cash advance from a subdistributor, the latter will charge and retain a larger distribution fee, because the payment of the advance obviously increases its risk. In fact, a distributor obtaining a large cash advance will usually not expect any overages after the subdistributor has deducted and retained its fee and expenses and recouped the advance from gross receipts.

A distributor who wants to set up a straight distribution arrangement overseas sometimes encounters difficulty because of government regulations restricting the remittance of money from a foreign territory. Some independent distributors will do all of their licensing of films in a territory through one subdistributor. In this kind of arrangement, the independent distributor will have day-to-day supervision over distribution effected by the sub-distributor.

ADVERTISING AND MERCHANDISING

A producer attempting to regulate distribution expenses may want to insert in the contract a ceiling on the amount a distributor can spend for prints and advertising of a film. Some distribution companies agree to manufacture no more than a given number of prints or to spend no more than a stated amount for advertising without the producer's consent, and these figures are generally so high that in all likelihood they will never be reached. But most distributors argue (perhaps correctly) that it is foolish for the producer even to try to place restrictions on the amount that they may spend on prints and advertising. After all, they will say, they know their business and will not spend money on prints and advertising unless there is a substantial likelihood that such expenditures will result in increased profits or at least be more than recouped.

The most important thing for a producer to do, if he has a choice, is to select the right distributor for the particular picture. As a practical matter, most disputes with distributors after a picture is released concern the distributor's accounting deductions and bookkeeping arrangements. Any argument over marketing policy is usually just an excuse for the producer's attorney to exact concessions or effect a settlement. Disputes will usually arise only over successful pictures—no one audits a flop. It is very difficult to document the speculative argument that the distributor could have achieved even higher grosses with a different sales campaign or release pattern.

It is, in fact, axiomatic that a distributor has complete control of advertising, publicizing, and promoting a film. Distributors do not want to give the producer the right of approval or even consultation on advertising. Once in a great while, a smaller distribution company may give the producer the right to develop an advertising campaign, subject to the distributor's approval, and will provide for this in the contract. Certain producers, who have their own ideas about advertising and some expertise in this field, can make a distribution deal that is conditional upon their having the picture advertised and presented in a way they envisage. Very few producers have such bargaining power however.

Most agreements give the distributor all ownership rights in the picture's advertising and publicity material, including rights to merchandise characters from the film. Merchandising involves the sale of articles (such as coffee mugs, T-shirts, and the like) that bear the likenesses of certain of a film's characters and/or objects. Sales of such items not only bring in money but also serve to promote the film. Such successful merchandising is not common in the movie industry and only a few major hits (such as *E.T., Batman,* and the James Bond, Disney, and *Star Wars* films) have generated much merchandising income. Many distributors do not have active merchandising departments, and merchandising rarely receives significant attention as part of the distribution process. There are independent companies that specialize in merchandising rights but they shy away from motion pictures as most do not lend themselves to character exploitation. Even when a picture does present merchandising opportunities, merchandisers are usually reluctant to make a deal with the distributor and to spend the substantial sums of money necessary to develop and market a line of products, unless they are fairly certain that the film itself will do enough business to attract a large number of people to those products. Some independent producers have a flair for merchandising and a distributor would be wise to let them negotiate agreements with merchandising concerns as freely as possible.

When a film seems to have substantial merchandising value, most producers will try to negotiate for a separate royalty covering income derived from merchandising. This means that no income from merchandising will be included in gross receipts; rather, the producer will receive a percentage of the merchandising income directly. This can be very advantageous for the producer, as only costs relating to merchandising need be deducted before the royalty is paid; in other words, the receipts and costs of merchandising are not cross-collateralized with the other receipts and costs of the film. However, you can be sure that if a studio is financing a film's production, it will, usually successfully, resist any attempt by the producer to receive a share of any revenues from merchandising until the studio has fully recouped its investment.

Ordinarily, a distributor will manufacture certain advertising accessories, such as lobby displays and billboards, to help promote a motion picture. The distributor tries in the P-D either to elect that revenue from the sale of accessories is gross receipts with respect to which distribution fees and expenses are deducted and retained (including the cost of the accessories) or that the distributor keeps all such revenue but cannot include the cost of manufacturing the accessories as distribution expenses. Most accessories, as well as trailers, are loss items, so a distributor would do better financially with the former election. However, since only a small amount of revenue is usually involved, to simplify accounting statements many distributors prefer to retain the revenue and not charge the expenses as deductions. Distributors preserve their right of election in the P-D because they may wish to take alternative positions in different territories or from time to time. In addition, a distributor that does not handle its own distribution overseas may find that its subdistributors insist that revenue from advertising be included in gross receipts and that advertising expenses be deducted as a distribution expense; in such a situation the distributor will try to impose that election on the film's producers.

The mechanics of preparing an advertising campaign are quite simple. The advertising department prepares a concept either by itself or in conjunction with an outside agency and ordinarily contracts the actual preparation of the artwork to one or more independent agencies. Sometimes more than one possible campaign is prepared, and the distributor makes a final choice. The concept selected is printed in various formats, which are then reproduced for a press kit that includes both sample ads and various publicity materials (star biographies, tie-ins, etc.). The press kits are sent to exhibitors, who use them to advertise and in general promote the picture. Since an outside company handles the manufacture of the advertising accessories and keeps the mats and plates for the sample ads in the press kits, all the exhibitor has to do is to pick up the phone and order directly whatever he wants.

ASSIGNMENT OF RIGHTS IN P-D AGREEMENT

In a P-D, consideration must be given to a clause limiting the producer's right to assign sums due him as net profits to third parties to obtain a loan, or for some other reason. Most P-Ds will provide that the producer cannot assign the net profits until delivery of the picture to the distributor. Otherwise, the producer has no incentive to finish the film and make delivery. Ordinarily, agreements will give the producer the right to assign receipts after delivery of the picture, provided that (1) the person to whom the assignment is made (the "assignee") signs an agreement confirming the distributor's rights in the photoplay; (2) if the distributor has a claim against the producer, the distributor will not have to pay the assignee but can withhold payment pending the resolution of the claim; and (3) the assignee has no independent right to audit. If there are multiple assignments to different people, the distributor will ordinarily have the right to require all the assignees to appoint one entity to receive statements, distribute moneys to the assignees, and audit on their behalf so that the distributor does not have to render accountings to several people.

Some distribution companies seek a preferred right to acquire the producer's interests in a film's net profits should he wish to dispose of them. The distributor of a hit film that promises substantial net profits for the producer will argue that it should have the right of first or last refusal to purchase those profits, since the distributor helped make the picture profitable.

Many of the concepts inherent in the negotiation of a production, financing, and distribution agreement that we have discussed here are also involved in alternate forms of financing a motion picture. An independent producer may not be able to interest a major motion picture studio in his production, or he may not want to be burdened with the restrictions imposed upon him by the major distributor. In that event, the independent producer can search for other forms of financing, some of which will now be considered.

6 OTHER FORMS OF FINANCING

T he advantage of dealing with a studio is that it provides all the financing for the budget of a film. The disadvantages are that the studio usually insists on total rights of approval over production matters and that its definition of net profits is so unfavorable to producers that most of them work for a production fee and have to regard any right to net profits as purely speculative.

However, there are alternatives to studio financing. These include financing by investors and banks and by government subsidies. Banks finance production by making production loans and, as the prime source for repayment of the loan, look to advances payable by licensees for grants of territorial and/or distribution rights in the picture. These licensees may be, for example, a home video company in the U.S., a pay cable service such as HBO, foreign distributors, and so on.

In some cases a studio, rather than financing a film in progress, agrees to pay the full cost of the budget of the film upon its completion. This arrangement is commonly referred to as a "negative pickup." The promise of the distributor (presumably creditworthy) to pay the negative pickup price basically is the collateral for the bank loan that provides the actual week-to-week production financing. This chapter covers investor financing, bank financing, and agreements with completion guarantors, which are companies that provide the bank and/or investors with the contractual assurance that the picture will, in fact, be completed. This is followed by a discussion of problems relating to the fractionalization of rights, which is what happens when different rights in the film are sold to a number of distributors. Finally, there is a discussion of coproduction agreements and types of government subsidies. It is important to note that no one method of financing excludes all of the others and that an independently financed picture may consist of investor financing, bank financing, and governmental subsidies, with the banks looking to a number of presales and to a variety of licensees for repayment of their loans. There is also the possibility of a foreign coproduction agreement whereby a film finds its producers in more than one country.

INVESTOR FINANCING

Our discussion proceeds from the investor's viewpoint since it is useful for a producer to understand the kinds of concerns an investor is likely to have and the kinds of arrangements that might have to be made to secure investor financing. The discussion does not deal with the structure of the investment (i.e., whether in corporate, joint venture, partnership, or limited partnership form) and the federal or state securities regulations that would govern such an investment, since we believe these matters are beyond the scope of this book.

The first kind of investment a producer may need is financing for the development or preproduction of the film so as to assemble elements (script, cast, director) to attract production financing. If an investor funds development or preproduction of a film only, how is he compensated for his investment? If money is to be raised to fund the entire cost of the film, provision is made in the budget for the development investor to be repaid his investment plus a profit when that money is raised. This investor also receives a negotiated percentage of net profits. If the cost of production is to be financed by investors, in whole or in part, the development investor also gets the opportunity to participate in the funding of the film's production along with, and perhaps on an even more favorable basis than, the other investors. For example, if a $500,000 investment entitles an investor to 1 percent of the profits, and if the development investor invested $500,000 in development and decides to invest an equal sum in the production of the film, the development investor might receive 1½ percent of the profits, rather than 1 percent.

Tax Advantages

The tax advantages in certain business development that have from time to time existed in the U.S. and other countries include a tax credit for a percentage of the investment that goes directly to reduce taxes and tax shelters involving various forms of accelerated depreciation which, coupled with the ability of the investor to borrow part of the investment on a nonrecourse (i.e., without personal liability) or limited recourse basis, give the investor a tax write-off of some multiple of the investor's investment. The latter form of tax shelter, which was very much in vogue prior to the Tax Reform Act of 1986, was, with some exceptions, of doubtful validity; the U.S. Tax Court has routinely disallowed investment coupled with nonrecourse borrowing as the basis upon which depreciation can be taken. The investment tax credit is now unavailable in this country. However, with new tax legislation the situation may conceivably change in the U.S. Moreover, tax shelters utilizing the above concepts are now available in some other countries, although the availability of a shelter may be conditioned on having principal photography of the film take place in the country providing the tax benefits and utilizing citizens of that country as talent. If the investment is going to be made by a foreign corporation, that corporation might be more interested in avoiding the imposition of U.S. tax and, in that event, might try to keep film rentals out of this country through the utilization of a tax haven then available. In any event, once the particular investor is identified, the producer should develop a corporate and tax structure for the production of the film that would best accommodate the wishes of the investor.

Investor Protection

This section assumes that an investor (whether a wealthy individual or a corporation) finances all or a substantial position of the cost of a film. If the investors are a group of individuals, their representative might have some or all of these rights which would be exercised by the representative. Typically, an investor in a single film production who finances all or a substantial portion of production wants to be presented with a package including principal cast, director, script, budget, and completion bond, and if the package is incomplete, probably wants the right of later approval of any elements missing from the package. The producer is therefore required, at his own cost, to assemble all such elements. If the investor is not contributing all of the financing, he is also interested in where the balance is coming from. He will want to know in advance, for example, if part of the budget is being financed by a bank loan secured by license agreements (see "Using Production Loans to Finance Feature Films," page 131), because he is then at risk if the bank forecloses its security interest on the picture, and to the extent that advances from license agreements are used for financing, those advances are not available to recoup his investment.

If the investor does not approve any element, such as a director, the investment agreement usually provides that the producer can submit additional directors for approval, and the investor retains the right to make the investment with the new element. A more difficult situation arises when all the elements have been approved but for some reason during filming an element of talent must be replaced due to incapacity or breach. In this situation an investor may have the right of consultation, but it would be difficult for an investor to secure the right of approval after filming has begun, particularly if lack of approval would give the investor the right to terminate his involvement.

Typically, an investor expects some financial protections: a completion bond naming the investor as a beneficiary (see discussion of Completion Bonds later in this chapter), becoming the named insured on production insurance policies, and perhaps, cosigning production checks. For his part, the producer wants assurance that the investment will in fact be made and usually asks the investor to deposit his money in a special account prior to the start of principal photography, with some mechanism that allows money to be transferred from the special account into the production account in weekly installments.

If there is bank financing, the bank insists that its money be the last used for the film, up to the amount of the budget; from the producer's point of view this is advantageous since production loans made at a later date carry correspondingly reduced interest charges. If there are a number of investors, each one wants to make sure that the money to be invested by all of them is in place. Sometimes, when all the investors are considered creditworthy, each agrees to contribute money as required but not to deposit those funds in an account prior to the start of principal photography. In such a situation an investor might want to provide that if any of the other financing were later not to materialize, he would have the option of replacing that financing with his own additional money, for which he would receive not only the recoupment and profit position of the other withdrawn financing but also some of the producer's net receipts. From the investor's standpoint, the justification for this is that the producer has a responsibility for seeing that all the necessary financing is properly in place.

Quite frequently in the course of shooting it is decided to spend extra money to enhance the quality of the film. The completion guarantor, as will be noted later in this chapter, is not responsible for enhancements but only for completing the film in accordance with the budget. Although the enhancement presumably improves the film, the additional production costs obviously delay profits and recoupment; therefore, an investor will usually want to approve all enhancements. If he does approve, a question arises as to whether the money for enhancement is to be recouped before or after recoupment of the original investment. This question is also of concern to the completion guarantor since if the guarantor is to recoup only after the enhancement, its recoupment inevitably will be delayed.

An investor in a feature film must be aware that the producer has to find distribution for his completed film and, in licensing rights in that film, must deal with the issues discussed later in this chapter under "Fractionalization of Rights." One such issue is that a distributor who acquires rights in a film will want to recoup its fees and expenses prior to remitting money to the producer; therefore, the investor's recoupment becomes second position financing (i.e., recoupment only after the distributor has earned back its fees and expenses). Of course, if the distributor agrees to give the producer certain advances, they would go directly to recoup negative cost and, thus, the investor's stake.

Typically, the money a producer spends to arrange for distribution is recouped first by the producer. Then the investor recoups his investment and, if there is more than one investor, usually all investors recoup in proportion to their investment. When a bank loan is used to finance part of the production cost, the loan agreement will provide that that loan is to be repaid first. Generally, the bank looks to specific presale agreements for recoupment of its loan with interest. However, if other presale agreements were entered into or other sums were received from exploitation of the film, any and all sums would go to reduce the bank loan. The completion guarantor is repaid after recoupment of bank and investor financing of the budget. This is followed by payment of any deferments to talent. Finally, the balance from film rental is divided between the producer and the investor. That division is a matter of negotiation, but the best a producer can usually do is to divide 50-50 with all investors. Any third-party talent participants are paid by the producer from his share. But when third-party participations are deducted "off the top," before division between producer and investors, the latter may receive as much as 80 percent of net profits, with that percentage possibly decreasing as the level of net profit rises. For example, on the first $1,000,000 of net profit investors get 80 percent, the producer, 20 percent, while on the next $1,000,000 the division will be 70 percent to 30 percent, and so on.

On occasion, an investor may request distribution rights in a territory or for a particular medium on terms and conditions advantageous to himself. If his investment is less than the total budget and the balance of the money needed comes from loans backed by presales, the investor may still demand a net profit participation equivalent to what he would have received if he had invested the entire amount of the budget, since the existence of presale financing invariably reduces the available markets from which the investor can recoup.

In some cases, the investor may request some rights of approval over distribution arrangements. To implement this, he may annex to the agreement certain minimum terms and conditions regarding sales of territories or rights with the proviso that if such terms and conditions are not met he must approve any lesser terms.

In a deal in which a sequel may be important, an investor will always want the right to invest in any sequel on the same terms and conditions as applied on the first film. With regard to such other ancillary rights as a television series and the like, the investor usually requires the right of consent before the producer can sell these rights. Most investors request and are routinely granted credit on the screen and in some cases in print advertising.

This book deals with the production of *individual* feature films and therefore investments with studios or distributors on a *number of films* is a matter only to be touched upon. In such situations the advantage to the investors is that with the studios as distributors, the investors can potentially recoup their investment along with the studios (i.e., the cost of production contributed by the investors is recouped pro rata with distribution expenses and the production costs advanced by the studios). In theory, distributors could reduce their fees and/or defer part of them until investor recoupment has occurred. In actuality, studios are generally unwilling to make such concessions. In addition, they are generally unwilling to let the investors participate in sequels and, furthermore, insist that only the standard video cassette royalty be credited to gross receipts and that film rentals include a percentage (usually 20 to 25 percent) of the wholesale selling price of videocassettes. As we have seen, this method of calculation benefits studios because with videocassettes, the manufacturing and shipping costs to be borne by the studio from its percentage are very small and most of the advertising expenditures are made during the theatrical release of the film and are thus treated as distribution expenses to be recouped by the studio.

As long as studios take the positions they do, it is unlikely that any investment in a slate of films could equal a market return on the investor's money—unless he gets very lucky and invests in a string of unusually profitable films.

USING PRODUCTION LOANS
TO FINANCE FEATURE FILMS

It is frequently possible for the producer of a feature film to enter into what are called "presale agreements" with one or more of the following: domestic theatrical distributors, a U.S. television network, a pay cable system, a home video distributor and various foreign distributors, any or all of which become "licensees." Pursuant to its agreement, each licensee will then contract to make payments of advances, guarantees, or license fees to the producer for the right to distribute or exhibit a film. To prevent losses from pictures that never get finished, licensees customarily make payments only on or after delivery of completed films. Payments may then be tied to exhibition of the films or simply scheduled in installments over a period of years. How, then, can a producer make use of the entire amount of all the above payments for production financing? The producer can attempt to borrow money from a bank with the guarantees payable under license agreements providing the collateral for the loan.

It is important to note how production loans run counter to traditional lending principles. Ordinarily a bank looks at a borrower's business on a "going concern" basis and decides whether the income from that business justifies making the loan. To do this the bank makes a detailed examination of the business's financial records, prospects, and related factors. The collateral the bank requires for the loan is a secondary consideration. In production loan financing the bank lends against collateral, namely, the payments represented by the presale agreements. In addition, the bank typically is granted a security interest in the producer's right, title, and interest in the film, and in the underlying literary or musical material created for it. The bank is not in the business of reading scripts or determining the merits of cast or director, and its credit decision is based solely on what it sees as the ability and creditworthiness of the licensee to repay the loan. As a matter of fact, the bank would probably prefer that a new production company, with no assets or liabilities other than the picture itself, be formed for any one new film. In this way, the company is not encumbered with liabilities relating to other activities. The loan rests on the premise that, regardless of any contingency, the value of the collateral is sufficient to guarantee repayment.

In the usual lending transaction, the borrower is a company with, theoretically, enough assets to repay the loan. In motion picture production financing, the production company—probably a corporate shell—will clearly not have any means to repay the loan, aside from the collateral. As a practical matter, therefore, the loan is nonrecourse (without recourse to any of the producer's assets, other than the film). The individual producer will generally not agree to guarantee his production company's obligations nor will he agree to utilize a corporation with substantial assets as the borrowing entity.

A bank traditionally contemplates a continuing relationship with a borrowing customer over a period of years. In contrast, most motion picture production loans are single transactions, though a producer might want to continue his relationship with a particular bank for financing other pictures. Each loan, however, is treated by the bank as a separate transaction, generally involving different collateral.

Most commercial bank loans are for a limited period, infrequently more than three years. (Long-term loans tend to be made by insurance companies or other institutional lenders.) Motion picture production loans often require a longer than average term—particularly if the presale agreements that represent part of the bank's collateral include network television or syndication deals. Payments under such agreements may not become due until five or more years after the first release of the picture, or six or more years after the date of the first loan. This delay in payment does not occur under agreements for distribution overseas, because there the advance is usually paid upon delivery of the photoplay to the foreign licensee, which occurs shortly after its delivery to the domestic distributor.

Finally, under traditional loan concepts, the bank considers the borrower to have the financial ability to pay interest on the loan on an ongoing basis. With a production loan, because its only asset may be the film, the borrower is usually unable to pay interest in that way. Therefore, the bank must lend not only the principal amount of the loan but the interest as well.

Clearly then, for a bank, film production financing is quite different from its customary financing. The loan seems riskier because the borrower has no independent assets and basically the bank must look to the collateral for repayment. However, in traditional financing, a bank faces the risk that the collateral of a going concern may tumble in value should that business go into liquidation. Conceptually, the collateral in a motion picture loan should always be sufficient to repay the loan with interest. As long as the collateral is in place, the bank can expect to be repaid. Thus, the bank must make sure that there are no defects in the collateral package that could prevent repayment.

Although a motion picture production loan has some of the characteristics of account-receivable financing, there is one crucial difference. In the typical factoring arrangement, the factor is lending against a borrower's existing accounts receivable. The goods or services have been duly furnished by the borrower and the borrower is due payment from the account debtor. If the account debtor does not pay for any reason other than inability to do so, collection becomes the responsibility of the borrower, not the factor.

In motion picture production financing, the problem is that the accounts receivable do not mature until delivery of the completed picture to the licensee(s). If circumstances arise that gives a licensee an excuse not to accept delivery and therefore not to pay, the bank, by definition, is exposed, because the borrower admittedly does not have the independent means to repay the loan. Therefore, the bank's concern is twofold. First, does the licensee have the ability to pay? Second, how can the bank be assured that any conditions precedent to payment under the presale agreement will be fulfilled so that the licensee will be required to pay?

In most cases, a bank can be reasonably certain that the U.S. licensee is creditworthy if it is a television network, a major pay cable and home video system, a film studio, or a large domestic theatrical exhibitor chain. But with foreign licensees, it may be more difficult for the bank to determine creditworthiness. The bank may also be fearful that, despite contractual obligations, a foreign licensee will refuse to pay if it doesn't like the film, which would force the bank to pursue its remedies in a foreign jurisdiction. If there is any doubt about a licensee's willingness or ability to pay, the bank may well require that the licensee's obligation to pay be secured by an irrevocable letter of credit.

In assessing the production loan, the bank first examines all the presale agreements that represent collateral so as to be sure that they contain no conditions to acceptance of a picture that cannot be fulfilled by a completion guarantor. (Some of these conditions will be covered in the next section of this chapter, "Completion Bonds.")

Typically, the bank requires the producer to expend any other financing he has arranged toward the film's production cost before the bank makes its first loan. Furthermore, prior to making that loan, the bank will insist that the completion guarantor certify that this other financing was properly expended. Otherwise, the completion guarantor could later take the position that funds had been improperly used and, therefore, that production financing up to the amount of the budget had not been provided.

Usually the bank makes loans in installments to cover production costs, first during principal photography of the picture and then throughout postproduction. The bank requires that each installment of the loan be conditioned on certification from the completion guarantor and the producer that all money previously advanced or loaned was promptly applied toward the production of the picture. There is generally a cutoff date beyond which the bank is no longer obligated to lend.

The bank usually charges a fee of anywhere from .25 percent to 2 percent (depending on the risks) for its commitment to make the loan. The loan itself bears interest at up to 2 percent over prime, although if the studio makes a presale agreement to cover the entire budget upon delivery of the film, the rate is closer or equal to the prime rate. The interest is usually payable quarterly. Thus the bank, in addition to making installment loans toward production, is also making installment loans to fund the interest payments.

Obviously, in deciding how much can be loaned against a particular presale agreement, the bank must make sure the license fees are sufficient to repay the bank's principal, its interest charge, its commitment fee, and its costs. This means that the bank can lend only against a percentage of the license fees, depending upon the interest rate, the commitment fee, the projected term of the loan, and taking into account that the loan will be paid in installments and adding a reserve to cover the possibility that the prime rate may increase over the term of the loan. This discount reserve factor will, of course, increase if the licence fees are to be paid over a number of years, since the longer a loan is outstanding the more interest there is to pay. There is risk to the bank if the prime rate increases so dramatically during the life of the loan that the license fees are no longer sufficient to repay the principal and the actual (now higher) rate of interest—resulting in an interest shortfall. This risk can be covered in three different ways. First, some presale agreements provide for license fees to be paid on alternate dates (e.g., either on the first network telecast or for a period of years after a network obtains the right to telecast, whichever date is earlier). In assessing the amount to be loaned, the bank must assume that the license fee will be paid on the later date, but if the film is then telecast earlier than expected, the bank is paid sooner, and the interest factor is reduced. Second, since the bank has a security interest in the entire film, the bank is entitled to receive not only the presale agreement fees, but any other money paid to the producer by a licensee or distributor of the film. These other funds are ordinarily contingent upon box office receipts, but if the film has any commercial value, some portion of them should flow to a producer from the distribution of the film, making them available to repay the loan. Third, the producer or distributor can voluntarily pay the interest shortfall to prevent the bank from foreclosing.

The bank's security documentation consists of an agreement in which it is granted a security interest in the producer's collateral (his right, title, and interest in the film, etc., as mentioned earlier).

In the event that a picture is to be produced in whole or in part overseas, the bank must perfect its lien under the laws of each appropriate foreign jurisdiction. Domestically, the bank's security interest is perfected both by filing financing statements in the state and county of the producer's principal place of business and in any state where principal photography of the film is to occur, and by filing a mortgage of copyright with the copyright office. It is not clear to what extent, if at all, the Federal Copyright Act might preempt the field so as to make state Uniform Commercial Code filings unnecessary and copyright office filings mandatory. The present Copyright Act permits recording mortgages in the copyright office but does not deal with the foreclosure or enforcement of rights in mortgages. Some recent decisions, however, hold that the proper place to perfect copyright mortgages is under the Copyright Act. Perfection can only take place if there is a copyright registration, priority is obtained if the document is recorded within one month after execution, and, because of the registration requirement, a filing cannot be made for after-acquired property; that is, intellectual property created after the date of the original registration. To obtain priority effectively, one must wait the month to see if anyone else has recorded. The copyright office is so far behind in its recordation that it is difficult to see how a search would reveal a prior registration during a thirty-day period. In the absence of definitive judicial interpretation, it is still prudent to file both under a state's UCC as well as in the copyright office.

A bank's lien is typically made subject to certain encumbrances. For example, laboratories are granted statutory liens that attach automatically. A bank will request that a laboratory execute a "pledgeholder agreement," under which the lab will subordinate its lien to the bank and, as pledgeholder for the bank, agrees to hold film material in the event of a default. Or, a bank might permit the lab to retain its lien but only to cover up to a specified dollar amount of unpaid services. The lab's lien would then be subordinated to the bank if it let its unpaid bills exceed that amount. In spite of a lien and prior to any default, the producer is permitted access to the film material for the purposes of cutting and editing the film.

The bank's requirement that it have a priority position conflicts with the SAG requirement that a producer grant it a lien to ensure payment of talent compensation and residuals. The bank is sometimes able to have that lien subordinated to bank financing or, if the presale agreement contemplates the grant of worldwide distribution rights to a distributor, to insist that the distributor execute an agreement with the Guild assuming the obligation to pay residuals in exchange for SAG's releasing its security interest. A bank may occasionally approve a presale licensee's request that if it forecloses, the bank will not disturb that licensee's rights so long as it fulfills its obligations under its presale agreement and remits any money payable to the producer directly to the bank.

It should be noted that if a bank does foreclose, the foreclosure would eliminate the unsecured profit participations not only of the borrower but of any unsecured third-party participants, including investors and talent. In the event any third party has a gross receipt participation in the film that is calculated from the first dollar of film rental, special care must be taken by the producer in carving those gross receipts from the advance because any advance from a licensee to be paid to the bank in reduction of a loan would normally be considered gross receipts to such a participant. Otherwise, if the participant claims entitlement to a percentage of those gross receipts being paid to the bank, where would the funds come from to pay the participant? Of course, to the extent participations are carved out of advances, the amount a bank can lend is lessened.

Assuming that presale agreements include a network or television syndication presale, the same problem potentially exists with respect to residual payments. If there is theatrical distribution in the U.S., the theatrical distributor will not assume responsibility for residual payments unless the distributor has also acquired television rights. But if the only funds left to pay the residuals mandated by U.S. television exhibition are from television revenue and foreign revenue, and if *those* revenues are utilized to repay a loan, the producer obviously faces a serious problem.

As can be seen, bank financing has certain risks not only for the bank but for the producer and third parties as well. In order to secure a bank loan, a producer has to enter into presale agreements.

But, particularly if his picture proves highly commercial, he would be far better off if it were financed without the necessity of presales. On the other hand, banks traditionally do not request an equity participation in the film's profits, and bank loans allow the producer to finance his film without investors, who *would* be granted an equity participation in exchange for their investment. Moreover, the availability of bank financing means that the producer need not deal with a studio, thereby avoiding the loss of artistic control and the overhead and other charges that a studio is likely to impose. Bank financing should be viewed then simply as one more mechanism for the financing of a motion picture, with certain advantages and disadvantages when compared to other financing arrangements.

COMPLETION BONDS

Banks and investors require assurance that a film will be completed and delivered in accordance with the terms of a presale agreement. This linchpin in the willingness of a bank to enter into a production loan or, in many cases, of an investor to advance funds is contained in a completion bond agreement ("the bond") between a completion guarantor and a producer, and a bank or investor, if applicable. A completion guarantor is a company that, pursuant to the bond, agrees either to advance all sums required to complete payment of the production cost of a picture if that cost exceeds the budget, or, alternatively, to repay the sums a financier—whether bank, investor, or financier/distributor—has loaned or invested.

Creditworthiness

For producer, bank, or investor, the first concern must be the creditworthiness of the completion guarantor. Unfortunately, most completion guarantors are not themselves substantial companies and therefore their creditworthiness might normally be a problem. However, some of these guarantors have made arrangements with insurance companies or other creditworthy commercial organizations to provide overbudget financing. In that event, the bank or investor receives the right to assert a claim directly against the company agreeing to provide the additional overbudget financing. Other completion guarantors will agree to provide overbudget financing only up to a specified maximum. If the cost of production were to exceed that limit, there would be no source for additional financing. However, if the limit is high enough, the chance that the cost of a particular film will exceed it is extremely remote. In each case the bank or investor has to make a judgment as to the creditworthiness of the guarantor and the sufficiency of any limit in the amount of the guaranty.

Fees

The completion fee charged by the guarantor in the bond is typically up to 6 percent of the budget of the film (excluding the fee). Obviously, the budget for the film must provide for the fee. Quite frequently, the guarantor will agree to return up to 50 percent of the fee to the producer if he is not called upon to advance money to finish the film. This rebate is normally payable to the bank as additional collateral for its loan or to the investor as recoupment. Sometimes the rebate is eliminated and the fee reduced to 2 percent or less if the guarantor is affiliated with a company providing some other service to the picture (e.g., payroll or production insurance), and depending upon the perceived overbudget risk.

Delivery Requirements

The completion guarantor must agree to deliver the film in accordance with the requirements of the presale agreement. This can pose problems to a bank and it is most important to reconcile fully any requirements contained in the presale agreement with the obligations of the completion guarantor. For example, the presale agreement may require that the film have a particular director and/or star(s). If any of these persons were to die or become incapacitated, the resulting loss would be covered by insurance. If, however, the director and the star breach their agreements with the producer and he wishes to terminate their contracts, such right of termination must be conditioned upon either finding replacements who are acceptable to the licensee or having the licensee agree to waive its requirement for a particular talent if that person breaches his or her agreement and is thereby terminated during the course of production.

Where there is a network or pay cable presale licensee, the picture may be subject to television "standards and practices"; these deal with certain determinations relating primarily to matters of obscenity and questionable taste. Prior to principal photography, it is possible to obtain from a television licensee an analysis of the shooting script that indicates the problem areas that may make the script unacceptable and that makes suggestions for changes in filming to avoid any difficulty. Should the presale agreement provide that the network must accept the picture if those suggestions are followed, the guarantor is responsible for seeing to it that they are.

If there are requirements that are subjective in nature, dealing with a film's artistic quality or commercial appeal, the guarantor probably would not commit to meet those requirements; in that event, a presale agreement containing them might simply prove unacceptable to the bank or investor. Tension often exists between the requirements of the licensee in the presale agreement and the commitment of the completion guarantor to fulfill those requirements, and it is crucial for the bank or investor to effect a reconciliation between both before agreeing to lend or to invest.

As we have seen, presale agreements may contain conditions regarding payment, even after delivery, that create problems for a lender or investor. Licensees may agree to make payments before or after delivery. When payments are made after delivery, the amount of interest on the bank loan obviously increases, and the bank's credit decision becomes more difficult if the loan is to be paid back over a long period.

There are even more serious problems, however. The completion guarantor's responsibility to deliver the film to a licensee ends when the film is delivered. Therefore, a bank or investor must scrutinize the presale agreement to determine whether a producer's failure to meet a postdelivery obligation might give the licensee grounds for nonpayment. For example, many home video license agreements require as a condition for payment of an advance: first, that the film be distributed theatrically by one of a named group of distributors and, second, that the distributor agree to expend a specified minimum on prints and advertising within a stipulated time period. What happens if for some reason the distributor fails to spend that sum? Unless a provision can be devised to satisfy the home video licensee (perhaps a requirement that the distributor remit to him any money it has not spent in prints and advertising), for a bank, at least, the only solution to its problem is to make the distributor directly liable to the bank for the amount of the advance that was lost because of its failure to meet the home video licensee's requirements. Clearly, theatrical distributors do not want to incur such a liability.

Another contentious issue centers around the so-called "windows," the time periods between the end of one form of exhibition and the beginning of another. Assume that a licensee agrees to pay an advance for television syndication rights and that this advance is to be payable during the period of syndication—a period that normally begins after the windows for cable and network licenses are over. If the syndication licensee makes the producer promise that he will not allow any pay cable or network television exhibition except during time periods that do not violate the windows and if the producer then breaches that covenant, the syndication licensee would have a reason not to pay. The investor looks to the producer's integrity for assurance that such a breach would not occur, but it is more difficult for the bank to protect itself. When presale licenses are used as collateral for bank loans, any provisions for postdelivery payments must be carefully reviewed by the bank's lawyers. To the extent that the investor relies on presale licenses for a return on his investment, he should realize that the licensees' obligations to pay are not ironclad and under certain circumstances may even vanish.

Finally, there may be a dispute between the completion guarantor, who claims to have delivered the film to the distributor, and the distributor, who claims that delivery is incomplete or not in accordance with the distribution agreement. Clearly, the distributor should not be able to release the picture without paying the advance. The bank may require a quick dispute resolution mechanism to resolve such conflicting claims.

Bond Exclusions

The typical form of bond, written not for banks but for investors, contains a host of items for which the completion guarantor assumes no responsibility. These items normally include, among other things, costs that should have been covered by insurance but were not; overbudget costs on items for which suppliers have agreed to accept a flat sum in payment, which sum is denominated as such in the budget; costs resulting from loss due to X-rays, radiation, or the like; and costs due to currency fluctuations. The completion guarantor argues that he should not be responsible for these items because they should have been provided for by the producer. Similarly, the completion guarantor should not be held responsible for losses due to the fraud or dishonesty of the producer.

From the viewpoint of the bank, however, the bond must be much more restrictive. The guarantor is typically responsible to the bank for all matters relating to the production of the film except (1) the obligation to provide financing as required up to the maximum amount of the budget; (2) the delivery of film materials in excess of those provided for in the presale agreement; (3) the technical quality of the film; (4) any defect in title; (5) problems in obtaining a specific film rating from the Motion Picture Association of America; and (6) any obligation to deliver *before* a specific date.

The bank attempts to reduce its risks with respect to the above exclusions in the bond as follows: (1) If the bank is lending money up to the budget, it can continue to do so (even if the producer is in breach) so as to trigger the obligations of the completion guarantor and ensure that the film is properly delivered. In any event, while failure to fund the budget does not void the bond, it does relieve the guarantor from financing costs that occur because of delays or other circumstances that arise due to the lack of financing. (2) The materials the completion guarantor is obligated to deliver as set forth in the bond should be the same as those materials required under all presale agreements. (3) Since there should be no obligation under a presale agreement for matters of artistic quality, this exclusion should not cause any difficulty. (4) If there is a defect in title, the bank does have a problem. This is the one area where it is conceivable for the bank to be exposed despite diligence. For instance, an author could conceivably have made a prior grant of the literary material to someone other than the producer. Other defects in title relating to claims of infringement, libel, and slander are covered by insurance, although the typical insurance limits would probably be far below the budgeted costs of the film. (5) With respect to an MPAA rating, it is possible to submit a script to the MPAA for a preliminary rating and to require the guarantor to guarantee that the film as photographed will receive that rating. Ordinarily, the presale agreement requires some minimal rating (usually at least an R) from the MPAA. (6) With respect to delivery prior to a certain date, the bank can simply insist that delivery must be made in accordance with the requirement of the presale agreement.

Progress Reports

The completion guarantor normally requires the producer to prepare various production reports on the status of each production. The financier should require that it receive copies of such reports from the completion guarantor. Since installments of the loan are being paid to the producer on a weekly basis during principal photography, the completion guarantor should confirm in the bond that all money loaned by the bank or advanced by the financier is properly applied to the budget. Otherwise, if the bank made an installment of the loan but conditioned an additional installment on acknowledgment by the guarantor that the prior installment had been properly expended toward the budget, the bank would have a problem if the guarantor took the position that the earlier installment had been improperly spent, since the guarantor could claim that the production funds constituting the budget had not been advanced as required.

Takeovers

One of the hotly contested disputes between the producer and the completion guarantor relating to the bond is the completion guarantor's right, customary in such bonds, to take over the film and deliver it if it appears that the film is going overbudget or is behind schedule.

The takeover threat, from the guarantor's point of view, is what keeps the producer honest. When the guarantor does take over a picture, it is contractually obligated to deliver the picture based on the shooting schedule and in accordance with the requirements of the specified presale license agreements. But, subject to these agreements (in the event of a takeover), the guarantor has the right to fire the director, the producer, and the cast, and the right, to the extent the picture is overbudget and the guarantor is advancing money, to advance that money on its sole signature.

Now let's look at the right of the completion guarantor to take over production from the point of view of the producer, the bank, and the investor. From the producer's point of view, he loses control of a project that he may have been working on for years. To protect himself he will try to provide that the right of takeover will only occur if the picture is either overbudget by a stipulated percentage (that includes the contingency sum in the budget) or is a specified number of days behind the shooting schedule for reasons other than an act of God. Sometimes the guarantor will agree that before an actual takeover he will advise the producer on how to eliminate the problem(s) causing the takeover threat. For the bank, which is not concerned about the artistic quality of the picture, it matters little whether a takeover occurs so long as its investment is protected. Finally, the investor is torn between wanting the producer to retain responsibility for production, in order to ensure the film's artistic quality, and the risk of having the film greatly exceed its budget, which would of course delay his recoupment and receipt of any profits.

A related problem concerns "enhancements." Quite frequently during the course of production, the producer decides to spend more money than budgeted, perhaps for special effects or for a scene not in the original script or for something comparable to improve the quality of the film. Vis-a-vis the producer, the completion guarantor is not responsible for the cost of enhancements. So if a producer wants to enhance a picture he must make sure that he has the available funds to do so and that the bank and the completion guarantor have agreed to the enhancement. For a completion guarantor it may be difficult to sever enhancement costs from the costs for which the guarantor is responsible. The investor may or may not agree to the enhancement, but in any event he will want to make sure that the enhancement does not in any way compromise the guarantor's obligation to pay other overbudget costs.

Recoupment

To the extent that a completion guarantor advances money toward the production of the film, he always recoups his contribution in second position after the budget is recouped. If the bank lends against presale advances, the guarantor must recoup from overages or unsold rights or territories. The completion guarantor's money bears interest usually at the same rate charged by the bank, and the producer's obligation to repay the completion guarantor is secured by a lien on the picture that is subordinated to the bank lien and those liens permitted by the bank. Sometimes the bank requires that the completion guarantor specifically subordinate his right to payment to the bank's rights and that he agree not to take any action to enforce his security interest rights until the bank has taken action to enforce its lien, or until the bank has given him permission to take such action. A bank-guarantor subordination agreement would terminate upon repayment of the bank loan. Subject to the foregoing, the completion guarantor's security documentation would be similar to the bank's.

FRACTIONALIZATION OF RIGHTS

Whether a producer licenses distribution rights in his film prior to or subsequent to the production of the film depends upon a number of factors. Obviously, he has no choice if the only way he can finance the film is to license some or all of the rights to a distributor on a negative pickup basis (whereby the distributor either (1) advances the cost of production or (2) guarantees to pay that cost on delivery and the guaranty is used as collateral for a production loan). However, if the producer has other sources of financing, he may face a difficult decision. Before a film is produced, it is anybody's guess how it will turn out, no matter how attractively it is packaged and marketed. A chance always exists that the director will not do his best work or there won't be any chemistry or spark between the actors despite how appealing they may be individually. The presence of such risks means that the producer will probably get less favorable distribution terms before production than after production of the film, unless, obviously, the film totally fails to realize its presumed potential. (In such a case, the producer would be better off licensing distribution rights prior to the production of the film, but who's to know?) As few producers are prescient, they must base their timing of licensing agreements on an evaluation of the elements of the film, the track records of the writers, director and actors, and on analysis of actual market demand prior to the film's production as compared to anticipated demand when the film is available for release.

Whether distribution rights to a film are licensed before or after the film is produced, the issues relating to the terms of the license will be similar. Licensing all rights to a film on a world-wide basis was discussed in Chapter Five. Sometimes, a producer will find it advantageous to license the various rights to the film separately— that is, the distribution rights in themselves and the different territories in which those rights may be exploited. As noted earlier, such separate licensing is known as the "fractionalization" or "segmentation" of rights.

To review: the individual distribution rights typically available are the theatrical rights, network television rights, pay television rights, syndicated television rights, home video rights, and nontheatrical distribution rights (that is, rights to exhibit a film on airplanes, ships at sea, military bases, hospitals, and other closed-circuit systems, 16mm film, oil rigs, and college campuses). The incidental rights that may bring in some income are the merchandising rights, the music (sound track and music publishing) rights, the print publication rights (usually this will involve only a novelization and/or photo-novel of the film), and, a newly developing area, theme-park rights. Most often the theatrical distributor acquires the merchandising, music, and print publication rights.

Any or all of the foregoing rights may be licensed to individual distributors in different territories. The "domestic" territory means the U.S. and Canada. Canadian laws, however, now require that under some circumstances a Canadian distribution company control the Canadian theatrical rights, although a non-Canadian company can distribute in Canada if it also distributes the film throughout the rest of the world. The "foreign" territories consist of each country of the world or sometimes a grouping of countries (for example, Southeast Asia) in which a particular company distributes.

When a producer fractionalizes the rights to a film, he may license the domestic theatrical rights to one distributor and the domestic video rights to another; all German rights to a German distributor; U.K. theatrical and video rights to one U.K. distributor; U.K. television rights to another U.K. distributor; and so on. As can be seen, the combinations of rights and territories appear to be endless.

Theatrical Distributors

The locomotive that drives the train of fractionalization is the domestic theatrical distributor. The producer must be extremely judicious in his choice of this distributor, both as to its presumed ability to maximize the profits of the film and as to the rights that it will (or may) insist on acquiring in addition to domestic theatrical rights. There are three types of domestic theatrical distributors: major theatrical distributors, "mini-major" theatrical distributors, and independent theatrical distributors.

The major domestic theatrical distributors are the studios that finance and distribute the majority of high-budget American films. Typically these distributors will have their own film exchanges, production facilities, overseas offices, and sources of financing. Today they include Paramount, Universal, Disney, Warner Brothers, Twentieth Century-Fox, MGM-UA, and Columbia (Sony).

The mini-major theatrical distributor does not have its own production facilities and distributes in foreign territories only
through subdistributors. It will do a few high-budget films, some
medium-budget films, and perhaps some "art," "classic," or im-
ported films. Examples of distributors in this category are Carolco
and New-Line.

Finally, there are the independent domestic theatrical distributors. Some of these companies distribute nationally, others distribute directly only in major marketing areas like New York and
Los Angeles and use subdistributors in other parts of the country.
Apart from the obvious disadvantage of not having the capital to
market a film on the same level as would a major or mini-major
distributor, the independent suffers from often being left with the
less desirable theaters in which to book its product. Additionally,
because the films they distribute are low budget and because
many independents distribute only a few pictures per year, their
leverage with the exhibitors is often minimal. This may well result
in an independent distributor having a severely diminished ability
to collect the sums owed to it by theater owners. As distributors
will always give accountings to producers based on the sums they
receive, as opposed to the sums they are owed, a producer will derive no benefit from even the most favorable agreement with an
independent distributor if that distributor is unable to collect
from the theater owners. Furthermore, a guarantee from some independent distributors is almost worthless as a means of financing the production of a film because the lenders may believe that
these distributors will be in bankruptcy before the film is completed. The disadvantages of dealing with an independent distributor,
notwithstanding, there are enough instances of success stories
among the independents to make them attractive to the more ad-
venturesome entrepreneurial producers. Besides, sometimes there
is simply nowhere else for a producer to turn.

Foreign Sales Agents

By far the most common example of fractionalization of rights is
the producer's attempt to assign all rights in the domestic territory
himself and to engage a foreign sales agent to sell all rights on a

territory-by-territory basis abroad. The agreement between the foreign sales agent and the foreign distributor will resemble a normal subdistribution agreement except that the foreign distributor will not be entitled to any net profits. Typically, the foreign distributor will take its distribution fee (which sometimes is as much as 40 percent or more of gross receipts), deduct its costs, and remit the remainder to the foreign sales agent. If the foreign distributor has provided an advance, it will, of course, recoup its advance from the money it would otherwise remit to the foreign sales agent. The foreign sales agent, in turn, takes a sales fee before remitting any money received to the producer. As with a distributor, a foreign sales agent often pays an advance to a producer for the right to function as the foreign sales agent. The amount (or existence) of the advance depends largely upon the foreign sales agent's confidence in his ability to market the film and to obtain advances from foreign distributors. The fee the sales agent charges will depend upon the size of the advance it has given to the producer. If the foreign sales agent takes the risk of offering the producer a substantial advance he will, in turn, charge a higher fee (sometimes as much as 30 percent or more of the gross receipts). The smaller the advance, the lower the sales agent fee (which is rarely less than 10 percent of the gross receipts). The foreign sales agent rarely receives a profit participation in the film.

Foreign sales agents usually market their products at film festivals such as those at Cannes, MIFED, and the American Film Market in Los Angeles. At these festivals, foreign distributors view many films and bid on those that interest them. Preparing and selling a film at the festivals can be quite expensive. The most advantageous arrangement for the foreign sales agent is to deduct its expenses from the producer's share of the receipts. For example, if the foreign sales agent takes a 25 percent fee, it will first retain 25 percent of the gross receipts; it will then deduct its expenses from the amount remaining. Next it will deduct an amount equal to any advance it has made to the producer (with or without interest, depending on what is negotiated), and finally it will remit whatever is left to the producer. If the producer has some leverage, the foreign sales agent may deduct its expenses "off the top."

That is, from the gross receipts the sales agent will first deduct all of its expenses, then its sales agent fee on the balance, then any advance paid to the producer, and then remit the remainder to the producer. In very rare cases (where the producer has very great leverage), the foreign sales agent may be forced to collect its expenses from its share of receipts. In this case, from the gross receipts the sales agent will first deduct its distribution fee, then deduct any advance paid to the producer, and remit the remainder to the producer, leaving the sales agent without a deduction for its expenses. Note that the advances made to the producer are always deducted from the producer's share because the advances are made against the producer's share of receipts.

Also affecting the economics of the producer's agreement with the foreign sales agent (or with any distributor) is the term of the distribution license. The sales agent (or distributor) wants to acquire the right to sell (or distribute) the film in perpetuity. The producer, on the other hand, will not want to risk being stuck with a sales agent (or distributor) who is not performing and will therefore want the term of the license to be as short as possible. Sometimes the agreement provides that the sales agent has the right to sell the film for a given period (often seven years) and the right to extend that term for an additional period if it has achieved some specified measure of performance, such as a stated amount of gross receipts. This is a fair compromise because it protects a sales agent against losing a film on which it has spent money and done a job good enough to have increased the value of the product, while it also protects the producer when the sales agent has either ignored the film or simply been unable to exploit it properly.

Problems With Fractionalization

While at first glance fractionalization of rights appears to be a fairly simple matter, that is usually not the case. Often a major or mini-major domestic theatrical distributor will simply not be interested in a film unless it is able to obtain all domestic rights. If the producer insists on fractionalizing the domestic rights, he may be forced to go to an independent distributor. Major and mini-major distributors are particularly reluctant to distribute a film theatrically if they do not control the videocassette rights. The reason for this is two-fold. First, video exploitation is extremely profitable for the distributor, who typically includes in gross receipts only 20 to 25 percent of the amount it receives from the video market. As most major and mini-major distributors either own their own video distribution company (sometimes in partnership with another company) or have a very favorable output deal with a video distribution company, it is very important for them to have video rights. Second, video distributors do relatively little advertising of their own. Instead, they rely on theatrical advertising of the film to propel the video exploitation. They can do this because nowadays films are available on video very soon after theatrical release. Thus, the major or mini-major distributor will want to derive the full benefit of its own advertising dollars, rather than losing that benefit to some unrelated third party. Accordingly, if video rights are not available, a major or mini-major distributor will either refuse to distribute a film or will greatly reduce its commitment to advertising and print costs.

This puts the producer in a catch-22 situation: video distributors may well demand from him a minimum guarantee of financing for theatrical prints and film advertising as a precondition of a video deal. Sometimes the producer is able to obtain such a commitment from the theatrical distributor, and sometimes he is forced to seek equity investment to provide this piece of the financing.

When a producer has access to an equity fund to finance the cost of theatrical prints and advertising, he will often attempt to make a deal with the domestic theatrical distributor whereby the latter puts up no money for prints and advertising and simply provides its distribution facilities and personnel. Under this arrangement, known as a "rent-a-studio" arrangement, the domestic theatrical distributor has few expenses, takes virtually no risk, and, accordingly, charges a very small distribution fee. On the other hand, a studio will consider this arrangement only when it has an unexpected vacancy in its distribution lineup that it is otherwise unable to fill, is having financial problems and cannot fund a production schedule, or can work with a producer who has a track record of enormous success. A studio is in business, after all, to take risks in order to reap great rewards, and even with a very successful picture, it receives little profit from a rent-a-studio arrangement.

When the producer fractionalizes the rights to his film, the agreements with the various domestic distributors will be very much like the foreign sales agent agreement we described: a distribution fee will be charged, costs will be recouped, advances will be recouped, and the remainder will be remitted to the producer. Sometimes the distributor will also receive a share of the net profits of the film. However, unless the distributor is making an equity investment in the film, the producer will resist this and argue that from its distribution fee the distributor is making all the profit it is entitled to given the risk involved. Sometimes a distributor of one set of rights will require the protection of having the producer cover that distributor's losses from the producer's share of net profits received from other distributors. Thus, even in a fractionalization of rights situation, the producer may end up cross-collateralizing certain rights for certain distributors.

Holdbacks on Distribution Rights

When fractionalizing rights, a producer must be careful to provide holdbacks on the various rights he has granted in order to give each medium an opportunity to be fully exploited without interference from competing media. Each medium, therefore, should have a window of exploitation during which time it will be the principal source of exploitation of the film. Usually the film will first enjoy theatrical exploitation that may continue for as long a period as the theatrical distributor is able to negotiate. About six months after the film's initial theatrical release, the video window will open. In other words, the film will not be available to the video distributor until it has been in theatrical release for six months, although sometimes it will have been released for as little as four months before being available to video distributors. Six months after the initial video availability of the film, the pay television window will open, usually for two years. After that two-year period, the pay television window will close (that is, no further pay television exhibitions will be permitted) and the network television window will open, usually for two to three years. At the end of that time, the network television window will close and a second pay television window will open for about one year. At the end of the second pay television cycle, the syndicated television window will open and remain open for between three and seven years.

The fractionalization of rights may be complicated and is becoming more difficult for the individual producer to accomplish. There is, for instance, a trend among pay television networks to enter into output deals only with large-scale suppliers and not to accept films on a title-by-title basis from independent producers. Nevertheless, for the producer who succeeds in fractionalizing rights, the rewards can be great. For one thing, if he finances his film in this way he retains virtually complete artistic freedom. Additionally, for a producer who succeeds in keeping distribution agreements for the various rights and territories independent of one another, the film's receipts and expenses as it moves from medium to medium and territory to territory will not be cross-collateralized. Thus, for example, a film's losses in theatrical distribution cannot be deducted from its profits in video if different distributors are responsible for the two media. In this way, the producer's profits are maximized.

FINANCING BY LABORATORIES AND STUDIOS

Sometimes to finance part of the cost of production a producer can find a laboratory anxious for the business that will do the head-end work—that is, the manufacture of dailies and other preprint materials—for a discount or for deferred payment of part of its cost. Suppliers of production equipment may do the same. Major film distributors, too, with studios that they wish to keep utilized, may offer their facilities to a producer on a basis that allows them to recoup some of their costs as deferments. In addition, any laboratory or studio that is willing to regard some production costs as part of its own overhead is, in effect, charging the producer less than the going rate and thus gives him a discount.

Alternatively, a laboratory or studio may actually provide a portion of a film's financing—or perhaps even all the financing needed after advances obtained from territorial sales—in return for the producer's agreement to use the facilities of that company.

FOREIGN GOVERNMENTAL FINANCING

From time to time some governments provide extraordinary tax advantages on films made, in whole or in part, in their countries and/or direct subsidies to the production financing of such films. The tax advantages make it easier to obtain financing from investors in those countries. A film will usually have to achieve a certain level of national "content" to qualify under the applicable law. For example, a Canadian law giving such tax benefits provides that a certain percentage of the film be of Canadian content. This is calculated by assigning numerical values to the various major elements of the film (writers, producers, director, actors, and screenplay). Added together, the numerical value of the elements that are of Canadian origin must equal a specified sum for the film to qualify for the tax advantage. A government may require that the theme of a film be particularly related to that country and/or that the picture be shot almost entirely (if not entirely) in that country. The national content requirements are often so stringent that they make achieving tax benefits in that country very difficult.

Some countries have treaties with each other that provide for tax benefits and/or subsidies when production entities from the two countries coproduce a film. While there will normally still be national content requirements under a treaty coproduction, the requirements are usually somewhat more relaxed and the prospects of actually financing such a film are easier.

CO-PRODUCTIONS: HOW
FOREIGN SUBSIDIES WORK

Some countries, eager to attract foreign (especially American) filmmakers, have set up governmental or quasi-governmental filmmaking departments (or ministries) or private companies to provide the goods and services to be used in that country at substantial savings. Some countries, through various quasi-governmental organizations, have entered into agreements whereby its facilities and personnel can be obtained at greatly reduced prices. The following is a typical example of the configuration of such a deal: The budget of the film is $10 million, $5 million of which is to be provided in local goods and services. The governmental agency would require the producer to pay half of the $5 million in cash, and would itself provide the other half of the goods and services free as its contribution toward the film. Thus, a $10 million film could be produced for $7,500,000 cash. (Keep in mind that the goods and services provided by the governmental agency for $5 million would cost a great deal more in the U. S. and thus, in and of themselves, represent a considerable saving to the producer.) In return for its contribution, the governmental agency usually gains the right to distribute the film in its country and receives a pro-rata share, along with the other financiers, of the net profits of the film worldwide.

It is sometimes hard to equate the value of services to a dollar amount. If a set is created, what is the actual cost to create it? What profit margin to the studio should be added to direct costs? If there is a completion bond, the bonding company should acknowledge, for the purposes of the bond, that the value of the goods and services provided equals a certain dollar amount. The same acknowledgment should also be made by profit participants.

Obviously, a producer has, at least theoretically, a wide variety of financing methods—alone and in many different combinations—available to him. It's up to him to determine the combination that works best for his particular project.

7 ARTIST'S AGREEMENT

O nce an independent producer has found the money to finance his film and has an approved budget, before principal photography can start he must deal with the various types of employment contracts that are required in the making of a motion picture.

SCREEN ACTOR'S GUILD
BASIC AGREEMENT AND OTHER FORMS

One of the most important contracts is the actor's agreement. Within the U.S., most experienced film actors are members of the Screen Actors Guild, and an independent producer must become a signatory to SAG and execute SAG's Basic Agreement if he wishes to use such actors. Aside from specifying salaries, the Basic Agreement describes in great detail the rights, duties, and obligations of actors, all of which relate to the amount of money they earn and the minimum time period for which they are hired. Certain actors are hired on a day-to-day or a week-to-week basis according to a form approved by SAG, and the only deviations permitted in this form are certain matters, such as billing, that are not covered by the Guild agreement. Most attorneys do not get involved in SAG-approved contracts for such actors; casting directors or production assistants will ordinarily prepare the contracts and have them executed as a matter of routine. However, an attorney may prepare certain riders to these agreements—for example, in the event that an actor is to receive billing on-screen or in paid advertisements and/or has bargained for items in excess of the Guild minimums. The SAG form incorporates references to the Basic Agreement, which must be consulted to determine working conditions, overtime, and other conditions of employment.

In dealing with lead actors who are paid more than the Guild minimum, the major motion picture distributors have to use a long form of actor agreement, since the Guild does not have an applicable standard contract for that purpose.

Periods of Service and Compensation

The elements of an actor's agreement are quite simple. An actor is hired for a certain consecutive minimum time period: he starts on a certain date and receives a stated salary, usually an amount per week for the minimum period, whether or not he is actually required to work during all of that period. Typically, the weekly compensation requires the actor to work five days in the studio or six days on location. If the actor has not completed his services within the minimum period, the producer has the right to extend the minimum period for an indefinite period of time, paying a certain sum for each additional week or part of a week (known as "overages"). Actors receiving large salaries are sometimes hired for the entire production schedule plus two to four weeks so that the need for overages can be reduced.

Sometimes there is a "free period" between the expiration of the minimum period and any additional extended period, during which the actor will work without pay. The concept of the free period is for the actor's benefit. If an actor's services are required for twelve weeks and he is to be paid $120,000, his agent may insist that he be hired for a minimum period of ten weeks plus two free weeks. In that way instead of being paid $10,000 a week for twelve weeks, he will get $12,000 a week for ten weeks. Aside from getting his money sooner, the actor also benefits if an additional period of employment follows the twelve weeks because traditionally the additional weeks are paid at the same *weekly rate* for which the actor was originally hired. And the agent can then say to third parties that his client received $12,000 and not $10,000 a week for his work, which is useful in negotiating the actor's next film job.

Although this point can be negotiated, an actor ordinarily renders services (subject to availability and after completion of principal photography) to do retakes or added scenes, to balance the sound in the event that his voice has not come through properly, and if necessary to rerecord some of the dialogue (known as "looping"). The first few days (depending upon what is negotiated) of such services are usually without additional compensation. Thereafter, he is paid his weekly salary prorated on a daily basis. Usually an actor will render services for a period of from two days to as much as two weeks prior to the start of the minimum period (also without additional compensation) for rehearsals, publicity, wardrobe fittings, and the like. A period longer than a week is the subject of negotiation both as to length of time and compensation. After completion of the principal photography of the film, if an actor is required for such publicity purposes as photo sessions and personal appearances, he usually receives only transportation and living expenses for his services.

An important point for a producer to consider is each actor's starting date. If the actor is a star or featured player who is needed throughout principal photography, his starting date is presumably the first day of shooting or whenever he is required to report for the preproduction activities described above. However, some actors are not needed for all of principal photography, and they may end up getting paid for doing nothing if their fixed starting date proves too early. Sometimes an "on or about" date is settled upon, with as big a swing period before and after that date as the producer can negotiate. As usually interpreted, "on or about" means twenty-four hours on either side of the starting date. Note that with actors hired by the day or from week to week, the starting date and any variation in it are governed by the SAG Basic Agreement.

According to the terms of most talent contracts, the producer can require the actor to work indefinitely to complete photography of the film—that is, for as long as his services are required—at his regular weekly compensation. Obviously, since such a commitment could force an actor to have to change plans previously made, he may try in his contract to specify that after a certain date (called a "stop date") he will no longer be required to report to work—whether or not he has completed his services. Sometimes the stop date is flexible in that a producer will receive an extension of the actor's services if additional shooting is the result of the actor's earlier disability or some event outside of the producer's control.

A stop date provision can prove disastrous for a producer or a completion guarantor should principal photography run behind schedule. With the actor gone, the producer will have to suspend production until he is available again. The alternative is to rearrange the shooting schedule in order to finish the actor's scenes first but it always increases costs to depart from the original plan. Consequently, most producers strongly resist any imposition of a stop date, and in fact, most conflicts of engagements are resolved informally by the parties involved. Usually an actor will try to schedule his commitments far enough apart so that he can be sure of completing one before he starts another. Sometimes, however; an actor is already committed to starting another film prior to the time the producer of the first film approaches him, and in such an event, he will either have to renegotiate his start date on the second film or insist on a stop date on the first film; otherwise, the producer of the first film could force the actor to breach his contract with the producer of the second film.

An actor's compensation is almost always paid weekly, on the regular payday of the week following the one in which services were rendered. If the actor works for a period of less than a week, his salary is prorated. Matters such as the number of hours an actor may be required to work and when the actor stops working on one day and resumes the next are regulated by SAG, as set forth in its Basic Agreement, though they can sometimes be bettered by negotiation.

Living Expenses

Besides compensation for services, an actor ordinarily will receive reimbursement for living expenses if he is working at a place sufficiently removed from his residence to necessitate overnight accommodations. This can be stated either as reimbursement to the actor for "first-class living expense" or in terms of a fixed amount of money per week. The living expense allowance will vary, depending upon where the film is being photographed. For instance, if principal photography is to be in both New York City and a community in upstate New York, the producer may argue that the actor should not receive the same living allowance for both places since the cost of living in the upstate community will be much lower. Generally, an actor's agreed upon living expenses will be much higher in metropolitan areas as compared to rural areas. Sometimes a contract allows one sum for the most expensive cities, a smaller sum for other cities, and a still lesser sum for towns and villages. In any case, a living expense allowance is often "non-accountable"; that is, the actor receives a fixed amount per week whether or not he actually spends it. The alternative form is reimbursement for actual, specified expenses up to a stated amount. Whether the expense allowance is accountable or nonaccountable has some significant tax consequences, and therefore the actor's business manager usually participates in deciding what to negotiate for.

In addition to his living expense allowance, the actor ordinarily will receive round-trip transportation from his residence to the place that principal photography is to occur and from one location to another. For all persons whose services fall within the jurisdiction of any guild or union, the agreement almost always provides that the transportation will be first class and by air if air transportation is available, unless the production is low-budget and *everybody* is flying in the same class.

Perquisites

In addition to transportation and living expense allowances, important actors can and do demand a host of other things. These can include round-trip transportation for more than one—perhaps the actor's spouse and family; a private dressing room or a private trailer for dressing on locations; a personal hairdresser, a makeup person, and a double; a chauffeured limousine to transport the actor to and from airports and locations; and so on. Some actors will ask for and get tickets to the film's premiere and a print (or videocassette copy) of the film. Sometimes more time is spent in negotiating these fringes than the actor's remuneration. A producer has to bear in mind that all of an actor's fringe benefits can add up to a significant sum when figuring the cost of production of the film. For an actor in a low-budget film, therefore, it is usually far more difficult to obtain the sizable living expense allowance and the accommodations that he may receive without protest on higher-budget, large studio films.

Dubbing

Up to now we have been concerned with the kinds of services that the producer and actor can agree the actor should render. There are, however, other services that the actor may want to render that the producer may not want to use. For instance, an actor's agreement will almost always allow the producer to use a substitute to dub the dialogue for foreign language versions of the film or even to dub in English should the original actor not be available or be unable to perform. While an important actor will almost always insist on the first opportunity to dub in English, there may be demands that he cannot meet—for instance, singing when he lacks that particular talent. Some actors want the right to dub their performances in certain foreign languages, and some agreements will require that the actor receive substantial prior notice as to when any dubbing in English is to take place so that he will have an opportunity to make himself available. For obvious reasons, an actor will not want his performance dubbed by an incompetent actor or someone whom he deems to be second-rate, and thus he may insist that if any dubbing is necessary he have the right to approve the person to be used. If the actor himself is to do the dubbing, the producer will want to provide that he do so without compensation, for in all probability his salary would be much more than would be paid to anyone else doing the dubbing. If dubbing is to be done abroad, the producer should not be obligated to pay for the actor's transportation to and from the foreign country, which could be very expensive. Dubbing abroad presents another consideration in that the agreement between distributor and subdistributor may permit the latter to dub the film into the language of the territory; having the original actor do the dubbing might violate such an agreement.

Doubles

The producer may also want the right to use a double for the actor to perform hazardous acts and perhaps to appear in scenes in which the actor would not be readily recognizable. Doing this can cut down the actor's minimum work period—and thus save the producer some money—and might also protect the actor from possible injury. Most actors will not object to a double, but there are some who insist on performing their own stunts. In such a case, the insurance company must be notified immediately and an additional premium may be required, because most cast insurance is based on the proviso that the principal actors will not be asked to do anything dangerous. Even if insurance is not a problem, most producers will not give the actor the right to perform stunts if the producer, in his reasonable opinion, considers them to be too hazardous.

Nudity

Another factor in which the doubling of an actor may become an issue is that of nudity. If the actor's role calls for nudity, the producer will want to have maximum discretion. Accordingly, he will want the right to use the actor in the nude scenes as well as the right to use a double for the actor if the producer is not satisfied with the actor's appearance. Some actors will agree to both. Other actors will not agree to appear nude but will agree to being represented as appearing nude by a "body double." Still other actors will require that they decide the degree of nudity and that the producer have the right to use a body double only with the actor's consent. Some actors will not agree to appear nude at all or even to be represented as appearing nude by a body double whom they have not approved.

This is, inevitably, a very sensitive area, one that is subject to delicate negotiations that involve balancing the artistic needs of the film, the moral values of the intended audience, and the sensitivities of the actor. The SAG Basic Agreement provides that the producer may not require an actor to appear nude or even to use a body double unless the actor gives his prior written consent. If the actor withdraws his consent to appear nude prior to the time the scene is shot, the producer is entitled to use a double. Once the scene is shot, the actor may not withdraw his consent.

Promotional Films

Usually an actor's agreement will permit the producer to incorporate footage of the actor in behind-the-scenes documentaries and featurettes relating to the film for no additional compensation, subject only to any minimum payments required by SAG (if applicable). Actors will generally agree to this, sometimes subject to their having the right to approve the footage (such approval not to be unreasonably withheld) in order to prevent an unguarded or embarrassing moment from appearing in a behind-the-scenes promotional film.

Rights to Services

All form agreements will contain variations of two key clauses, which may be considered together. The first key clause provides that all rights to the results and proceeds of the actor's services belong to the producer, and the producer may do anything he wishes with those results and proceeds. An actor will try to limit this right to use of the results and proceeds of his services to the film in question and its advertising and exploitation, in this way denying the producer the right to utilize footage containing his services in a sequel to the film or in any other motion picture. SAG prohibits this practice anyway, absent a negotiated agreement with the actor.

The second key clause is the "pay-or-play" clause, which provides that as long as the producer pays the actor the compensation required under the agreement, the producer is under no obligation to play the actor. That is, the producer is free to decide not to use the actor in the film at all or to use only selected portions of the footage in which the actor appears. This is why it's possible for an actor to sign for a leading role and find that most of his performance has been left on the cutting room floor. If an actor is hired for a role but during shooting is found to be unsuitable, the producer can, in essence, fire the actor merely by paying off his contract and finding another actor to play the role.

A hidden issue in the pay-or-play clause is that of mitigation. If an actor guaranteed six weeks work is used for only one week and then fired but paid his full salary, should his compensation for the five weeks he did not work be reduced by any payment he receives for his services from third parties—that is, for example, if he acts in another film—during this period? The producer will try to leave the agreement silent on that point, since by law mitigation will apply if not specifically provided to the contrary. The actor, of course, will wish to provide that if he earns money during the applicable time period, no mitigation will apply.

Rights of Approval

To protect the importance of his role and to ensure the artistic quality of a film, an important actor may insist on and get certain rights of approval from the producer. A star may want to approve the final script, the director, and possibly the other principal actors, or at least the other lead actor. Various schemes are employed to secure the actor's approval. The producer may suggest a number of names from which the actor will select one (or the actor may suggest and the producer approve). Sometimes the producer and the actor mutually agree on a list and the producer can hire anyone on it.

Actor approvals create special problems for the producer even if he is willing to grant approval in principle. For instance, if an actor with the right of script approval approves a final script, what happens if some rewriting is done during the course of the production, as is often the case, and the actor does not like the rewrite? Has the producer breached the agreement? (Of course, minor changes occurring in the course of production must always be permitted.) One compromise is to provide that the importance of the actor's role will not be significantly or substantially diminished during the filming or cutting. Such a subjective test could, however, result in litigation if actor and producer disagree about the effect of a change. If the actor has approved the director or costar but this person must be replaced because of death, disability, or default, does the actor have the right to approve the substitute director or costar? Could the actor leave the production on the grounds that his approval of a replacement has not been obtained? One solution to this problem is to have the actor agree that the approval must be given if certain objective conditions are met: for instance, he must approve any substitute director who has at least two films to his credit, each of which has earned a certain amount in gross receipts or had a budget of a minimum amount; or he must approve any substitute actor who is of a stature—as measured by customary salary and/or credits—comparable to that of the actor who must be replaced. Another compromise here is for the producer to grant the actor the privilege of consultation rather than approval, with the producer having the final say.

All solutions to the approval problem must take into account the fact that when a producer (or financier) is investing large sums of money toward a production, he must have a star's total commitment. How can he be sure of that commitment? Practically speaking, with regard to script approval, the actor exercises that right as soon as he reads a more or less complete script: if he doesn't like it, he simply doesn't take the job. Later, it is customarily understood in the industry that revisions can be made in a script during principal photography without the actor's approval.

Most actors resent the pay-or-play clause that gives a producer the right not to use all or part of a performance. If an actor can get a producer to agree that the script cannot be changed materially without his approval or that the importance of his role cannot be diminished in relation to the role of some other actor, then he will have some assurance that his performance will be preserved after principal photography has been completed. Such rights of approval by a star are very, very rare, however, and ordinarily an actor must make a commitment with awareness that his performance may be cut and that he cannot control which take or portion of a scene will be used.

Merchandising

Among the rights commonly granted in the actor's agreement are commercial tie-in and merchandising rights discussed in connection with the P-D agreement. However, the actor will always insist that his name or likeness not be used in connection with an *endorsement* of a product or service. Moreover, the actor will usually require a separate royalty on income obtained from merchandising. The standard royalty is 5 percent, reducible by royalties payable to other actors appearing on the same item of merchandise, usually to a floor of 2.5 percent. In other words, if an actor's merchandising royalty is 5 percent and if he and his two costars appear on one T-shirt and the costars each receive 2 percent, then the actor's percentage is reduced by the royalty payable to the costars to the 2.5 percent floor. Additionally, the actor will insist that the producer have the right to merchandise him only in character—that is, in the role in which he appears in the film.

Force Majeure; Disability; Breach

The actor's agreement always specifies certain circumstances under which an actor need not be paid. These are matters of *force majeure* or acts of God. Production of a film may be halted by such events of *force majeure* as a strike, riot, insurrection, war, or other occurrence, including the death or disability of the director or star; or by an act of God, which is narrower and relates to natural causes like an earthquake, fire, or a flood. Most talent agreements generally provide that the actor's performance and salary are suspended during the period of the event and for a reasonable period thereafter while the elements of the film are being reassembled. An actor will attempt to provide that the pertinent events set forth in the agreement be in fact restricted to the narrow act of God events and not include *any* act beyond the control of the producer, whether or not an act of God.

Theoretically, during the period of a *force majeure* event the actor may work for a third party, but as a practical matter it will be difficult for him to arrange other employment on such short notice. In any case, the producer will want the actor to be subject to recall on short notice when the event has ended. To protect the actor, his agreement commonly provides that if a suspension lasts for a stated number of weeks, either the producer or the actor has the right to terminate, except that the actor cannot do so if the producer has resumed payment to him under the terms of the agreement. The number of weeks is usually four to eight, depending upon the bargaining positions of the parties. If an agreement is terminated by such an event , ordinarily the actor receives only such compensation as has accrued up to the time of the suspension. Sometimes, however, an actor will insist that the full pay-or-play fee be paid if the event is the death or disability of another actor or the director. The reason for this is that the producer will have obtained insurance covering the cast members and the director for death or disability, and therefore, he will be reimbursed by the insurance company when paying the salaries of non-disabled actors.

The actor will usually insist that he not be suspended or terminated for such an event unless all other principal cast members and the director are also suspended or terminated. The reason for this is that the actor will not want the event to be used selectively against him, as a means of getting rid of him.

The agreement provides that if the actor cannot render his services because of illness, disability, or other incapacity, the contract can be terminated if the disability lasts for a specified period of time. The shorter the time period, the better for the producer. It is

usually anywhere from three to ten consecutive days for one incapacity and from seven to twenty-one days in the aggregate of all
illnesses during principal photography. The agreement also provides that during an illness or disability the actor is not entitled to
receive compensation or render services for others, though if he remains on location during the incapacity he is entitled to living expenses.
In the event of a dispute between producer and actor as to whether or
not the actor is ill, the producer usually retains the right to have the actor
examined by the producer's doctor, although the actor's doctor may attend the examination at the actor's expense. Ordinarily, the cast insurance company's doctor will also want to examine the actor. To the extent
that the actor's services are covered by cast insurance, if the actor is disabled that insurance would compensate the producer for the full guaranteed payment to the actor.

If the actor breaches the agreement, the producer usually has
the right to suspend the actor for the period of the breach. If the
actor takes several days off and does not show up on the set and
for that reason the producer must suspend production of the film,
then the mere fact that the actor later returns ready to perform
usually does not obligate the producer to put him back on salary
immediately unless the producer is actually ready and willing to
proceed with the production. During any actor-caused period of
suspension, the producer will insist upon the right to terminate
the actor's agreement, obtain injunctive relief in the event the actor tries to work elsewhere, recover damages caused the producer
by the actor's breach, withhold compensation, and eliminate the
actor's billing credit.

What constitutes a breach by the actor is not always easily determined. It is necessary to distinguish between a material breach
of the agreement and a nonmaterial breach. A nonmaterial
breach, for example, might be the actor's reporting fifteen minutes
late for a day's shooting. Even though the producer ought to have
all of his remedies at law, a nonmaterial breach should not be
grounds for termination of the agreement. Sometimes an actor's
agent will try to provide him with a twenty-four hour period to
cure any breach. But how can he cure a breach like showing up
drunk on the set or not showing up at all? Moreover, with a twen-

ty-four hour grace period, the actor could fail to show up every other day and still not be in breach of the agreement and, indeed, could be considered in breach only by refusing to render his services or by violating such clauses as the morals clause, which will be discussed later in this chapter. For this reason, if the producer grants the actor the right to cure a breach, it will usually only be for those breaches that are inarguably curable, and the actor's right to cure will be on a one-time basis only.

It is more difficult to establish that the actor is breaching an agreement should he forget his lines or have to have an inordinately large number of takes for each setup. For this reason, no matter what the agreement provides, the producer is generally at the actor's mercy. If the actor attempts to win a dispute with the producer by fluffing lines, he will usually succeed, depending of course on how badly he is needed by the producer.

Producer's Remedies

The actor's agreement generally gives the producer the right to obtain injunctive relief against an actor in the event of his breach, but for how long should that right continue? The actor will want to provide that the producer's right is merely to *seek* injunctive relief—in other words, the actor will not consent to an automatic injunction. If the actor wants to render services to third parties *after* the period during which the producer had a right to those services, should the producer have the right to prevent his working at that later time? The producer's position is that, as long as the actor is not rendering services for the producer, the actor should not render services for anyone else.

The actual damages the producer will try to claim for an actor's breach can be astronomically high if that breach causes production to be suspended. A producer will definitely not want to give the actor any compensation in the event of a breach of the agreement, no matter what its repercussions may be. But a big and frequent problem arises when producer and actor disagree as to whether or not the actor is in breach in the first place. The actor will rarely admit that he is. Given the likely possibility of such a dispute, the producer will want to provide contractually that pending its outcome, he can withhold the actor's money or deposit it in court or in a special bank account in trust. If the producer does not pay the actor, and has no right to withhold or deposit, he faces a dilemma. For if a court later decides he was wrong and should have paid because the actor was not in breach, he will be considered in breach himself. On the other hand, if he does pay and a court later rules that he was right and need not have paid, he may never get his money back. It may be very difficult to collect money from someone who is not working steadily. This is another of the many possible disputes in which settlement depends upon the respective parties' bargaining power. Of course, if SAG has jurisdiction over the actor's services, the producer will be in violation of the SAG Basic Agreement if he withholds salary from an actor simply by claiming breach.

What happens in the event the actor is entitled not only to fixed compensation but also to contingent compensation (such as a deferment or a profit participation) and his services are terminated after he has completed a small part of his role? Does he receive, in addition to the prorated portion of compensation due for his services prior to the termination, a prorated portion of the contingent compensation, assuming the film is completed and released? In other words, do part of the contingent payments become vested if services are performed but terminated for reasons other than a breach prior to their completion, or must all services be completed before the contingent compensation vests. Some agreements provide that if the actor merely appears on the screen recognizably to the public, he must be paid in full, including all contingent compensation.

When the termination of production is caused by an act of God, which is not covered by insurance, the producer will have lost money and there is good reason for him to take the position that the actor should also lose. Ordinarily, in the event of *force majeure* that causes production of the film to never be completed, the question of paying contingent compensation based on the release of the picture becomes academic. But this is not true if suspension or termination is caused by a cast incapacity, particularly if the incapacity takes place at the beginning of a production when it is usually possible to find a substitute for an actor or director and to continue with the production of the film. As noted, the decision to continue with production or to terminate, although made by the producer, is to a large extent influenced by the cast insurance company.

Cast Insurance

Cast insurance covers the production from losses due to the death or disability of an insured actor or director. Most actor's agreements provide that the actor must be covered by cast insurance and that it be obtained from the insurer without special conditions and with no more than the normal deductible for policies of that type. While almost anyone can be covered by cast insurance, the insurance policy may exclude compensation for known illnesses or other disabilities. For example, if an actor has a history of back trouble, the cast insurance policy may exclude from coverage any losses resulting from that bad back. (In such a case coverage would not include the one thing the producer would want most to be protected against.) Although the cast insurance policy may not have any special exclusions, the deductible or the premium may be unusually high because of some presumed special risk. If an actor has had claims on previous pictures, for example, this would affect the rate.

All actor's contracts should contain a provision requiring the actor to complete truthfully all insurance forms and to cooperate with the producer in any way necessary for him to obtain insurance. The agreement should also state that cast insurance must be obtained before the actor starts rendering services, and if for any reason the usual cast insurance cannot be acquired and the producer therefore wants to terminate (and he should have that right), termination must take place within a short period after he is notified of the failure to obtain insurance; otherwise he forfeits his right to terminate the agreement. If the cast insurance policy can be acquired only by payment of an additional premium, the actor should have the right to pay the additional premium to keep the agreement in effect. In the event the policy specifies an increased deductible, the actor might want the right to pay the producer the difference between the regular deductible and the higher figure.

The cast insurance policy will usually provide that while rendering his service the actor cannot engage in any extra-hazardous activity or fly on any nonscheduled airline without the written consent of the cast insurance company. If the actor is called upon to engage in such hazardous activities, a special policy is usually written. Special policies can also be obtained that cover transportation on airlines whether scheduled or nonscheduled.

Wardrobe

Some agreements state that the actor must furnish present-day wardrobe items to the extent that he has them in his possession, and he must return to the producer any costumes furnished to him. Ordinarily, however, the producer will furnish all clothing, and it is not unusual for the producer to allow the actor to keep that clothing, assuming it has not been rented.

Publicity Releases

Most agreements provide that an actor not issue publicity releases about a film without the prior approval of the producer or distributor. The reason for this is simple: if the distributor has planned a national advertising and publicity campaign, one that the actor may be totally unaware of, a casual statement by the actor to a reporter might rob the whole campaign of its impact. However, most agreements do permit the actor to make incidental references to the film during interviews (such as talk show appearances), so long as such references are nonderogatory to the film and any person or entity connected to it and do not disclose any information that is confidential.

"Morals" Clauses

Most talent agreements contain a "morals" clause, which grants the producer the right to terminate in the event an actor commits any act that is contrary to or ridicules public morality or tends to shock or offend the community. The clause, which protects the producer against adverse publicity that might affect the box office success of a film, is generally written to cover not only criminal acts but also political activity and other conduct that would not constitute a crime. The clause is rarely implemented, and in bargaining, the actor will try to make it as specific and narrow as possible. To the extent that the clause refers to acts that might "tend to" subject the actor to public disrepute or ridicule, he will try to eliminate such "tend to" language. Also, instead of being granted a termination right for reasons of morals, the producer is sometimes limited to the right to deny the actor screen and advertising credit while still being obligated to pay him. Some actors object strenuously to the whole concept of a morals clause and insist on having it removed completely, regarding it as a personal insult. Whether a producer agrees to that usually depends upon the actor's reputation and whether the producer believes that the actor is likely to be guilty of misconduct that could affect the film's performance at the box office.

Visas

On films to be shot abroad, the agreement usually provides that the producer has no obligation to the actor if necessary passports, visas, work permits, and other similar documents cannot be obtained. While the producer may attempt to impose upon the actor the responsibility to acquire these items, that duty probably belongs with the producer, so long as the actor assists him in his efforts.

Tax Indemnification

Another provision relating to productions outside the country is that of foreign tax indemnification. The actor will want to be indemnified by the producer against any additional income tax he may have to pay as a result of rendering services abroad. At one time, producers readily agreed to such a provision, but as the substantial adverse economic consequence of such an agreement has increased (since foreign taxes are frequently higher than those of the U.S.), resistance to foreign tax indemnification has grown to the point where such a provision is almost never granted.

Billing

The question of billing credits is usually as complicated as it is important to the actor. Billing credits include those on the screen and those in advertising.

Having billing credit on the screen means that the actor's name appears on all positive prints of the film. Here it is important to define two of the terms used in the industry in connection with billing credits. The "main titles" of a film are the credits that ordinarily appear at the beginning, together with the film's title, while the "end titles" of the film, as one might guess, are the credits that appear at the conclusion of the picture. In the distant past, all of the credits customarily were in the main titles, and the end titles were limited to the names of the cast members, indicating the roles played by each, and often a studio credit.

Today, the most important credits tend to be interspersed with the action at the beginning of the picture, and where permitted by guild agreements, the less important credits tend to appear at the end of the picture. It seems that more and more people are becoming entitled to credit, whether by guild agreements or by custom, and the end titles seem to be getting longer and longer each year.

One of the first considerations to be dealt with then is where the actor's credit will appear—on-screen, whether in the main titles or the end titles. While SAG requires a listing of the full cast in the end titles, a prominent actor is sure to have his credit in the main titles as well. The crucial question is whether the credit will appear "above" (before) or "below" (after) the title of the film. The main star can bargain for credit above the title, and in first position of all cast members, while a less important actor may have to settle for below title credit, but perhaps in first position among cast members receiving such credits. Actors often attempt to link size and placement of credits to those of other actors.

While the issue of the actor's credit in relation to the title is fairly simple in the on-screen context, in advertising it is somewhat more complicated. Nowadays, a typical movie advertisement will consist of a large visual representation of one or more actors in their roles in the film along with the title of the film known as the "artwork," and a smaller section below the artwork listing credits to various people and entities, known as the "billing block." Typically, the title of the film will appear in huge type in the artwork, known as an "artwork title," and will appear again in smaller type in the billing block, known as the "regular title." A distributor will usually sell a movie by prominent use of the name of the star(s), and will accord a credit to the star(s) in the artwork, above the artwork title and in type approximately equal in size to that of the artwork title. Thus, when the star demands that his or her credit appear in the artwork, distributors will usually agree. But when others ask for credit in the artwork they will be fiercely resisted because the distributor wants maximum flexibility to promote and advertise the film any way it wishes. When mention is made of an actor's credit being above or below the title, the actor's agreement will usually provide that the title referred to is the regular title, not the artwork title, unless the artwork title is specifically cited.

Another sensitive issue in the area of credit placement is how many other actors will be accorded advertising credit prior to the actor in question, and on-screen how many other actors will receive credit on the screen at the same time as the actor. Each sequence of credits that is visible on the screen at one time is called a "card." Thus, for example, an actor may receive credit on a separate card *and* as the third credit of all cast members. Another actor may receive credit as the seventh member of all cast members on a card he shares with no more than two other actors and on which the actor in question is in first position. As can be seen, there is an infinite number of permutations of these factors.

An actor will try to protect his advertising credit by attempting to define its size as broadly as possible, including not only size of type but also such considerations as its prominence, color, boldness, style of type (the typeface used may contractually have to be the same as that of the title or the name of any other cast member), and spacing between credits. The distributor will want to define size as narrowly as possible (for example, height and width of type only). Color and style of type are fairly objective matters, but prominence and boldness are certainly subject to interpretation. A credit can be given additional prominence by appearing after the word "and," or "as" followed by the name of the character portrayed, or by having a box around it. If an actor is able to get the producer to agree that his credit will be no less than 100 percent of the size of the regular title, in a small newspaper ad the title and that credit could both end up almost, if not completely, illegible. Consequently, the actor will bargain for a requirement that in no event will his credit be less than a specified percentage (for example, 20 percent or 25 percent) of the artwork title.

Rarely will a contract contain a provision obligating the distributor to use an actor's picture in connection with advertising of the film. This is called a "likeness" clause and it leads to enormous problems, particularly if a film has more than one star. Are the sizes of their likenesses to be the same? What relative position does each get? The contract of an important actor will commonly provide that if anyone else's likeness is to be used in an ad, the likeness of that actor must also be included. An actor's agent always fears that after a hard bargaining session for proper billing for his or her client, ads will appear that feature some young star whose picture undoubtedly draws people to the box office but detracts from the billing of the client. Sometimes, however, an important star with a cameo bit role in a movie will not even want billing or the use of his or her likeness in the film's advertising.

Ordinarily an obligation to the actor for billing credit will contain exclusions for certain types of advertising. These exclusions include ads in newspapers and magazines that are smaller than eight, six, or four column inches. Group ads in which a number of pictures are listed together are usually exclusions, as are "teaser" or "coming attractions" ads. Billing in trailers is often also excluded. Other exclusions are Academy Award advertising in which an actor who has received an Oscar nomination is featured, an institutional ad that particularly relates to the distribution company, and advertising in narrative form. Radio and television commercials are excluded from billing requirements, as is the mention of the actor's name in publicity releases. If an actor has sufficient bargaining power he can sometimes insist that he be billed even in excluded ads, or that if any other person connected with the film is mentioned in any of the excluded advertising or publicity, his name must also be mentioned. Of course, even if the actor obtains the right to be accorded credit in excluded ads, the producer will never be required to include the actor's name in award or congratulatory ads relating to other persons. Some agreements provide that a casual or inadvertent failure to comply with the provisions of the advertising agreement will not be considered a breach but will be corrected in future ads.

An important provision relating to advertising and publicity is the actor's right to approve photographic and nonphotographic likenesses. When, as often happens, publicity and advertising make use of stills taken during production of a film, the actor may require the right to approve the stills that are used. The producer can protect himself by requiring that the actor approve at least some prenegotiated percentage (usually 50 percent) of all the stills submitted. In turn, the actor will require that enough stills (usually fifty to one hundred) are included in each submission. The approval process will apply also to nonphotographic likenesses such as an artist's rendering of the actor. The approval process for nonphotographic likenesses, used far less often than photographic ones, is both more complicated and more dangerous for the producer. An actor will usually be entitled to disapprove a nonphotographic likeness one time only and must state in reasonable detail his reasons for disapproving it. Finally, with respect to both photographic and nonphotographic likenesses, the actor must exercise his approval rights within a specified period (usually seventy-two hours); otherwise, all likenesses submitted will be deemed to have been approved.

"Most-Favored-Nations"

As a catch-all technique, some actors try to negotiate a "most-favored-nations" clause, which specifies that if any other actor receives terms more favorable than those accorded to the actor in question, the latter will receive those more favorable terms as well.

ARTIST'S CORPORATION

Sometimes for tax purposes, beyond the scope of this book, and depending upon the vagaries of then current tax laws, the actor, like the producer, will not want to be an employee but will have set up his own corporation that will then lend the production company his services. The loan-out agreement obligates the corporation to cause the actor to perform the various services for the producer. A loan-out agreement will ordinarily contain a provision warranting that the actor has entered into an agreement with the corporation pursuant to which the corporation has the exclusive right to lend the actor's services. In addition, since it is only the corporation that signs directly with the production company, the actor will be required to sign a loan-out ratification in which, among other things, he makes the same warranties, representations, and agreements as the corporation, agrees to look solely to the corporation for compensation, and agrees that if the corporation does not do what it is supposed to do or is dissolved, he will work directly for the production company.

As a practical matter, from the producer's point of view, agreements with an actor or his corporation are the same, and the only reason for entering into a loan-out agreement is to accommodate the actor. From the actor's point of view under the loan-out agreement, the lending company is responsible for any guild pension and welfare payments, social security, and the like. The actor will ordinarily insist that the production company either reimburse his lending company for these payments or make these payments directly to the guild on behalf of the loan-out corporation. The producer will not, however, be required to pay any employer's share of the pension, health, and welfare contributions to the guild in excess of those contributions that the producer would have been required to pay had the actor been employed directly by the producer. Increasingly, the guilds and unions are looking directly to the producer for these contributions in the event the actor's loan-out corporation does not pay them.

PRODUCER'S BREACHES

Every agreement for services will contain at the insistence of the producer and distributor a provision that in the event of a breach on the part of the producer, the actor's rights and remedies will be restricted to an action at law for damages; he will not have the right to enjoin distribution of the film or its advertising and promotion or to terminate or rescind the rights granted. The reason for this clause has been discussed in connection with P-Ds (see Chapter 5 under "Default and Termination Rights").

There are various ways that actors will try to modify this clause. The actor may try to get the producer to agree that if the actor's advertising billing agreement is breached, he will have the right to enjoin the offending ad. He will argue for such a clause because it would be virtually impossible for him to prove later that billing of only 50 percent of the size of the film's title instead of the 75 percent he was promised caused him monetary damages. The actor, however, will almost never be successful in modifying the waiver of injunctive relief in this manner. The most he can hope for is an agreement that the producer will correct the billing error or omission on a prospective basis. The producer will insist that no breach by a third party be considered a breach by himself and that in no event will he or any third party be required to recall any prints or advertising materials to which such party has been irrevocably committed.

It is, of course, possible for the agreement to provide for an amount of liquidated damages in the event the billing clause is violated, but any such provision no matter how artfully drafted might be determined by a court to be a penalty clause, which under the law is unenforceable.

As previously stated, it is common for exhibitors to completely ignore the approved advertising billing. When and if an actor's advertising billing agreement has been violated, the costs involved in rectifying this by creating new ads and reprinting the press book would be quite substantial. Moreover, there may not even be time to have new ads prepared if newspaper or magazine space has been purchased in advance and deadlines must be met. If the error in billing occurs in the main titles of the photoplay, correction is even more difficult, if not impossible.

The agreement also provides that its termination cannot deprive the producer of his rights to the results and proceeds of the actor's services. In other words, if the producer is forced to terminate an agreement for any reason, he always wants to own that portion of the actor's services that has been completed. There is a chance that the actor's performance may still be salvageable, and after all, it has been paid for.

8 DIRECTOR'S AGREEMENT

In many respects the director's agreement with the producer is similar to the actor's agreement. Clauses dealing with billing breaches (with the exceptions to be mentioned here under "Credit"), reasons why the producer may withhold payment, illness, publicity, acquisition of rights, waiver of injunctive relief, and the like are pretty much the same. The principal differences relate to the start date, the scope and duration of services (for example, it is quite rare these days for a director, unlike an actor, to be hired for a specific number of weeks), payment of compensation, and the degree of creative and/or business control.

DEVELOPMENT

While a director may be brought into a project at any stage of its development (sometimes a director even comes in after the commencement of principal photography to replace another director), typically the director will be engaged at one of two stages: (1) at the point when the financier is interested in (but not committed to) financing production of the film and more development of the screenplay is required; this is known as a "development deal"; or (2) at the point when the financier has committed to financing production of the film, a start date for principal photography has been set, and no further writing is contemplated (with the exception of minor changes that the director may require). In the latter type of arrangement, the director becomes pay-or-play for the full directing fee upon entering into the agreement with the producer.

The reasons for structuring a development deal are numerous. Since directors today have more and more artistic control, they are vitally interested in the development stage of the film, and have very definite ideas about casting and the script. By the same token, a producer will not want to make a commitment to a director on a pay-or-play basis, in which all of the director's compensation vests, until the producer knows that the film will definitely be made. In a development deal, the director agrees to work (on a nonexclusive basis) for a stated compensation in the development of the screenplay and in the casting of the film. From the director's point of view, the problem with this arrangement is fixing a time when he can be sure he will be directing the film and when the producer will become responsible for paying his fixed compensation—whether or not principal photography has commenced.

This may be resolved in a number of ways. The development deal may provide the director with the right to make other commitments if he has not been given a starting date by a certain specified time. In this event, the producer must wait until the director has completed the other engagement before fixing the starting date, or the agreement terminates, and the producer must hire another director. As a variation, the agreement may provide that the director can take other engagements after a specified date, except that before doing so he must so advise the producer, who would have the right to preempt the engagement. If the producer does preempt, the director is given a starting date and his compensation becomes vested. Then if the film does not start principal photography by the specified date, the agreement automatically terminates and the director is paid his full fee. On the other hand, should the producer elect not to preempt the outside film, the director has the right to begin work on it.

Depending upon the relative bargaining power of the parties, the agreement might provide that even if the producer desired to go forward with his film while the director was engaged on the other project, he would have to wait until the director was available. Alternatively, the agreement may provide that the producer would either be free to proceed with his film without that director (if he wished to do so) or wait and engage the director for his full pay-or-play fee as of a starting date when he would next be available. This type of arrangement gives the producer the advantage of having the director participate in the development work (script, budget, cast and so on) for what is usually a limited sum of money, and minimizes his risks. Of course, if the director were to leave the project and another director with different ideas were to be hired, the earlier preproduction work might prove of limited or no value.

The development deal will usually provide that the director becomes pay-or-play for his full fee at such time as the film is set for production (as discussed in Chapter Five on the P-D), though the director will usually attempt to modify this by providing that if any other person is made pay-or-play for his fee prior to the time the film is set for production, then the director will also become pay-or-play at such earlier time.

After a director begins working on a film, he may find that there are problems with the script that he did not anticipate or that his concept of what the completed photoplay should be does not coincide with his producer's, and they may both want to be relieved of their obligations.

CREATIVE CONTROL

In the event that the director obtains artistic controls over the photoplay (and a director as well a producer can have these controls), they are spelled out in the provision of the agreement that otherwise normally gives the producer supervision of the director's services. Artistic controls and the exercise of them are similar to the types of controls a producer has in the P-D. Of course, if the director and producer both have artistic controls and rights of approval, their contract must contain a method of resolving disputes between them.

A strong director will have a great deal of creative control over a film. As the single most important element of a film is usually the star, a strong director will usually share approval with the producer over his or her selection. In some cases, the agreement will provide that if mutual approval cannot be reached and the director does not want to make the film with the actor selected by the producer, the director has the right to terminate the agreement and keep whatever compensation has been paid to him up to that time. Other contract provisions over which there may be heated negotiations concern the right to select principal cast members, the script, the budget, production and postproduction schedules, key crew members (director of photography, unit production manager, editor, etc.), the composer, principal location sites, and advertising and release campaigns. Contract provision for resolving disputes may range from final "say so" by the director, to mutual approval by the director and producer, to decision by the producer with the director having a right of consultation only. It is interesting to note that the one person a producer will almost always demand the right to designate is the production auditor. Because the producer must have accurate day-by-day information as to how much the film is costing and whether or not it is over-budget, he will almost always insist on having someone he trusts in that important position.

PRODUCTION SERVICES

After the development stage has passed and the director has been given a firm starting date, the other parts of the director's agreement become effective. Ordinarily the director must work exclusively on a film from the beginning of the preproduction period, somewhere between six and ten weeks (usually eight weeks) before the commencement of principal photography, which should be enough time to complete casting and generally get the production into shape. The director's services continue to be rendered on an exclusive basis until either the completion of principal photography or the delivery of his first cut of the film. Thereafter, the director's services will be on a nonexclusive but first priority basis (i.e., the services to the producer must have priority over services to others) until delivery to the producer of the release print of the film.

COMPENSATION

Although occasionally agreements entitle the director to payment for working additional weeks of principal photography beyond a certain stated number, most agreements now provide for a flat fee for the entire shooting period. The reason for this is simple: If there are problems with principal photography, it is usually the director's responsibility. If he is slow in shooting or requires many retakes and principal photography goes over schedule, it seems unfair to permit him to benefit from his own inefficiency by paying him for overweeks.

METHODS OF PAYMENT

Payment of compensation to the director is usually handled differently from payment to an actor. If the agreement with the director is a development deal, the development fee is usually applied to the first installment of the directing fee at such time as the directing fee becomes vested. This occurs either on the date the producer has set for start of production or possibly when any other person connected with the film (other than a writer) becomes pay-or-play if that date is earlier. If the deal is not a development deal, the director will become pay-or-play on signing.

The directing fee is usually paid in the following manner: 20 percent in equal weekly installments over the scheduled course of preproduction, 60 percent in equal weekly installments over the scheduled course of principal photography, 10 percent upon delivery of the first cut (see "Cutting and Editing," below) to which the director is entitled (sometimes that is paid when the music is recorded), and 10 percent upon delivery to the producer of the release print of the film. Some important directors will demand (and receive) the first percentage of the directing fee upon entering into the agreement with the producer (with the remaining installments paid as described above).

It should be noted that if the director's services fall within the jurisdiction of the Directors Guild of America, and if the producer is paying only the minimum amount required by the DGA, then the director's services will not, in fact, be on a flat-fee basis. The DGA requires that a director be given a certain minimum number of weeks for preproduction, a minimum number for principal photography, and a minimum number for postproduction. Under the DGA agreement, compensation is stated in terms of salary per week, and the director must be guaranteed the minimum salary times the minimum number of weeks. Thus, if the director's services are required beyond the minimum amount of time required under the DGA agreement, the director will simply be employed on a minimum-per-week basis.

An issue that often arises is what happens to the director's fee if principal photography of the picture is delayed or canceled. Usually, if principal photography is delayed by no more than a specified time (usually two to six weeks), the directing fee is paid in accordance with the foregoing schedule. If the film is abandoned, however, and production terminated or delayed for a longer period, the entire directing fee usually becomes payable when the decision to terminate or to delay production is made; the director then has no further obligations to the film unless he receives additional "holding" compensation for the additional period of delay (except to the extent discussed below).

Of course, this raises a new issue. If the director earns money from a third party during the time he would have been working for the producer, the producer will in the absence of contractual resolution, be legally entitled to reduce what he owes the director by the amount the director earns from the third party. On the other hand, the director will not want the money owed to him by the producer to be reduced at all. The concept of such a reduction is known as "mitigation." This disagreement is commonly resolved by allowing the producer to apply only the money earned by the director for his *exclusive* services to the third party against what the producer would have paid to the director during the time the director's services would have been *exclusive* to him. This compromise is more likely to be used with directors than with actors, as actors' services are almost always exclusive.

Also, if the producer has paid the director his full fee, he will often want the right to use the director without additional compensation if the film is started within a specified period (usually between six months to one year). If the director agrees to this, he will usually make his obligation to the producer subject to his (the director's) availability.

Quite frequently, the director, like an actor, will be entitled to receive a deferment or a profit participation or both. In addition, the breach, disability, and act of God provisions of the director's agreement will be almost identical to those of the actor's agreement. If there is a termination of services, the payment of deferments and profits sometimes vests in the same proportion as the footage shot by the director and used in the final version of the film bears to the total footage. Sometimes any profits paid to a replacement director are deducted from the money due to the original director. And sometimes the original director's rights to contingent compensation depend upon a minimum filming having taken place.

DISABILITY

The length of time a director can be ill during shooting without causing a termination of the agreement is somewhat more generous than the illness provision for an actor, since the director will render services for a much longer period of time. Sometimes, however, those time periods are shortened if the disability occurs during principal photography.

CUTTING AND EDITING

Under the present DGA agreement, after completion of principal photography the director has the right to do one cut of the photoplay, and there is a minimum of time the producer must give the director within which to complete his cut. Scenes are shot many different times from varying angles and, ordinarily, not in sequence. After shooting has been completed, editing must be done—scenes cut and assembled—to make the most effective motion picture. Although editors are specialists in what they do, no matter how well the actors have been directed and the scenes photographed, the director can lose control of the finished project if he does not retain the right to supervise the cutting and editing of the film. The DGA requires the director to have at least one cut, but it is not unusual for a director to request two or three cuts and to be granted more than one, though rarely more than three. While almost invariably the producer (or the studio) will have the right to recut the film after the director has delivered the last cut to which he is entitled, in a few very rare cases a director may be accorded "final cut"—that is, once the director has delivered his version of the film, no one else may touch it. (But even in such a circumstance the film may be cut again for reasons of censorship or time continuity.)

Since a film is usually scanned for wide-screen theater projection, either one side or the other may need to be framed for television viewing (the TV screen being squarer), or it may be speeded up to avoid cutting (some films scan a little faster for television or home video). The director, therefore, may also want to control the adaptation of his film for the small screen. Emerging concepts of "moral rights" that prevent the mutilation or alteration of a creator's work without his permission may in the future prevent the alteration of a feature film, depending on whether the "creator" of such a collaborative medium is considered to be the writer, the director, the producer, or the actors.

It is most important for a producer to make certain that the cut is completed within a specific period of time. With the high cost of money today, the longer it takes to release the film, the more the interest will run, and the more difficult it will be for the film to earn a profit. Also, the producer may have entered into an agreement with a distributor that commits the film to specified play dates.

It ordinarily takes anywhere from six to twelve weeks to complete the first cut, depending on how fast the director works and how complicated the shooting was. Some directors will cut while they are shooting. The DGA requires not only that the director be given at least one cut of the film but also that no cuts be made by anyone else until the director has finished his. (The practice of others cutting the film while the director is completing his cut is known as "cutting behind" the director.) The DGA has established a hotline as further protection to quickly resolve disputes over cutting and other creative control issues.

The director is also usually given the right to show each cut of the film he has made to an audience in order to gauge public reaction and decide whether further editing is required. These showings are known as "previews." The director will often bargain for their being "paid public previews," which means that the producer must rent a regular movie theater and advertise that a "sneak preview" is to be held at a particular date and time, and that people pay the regular admission fee to attend. After the preview, each person in the theatre is asked to complete a questionnaire designed to give guidance to the filmmakers as to audience reaction to various elements of the film. The director will argue that the response from this type of preview is far more accurate than from the "invited preview," where the producer simply books a screening room on the studio lot and invites an audience to attend, usually through some type of service. The invited preview is, however, much less expensive and the producer therefore will usually indulge in hard bargaining for it.

SEQUELS AND REMAKES

Typically, the director will bargain for the right to direct any sequels and remakes of the film. This is structured so that the director has the right of first negotiation to direct any such productions, with the terms of his directing agreement for theatrical sequels and remakes being no less favorable than those relating to the original film. A strong director will also bargain for the right to function as the executive producer (on an exclusive or nonexclusive basis, as he may elect) on any television series based on the film. If the producer agrees to the television provision at all, he will insist that it be made subject to the approval of the applicable network or other buyer. Although such a provision is quite rare, a very strong director may be given a passive royalty even on episodes on which he does not render services.

CREDIT

The traditional form of credit for the director is a "directed by" credit, located on a separate card as the last credit in the main titles of the film. The credit and its placement are required by the DGA, as are certain specifications regarding its size. The DGA also requires that the "directed by" credit appear in all paid advertising (except award and congratulatory ads) in which any other person or any entity other than two actors receives credit.

A more recent form of credit to the director is a "possessory" credit. For example, if the director's name is John Smith, the credit will read either "A John Smith Film" or, less commonly, "A Film by John Smith". This credit by and large is not protected by the DGA. The director, therefore, must bargain contractually on all factors relating to it (size, placement, and so on). Typically, this credit will appear above the title in the main titles, and above the regular title in paid advertising. A very strong director may persuade the producer to also accord the possessory credit above the artwork title in paid advertising.

MISCELLANEOUS ISSUES

The DGA agreement deals mainly with the director's compensation, creative rights, cutting, credits, pension and welfare plans, and residual payments. It is not concerned with the day-to-day work rules to the same extent as is the SAG agreement. For example, a director's contract will almost never provide that he must work a stated number of hours or days in a week. Most directors understand that it is necessary to work most of the time. In the morning they must be ready to set up the first shots, and in the evening they usually view the film recently shot (known as "dailies" or "rushes") as well as prepare for the next day's work. It is quite routine for a director to work unusually long hours.

The director's agreement will, however, also cover a number of other less major though nonetheless important issues, such as the living expenses to be paid while on location, the manner of travel to be provided (the DGA, like the other guilds, requires first-class travel), an office and secretary, a motorhome and a car and driver while on location, and a videocassette and/or print of the film once it is completed.

9 PRODUCER'S AGREEMENT

In the event that an individual producer does not have his own production company, is not employed by a production company, or is not responsible for packaging, then an individual producer's employment agreement form will be used instead of a P-D. The differences between this agreement and a director's or actor's agreement are relatively few.

If the producer brings the literary property to the financier, their agreement should contain a turnaround or reversion provision in case of abandonment; this gives the producer the right to repurchase the property should the film not proceed as provided in the agreement. (See Chapter 5 under "Abandonment.") Terms of the producer's rights of approval or selection—of script, director, cast, etc.—must be spelled out in the agreement just as they are with a director.

Sometimes, without a producer's participation, a project is developed by various parties (such as a financier or a studio), a director and cast have been selected, and the film is ready for production. At the point when production is about to start, a financier may hire a producer to oversee the physical production of the film. This type of a producer, known as a "line producer," will enter into an employment agreement much like that of a director. Alternatively, the producer sometimes is brought in at an earlier stage to help develop the film to the point where the financier can set it for production. In this situation, the producer will enter into a development deal with the financier that is structured in a manner identical to a director's development deal. The agreement with the producer, whether a development deal or a production deal, must state when payments are to be made and when the producer's total fee and contingent compensation become vested. As with the director's agreement, this one should make provision for what happens if production of the film does not begin within a stated period of time. Would the individual producer be free to take on other assignments, and how would a conflict of assignments be resolved?

PRODUCER CREDIT

An interesting question that relates most commonly to a producer's agreement is that of vesting of credit.

Most unions and guilds protect the credit to be accorded their members through collective-bargaining agreements. A producer, on the other hand, has no such protection and thus is very vulnerable in this area. Consider, for example, the case of a producer who brings a project to a studio without any other elements (such as a director) attached. The studio enters into the standard development deal with the producer that requires a small development fee be paid and that the producer become pay-or-play for the producing fee when the film is set for production. Typically, the studio will attempt to grant the producer his "produced by" credit only if the film is completed under his supervision. Under this scenario the studio could acquire the project from the producer, have him develop the project to the point where it is ready for production, and then pay him off without ever giving him any form of credit for his work. This happens most commonly when an important director or actor is subsequently hired who insists on having a different producer on the film, and that producer insists on getting sole producing credit.

Accordingly, it is important that a producer bargain for a provision requiring the studio to give him credit whether or not he actually produces the film—so long as he is not in breach. Frequently the studio agrees to give the producer sole "produced by" credit if the film is produced under his direct supervision and shared "produced by" credit or "executive producer" credit if another producer is brought in.

The most important producers will also receive a possessory credit, as more fully discussed in the chapter on the P-D.

PRODUCER'S PROFITS

As discussed in connection with the P-D agreement, sometimes a producer and a studio agree to split the profits of a film 50-50, with the producer bearing all creative third-party net profit participations, and with gross participations being converted to net profits on a dollar-for-dollar basis or some artificial formula. It is rare for a studio to grant the producer the right to approve the third-party participations to be awarded. Thus, the producer will have to protect himself against the possibility that the studio will simply give away all of his share of net profits. This is done is by providing that the producer's obligation to bear third-party participations will be subject to a "floor."

The producer's agreement will usually deal with two types of floors: the "soft" floor and the "hard" floor. It requires the producer to bear all of the third-party profit participations until his 50 percent has been reduced, point by point, to a soft floor of, for example, 20 percent. Thereafter, the producer and the studio will in some manner share additional third-party participations until the producer has reached a hard floor such as 15 percent. After that the studio alone will bear all further third-party participations.

The manner in which the studio and producer share the bearing of third-party participations between the soft floor and hard floor is naturally the subject of some discussion. The studio will usually take the position that third-party participations should be borne 50 percent by the studio and 50 percent by the producer. The producer, on the other hand, will argue that the third-party participations should be borne by the studio and producer in proportion to their respective profit participations.

To illustrate, let us assume that the studio and producer agree to split profits 50-50, with the producer bearing third parties to a soft floor of 20 percent and a hard floor of 15 percent. As the studio and the producer each start at 50 percent, the first 30 percent of all net profits given away to other profit participants (such as the director, writers, and actors) will be borne by the producer. At that point, the studio is entitled to 50 percent of the profits and the producer is entitled to 20 percent of the profits. Once the 20 percent soft floor has been reached, however, the studio begins to bear some of the third party participations. If, for example, another 7 percent of the profits are to be given away, the studio will argue that the studio and producer should bear those participations equally, 3.5 percent to be borne by each (bringing the studio down to 46.5 percent of the profits and the producer down to 16.5 percent of the profits). The producer, on the other hand, will argue that those third-party participations should be borne on a pro-rata basis. As together the studio and producer at that point are entitled to 70 percent of the profits (50 percent to the studio and 20 percent to the producer), the producer will argue that the studio should bear five sevenths of each point and the producer should bear two sevenths of each point. If the producer's argument prevails, of the 7 percent to be given away, the studio will bear 5 percent (bringing its profits down to 45 percent) and the producer will bear 2 percent (bringing his down to 18 percent).

However the reduction is calculated, once the producer has reached the hard floor, the studio must bear all the rest of the third-party participations.

The discussion of producer's profits assumes that all profit participants receive a percentage of gross profits and discusses how those profits are allocated between the producer and the studio. What if some of the participants receive a participation in the gross receipts? As we have seen in Chapter 4 under "Participations in Gross Receipts," some well-known talent and directors receive a gross receipts participation from the first dollar. In these instances, their compensation is usually treated as an advance against the gross receipt participation. Therefore, if an actor is paid a salary of $5 million and receives 5 percent of the gross, the $5 million is an advance against the 5 percent of the gross and the gross film rental will have to exceed $100 million before the actor receives additional compensation. In other cases a percentage of gross receipts is payable after some artificial breakeven point. In both cases, how are these participations shared between the studio and the producer?

Participations in gross receipts are almost always treated as a cost of production and usually bear interest and overhead. The effect of this gross participation is to push back the breakeven point after which there are net profits, and therefore, the gross receipt participation is borne by all net profit participants including the studio. The studio may try to have the producer bear this cost out of producer's net profits. In some cases, gross participations are converted to net profits on a dollar-for-dollar basis. For example, if the gross participation was $1 million, that sum would be deducted from the first million dollars in net profits payable to the producer. In other cases, there is a negotiation of an artificial formula for converting the gross participation to net profits. If the gross is paid after an artificial breakeven point, two gross points after that breakeven might be deemed to be worth three net profit points. Of course the studio should not have it both ways. If gross profits are being recouped as part of the cost of production and being treated as production costs they should not be treated as profits to a producer. This is one of the reasons why participants request of a studio that a particular cost only be deducted one time. It would seem that such a provision would be unnecessary since, one could argue, how could a cost be deducted twice? This is, however, one instance where a double deduction is at least a possibility.

EXECUTIVE AND CO-PRODUCERS

In today's movie world, there are many types of producers. For example, a person may function as an "executive producer," an "associate producer," a "supervising producer," "a line producer," or a "co-producer." These titles have no set meanings and are frequently the subject of negotiation. An executive producer, for example, can be one of many things: a person who provides some portion of the financing for the film; a person who acquires the underlying rights to the film and then sells them to the financier but, not having had enough experience to actually oversee the production, cannot be accorded the title of "producer"; or a person who is developing and producing a number of projects at the same time and does not have the time to devote his attention fully to any one film.

An executive producer's agreement will be similar in form to an individual producer's agreement, except that the executive producer performs only a supervisory function and does not have day-to-day responsibilities for production of the film. For this reason, the duties of an executive producer are almost always nonexclusive and he has the right to be engaged in other projects. In some cases, the executive producer has no duties in connection with the film, in which case his billing is no more than an honorary credit.

More and more frequently we see producing *teams* entering into agreements with financiers. Such teams usually consist of two persons. Under such arrangements, the compensation (both fixed and contingent) is paid to the team in the aggregate and divided between the team members as they see fit. This division may change if one producer breaches or is disabled. Usually the team has the right to designate one member to render services on the film on an exclusive basis, the other on a nonexclusive basis. The most dangerous aspect of such an arrangement to the team members is that the financier will invariably insist on cross-liability; that is, if one team member is in breach of the agreement, the other member is also deemed to be in breach and thus fully liable. Also, in the event that the coproducers disagree about something, the agreement must provide for dispute resolution vis-a-vis the financier/distributor. Presumably, if one of the producers becomes ill or disabled, the other one carries on alone.

In most other respects, the individual producer's agreement, even if for coproducers, contains terms that closely resemble the rights and obligations of the producer under a P-D agreement.

10 FACILITIES AGREEMENTS

Most motion pictures, whether or not produced in this country, are made at least in part in a studio. Even those that are filmed largely on location generally have some interior shooting and this is usually done in a studio.

There are two types of studio agreements in general use. The first is a "studio facilities agreement" in which a major producer-distributor owning its own production facilities enters into an agreement with an independent producer for the use of those facilities. If the major producer-distributor is financing the film, you may rest assured that under normal circumstances the P-D will require that the film be produced at the distributor's studio to the extent it is not to be filmed on location. In such a case, either a specified percentage overhead charge is made for the use of the facilities or, more rarely, a heavily detailed facilities agreement, one that breaks down the specific charges, is embodied either in the P-D or in separate agreements between the producer and the distributor. Sometimes both a percentage overhead and specific charges are imposed. To the extent that the studio does not provide value equal to the overhead charged, the differential is a hidden financing cost.

The other type of facilities agreement covers the use of independent studios. Such studios exist in most major cities where a substantial amount of television or motion picture production occurs, and such an agreement of course contains specific charges, to be negotiated and detailed, for the use of the various facilities.

In the case of a studio facilities agreement, the producer's cost will, obviously, depend upon the parties' respective bargaining power, and in this situation the producer will have very little. If he wants to get his production financed, and the distributor includes studio facilities as part of the production cost obligation, the producer can do no more than determine to what extent the percentage to be charged is realistic and reflects the actual cost of the services that the studio will provide. Barring the unusual, the financier-distributor is sure to insist that all studio work be done at its facilities, with the agreement setting forth exactly which facilities will be made available. If the producer does not know precisely what he will need, he would be well-advised to engage a production manager to make certain that the studio will have all essential equipment. Only if the studio cannot provide what is required will it permit a producer to go elsewhere for stage and production office facilities, equipment, or material. Should the financier-distributor try to assess unrealistic charges for what it is offering, the producer must evaluate them before deciding whether the P-D deal is worthwhile or whether the many artificially inflated costs will only ensure that the film can never, practically speaking, become profitable.

With an independent studio facility, the producer can bargain differently and can shop around more freely to see whether one studio deal is as favorable as another. He can also compare the facilities of the various available studios to see which is best suited for his particular needs. In other words, in dealing with the independent studio the charges are always negotiable, and the bargaining power of the parties involved is dependent upon the number of independent studios in the vicinity and how busy they happen to be at the time. If the studios are loaded with work, the producer can bargain very little, but if they are idle, he will be in a strong position to work out quite a desirable agreement.

The issues that most frequently arise in facility agreements relate to access to the facility; the security to be provided; which party is liable in the event of damage, destruction, theft of equipment, or injury of persons; and the incidental items that will be provided to the producer and whether they will be included in the basic cost or constitute an additional charge. Obviously, the prudent producer will make sure he has proper and adequate insurance covering production liability and equipment and sets.

Certain contract provisions may be the same in a facilities agreement with a major studio and that with an independent. Either may require the producer to execute guild agreements and to use the studio's employees (who will be guild members). If the producer wishes to use specific personnel of his own choosing, he must make this known and so provide in the agreement. Another common provision relates to the period of the lease. Exactly when will the studio facilities be required, and will there be a fixed termination date? May the studio or the producer terminate or extend the lease if an event outside the parties' control affects one or the other of them? The studio will ordinarily charge a different rate for construction purposes, for shooting purposes, and for striking purposes (i.e., removal of the sets after completion of shooting). It should be borne in mind that within the period of the lease, rent is charged for each day, whether or not the studio is used on that day, so the producer should plan carefully. In fixing a termination date, the producer must protect himself against the possibility that principal photography will last longer than anticipated, requiring use of the studio for additional periods of time. Under most circumstances, the agreement will provide an outside cutoff date so that the studio will know when it can rent its facilities to another producer.

In either agreement it is important to consider exactly what areas of the studio and what items of equipment are to be rented. Ordinarily, these will be enumerated in a schedule, but in addition to the particular sound stages and other major shooting facilities the studio provides, there must be arrangements for access to and use of offices, makeup rooms, dressing rooms, carpenter shops, and possibly parking facilities. If there is a particular time of day that the studio must be used, or if the producer wants the studio available at all hours on a seven-day-a-week basis, the agreement must so provide and must require that electricity, heat, security, and so on are available during those periods.

Most studio leases will contain a clause requiring the producer to pay any sales tax due on the rental covered by the agreement. There may be a question as to whether or not the sales tax is payable on the entire cost of the rental or whether part of the cost should be apportioned between real property, services provided, and personal property. Since some of the services and/or items provided may be exempt from sales tax, if the studio insists on inserting a clause obligating the producer to pay the tax, then he may choose instead to indemnify the studio for taxes actually paid or to pay whatever taxes are due directly to the government. If the studio's charges are deemed to be manufacturing costs, an exemption certificate from the local jurisdiction can be obtained, in which case the studio will not collect a sales tax.

Usually the studios require the producer to obtain liability insurance, insurance against loss or damage to the equipment, fire insurance, and worker's compensation. Normally, the producer is obligated to repair or replace lost or broken equipment unless the breakage was due to normal wear and tear or to a defect in the equipment when the producer received it. The studios will also try to limit their liability to matters of negligence or even gross negligence.

Finally, the producer must be sure to provide that if other parts of the studio are being used by other producers, there will be adequate control over noise and interference. The producer must rely on the studio to supervise shooting so that one production in no way prevents another production from proceeding efficiently.

11 TECHNICAL AGREEMENTS

TECHNICAL PERSONNEL

Most technical personnel engaged for a picture will receive weekly checks and will not be hired for any particular minimum period of time. If they are experienced they are likely to be guild members so that their guild agreements will govern their services, providing for compensation, for overtime, for occasional billing credit requirements, and the like. On rare occasions, a technical person particularly well known in the industry may insist on a special contract. He may then negotiate for a fixed number of weeks as a minimum, no matter how long his services are actually required, instead of settling for employment on a week-to-week or day-to-day basis.

The form of most employment agreements for technical personnel is substantially similar to the form of the actor's contract with many of the same terms and conditions, except that usually the technicians's agreement will be much shorter and much less detailed.

Essentially, the agreement should provide that the producer is granted the results and proceeds of the employee's services as a work made for hire and that the producer has the sole right to direct, supervise, and control those services while the film is being made. The agreement should also state a minimum time period for services, with a provision that if the employee's services are needed for additional weeks, compensation continues at the same rate for the additional time. By and large, most contract terms are governed by the appropriate guild agreement, which is incorporated by reference into the employment agreement.

SPECIAL EQUIPMENT

In addition to employer-employee technical agreements, occasionally special agreements are required to cover use of extraordinary lenses or other photographic equipment, such as Panavision. These agreements are usually in the nature of a leasing agreement, with the lessor leasing specified equipment to the producer at a specified cost. Lessors will generally require billing credit and will detail the rights and obligations of the lessee, particularly providing for rights and obligations if the equipment becomes lost, damaged, or stolen. It is usually difficult for a producer to achieve any substantial change in the lessor's clauses in this type of agreement and, by and large, extended negotiation is not necessary just as long as it is clear what the costs are and as long as most of the producer's risks can be covered by insurance.

SPECIAL EFFECTS

As motion picture technology has developed so has a new genre of film: the "special effects film." The term "special effects" used to relate only to the preparation and execution of stunts and spectacular events, such as explosions and floods. Now, however, it has been expanded to include the realm of visual effects that are optical in nature. With the growth of the special effects film, a demand has been created for businesses that specialize in the design and production of these extraordinary optical effects. Thus, if a film requires any special visual effects at all—and today some films allocate to them as much as 30 percent or more of their budgets—the producer will probably have to enter into an agreement with a special visual effects house.

A visual effects house performs such work on one of two bases: a cost-plus basis or a fixed-price basis. With the cost-plus basis, the producer and the visual effects house agree that the producer will pay for whatever the effects actually cost to create. This includes the personnel, equipment, materials required, and some prenegotiated figure for general overhead, plus a markup on those costs (usually between 7.5 percent and 15 percent) that constitutes the profit margin of the visual effects house. With the fixed-price basis, the visual effects house agrees to deliver the agreed upon effects to the producer for a set cost that includes the intended profit of the visual effects house.

Both arrangements have advantages and disadvantages. A cost-plus basis imposes on the producer the risk of going over budget but gives him the benefit if the effects are ultimately produced for a cost less that originally anticipated. As the visual effects house assumes no risk under this arrangement, it is limited in the profit margin that it can justifiably charge the producer. On a fixed-price basis, the situation is reversed: The visual effects house assumes the risk of the effects going over budget, but garners the benefit if the effects are produced for less than anticipated. Since for them an element of risk is involved under this arrangement, the visual effects house will usually build into the agreement a more substantial profit factor (usually 20 percent to 25 percent). This is both their reward for assuming the risk and a contingency reserve in the event the effects cost more than anticipated. In most situations involving independent producers who have obtained or must obtain a completion bond, the producer will usually opt for the fixed-price basis, if only because the bonding company is likely to insist on a fixed and reliable budget for the film.

12 MUSIC

Several types of music may be used in a motion picture. First, an original score may be written specifically for a film by a composer selected by the producer. Second, music that has already been composed and recorded can be rerecorded and used in the motion picture if a synchronization license is granted by the music's publisher. Such music, sometimes including the original hit records, is commonly used, for example, in trying to establish a time period: for a picture set in the 1930s, music from that era can help to create the appropriate mood. Third, there are some music publishers who will provide a producer with "canned" music—that is music that has already been recorded, to insert into the picture as desired. For this, a master use license will be required.

MUSIC ORIGINALLY WRITTEN
FOR A MOTION PICTURE

Ordinarily, the composer of a film's score is not hired until after principal photography has been completed, at the point at which the director must cut the film. The music serves to highlight certain aspects of the mood, action, or message of specific scenes or the film as a whole. Although a composer could begin to write prior to any cutting, it is customary for him to wait until there is at least a rough cut so that he may have some idea of what the picture is about, what type of music is suitable, and where in the film it is required. After the rough cut is completed, the composer can begin working out his main themes and considering the sequences in which background music would be desirable, but he cannot actually match the music to the picture until there is at least a "fine cut," the completion of the next cut after completion of the rough cut.

Working with the director (and probably the producer), the composer will decide upon the various approaches the score should take. Once a fine cut of the film has been prepared, the composer, the director, and the music editor will spend at least a full day, and sometimes two, going through the film scene by scene, deciding which sequences need music, what the music is intended to accomplish, and where the music will begin and end. This process is known as "spotting."

Generally speaking, the music contained in a film will be of two types. One is the underscore: music that appears out of nowhere and "plays" the scene, and which could also be an audio-visual use—i.e., an actor singing the music. The other is "source" music: music for which there is an identifiable source on-screen, such as a radio or television set. Both types of music may be the original compositions of the film composer.

There is usually a four- to ten-week period between the completion of the fine cut and actual recording of the music. Then a number of recording sessions may be necessary to fit the music into the appropriate segment of the picture.

Although agreements will vary, the composer is quite often responsible for composing, arranging, and orchestrating the music and for conducting it, or electronically synthesizing it, at the recording sessions. There is no collective-bargaining agreement governing the services of a composer (although the American Federation of Musicians—the AFM—has jurisdiction over the composer when he serves in certain capacities, such as orchestrator). The agreement generally provides that the composer is an employee of the production company, and as employer the production company will own the score and hold all copyrights in the composition. To the extent that a score is published by a music publishing company (usually the publishing arm of the financier-distributor if there is a P-D, or a publisher selected by the producer or distributor, depending on the deal), the composer will receive the same author's royalty scale as would any published songwriter, and the producer or distributor (or the publisher designee) will receive the publisher's share. Some well-established composers have sufficient bargaining power to insist that they copublish their scores with the music publisher chosen by the producer and thus receive part (usually half) of the publisher's share as well. Such a provision is solely a matter of bargaining and no rule of thumb is applicable.

When a composer is hired and regarded as an employee, the studio will generally be responsible for providing and paying for all recording and editing facilities, musicians, and incidentals. If, however, a composer is hired on a "package" basis, for a flat sum he is obligated to compose, orchestrate, arrange, copy, record and mix the score, and to deliver to the producer a finished tape ready for synchronization with the film. Under such an arrangement, just as with a fixed-price visual effects agreement, the composer will bear the risk of any overbudget costs and will reap the benefit of delivering the score under budget.

While enhancing the picture is always the main purpose of the score, the producer and the distributor are always hopeful that it will contain one or more hit tunes, thereby making their publishing rights much more valuable.

Length of Services and Compensation

As an employee of the producer, the composer agrees to render exclusive services (or at least agrees to give first priority to the film project) for a stated period and as long thereafter as the producer deems necessary for writing the finished score. Sometimes the composer's compensation is based on a minimum number of weeks and he is compensated for overweeks. Usually, however, he works for a flat sum, no matter how long it takes him to complete his services.

The composer agrees to confer with the producer and director when and where the producer requires. It is sometimes difficult to fix a start date for a composer's services because it depends upon when the fine cut of the photoplay is ready, which is not always easy to predict. Sometimes, therefore, the agreement provides that the composer's services are to be nonexclusive during the period from the rough cut to the fine cut. In this period of time, the composer may be able to write the themes and other major parts of the music, although the actual scoring, as stated, will begin after the fine cut.

The amount of time the composer takes to write the score directly affects the postproduction schedule of the film. The faster the composer completes his work, the sooner recording sessions begin, and the sooner the film will be completed. In some agreements, the amount of music the composer is to write is specified by number of songs, number of minutes, or both. In setting up the postproduction schedule, it is always a good idea for the producer to provide for the possibility that the composer may be late or that his material may not be satisfactory by allowing time to obtain music from another source. Of course, the composer's agreement may provide that if his music is considered unacceptable, he will compose different material until the producer is satisfied. Such a clause will ordinarily put a limit on how much additional music the composer may be required to write.

It is not uncommon for a producer to underestimate the amount of money required for the music in a film. Remember that an original score is going to require a substantial number of recording sessions. (Many scores are recorded overseas where costs of recording may be cheaper.) Ordinarily, one or more sessions involving a large number of musicians will be needed for that portion of the score written for a full orchestra, while the balance of the sessions will be limited to a smaller group unless the score is electronically synthesized. In addition to his compensation for writing the score, the composer will be paid at least union scale (that is, minimum) if he conducts, orchestrates, or copies, and union scale if he actually performs as an instrumentalist. Sometimes union scale payments are applied against the composer's overall fee.

Many of the provisions that are found in talent agreements will also be in the composer's agreement. In addition, the composer's agreement ordinarily permits the producer to have lyrics written for any music written by the composer, or to use new and different music in lieu of, or in addition to, that written by the composer.

Composer's Royalties

Usually the writer and the publisher divide equally the royalties from record sales ("mechanical income") and audio-visual uses other than use of the music in the film ("synchronization income," on which no royalties are paid since the composer's compensation is intended to cover that use). The composer and publisher each get paid performing rights revenue directly from the U.S. performing rights society (ASCAP or BMI); foreign performing rights revenue is generally divided equally between the publisher and the composer, with the latter's share collected either by ASCAP or BMI, or by the publisher and then disbursed to the writer. Royalties for printed editions are by and large the standard songwriter royalties of $.06 to $.10 per printed edition of a single song, and 10 to 12 percent of the wholesale price of the folios—i.e., printed collections of several songs—prorated by a fraction, the numerator of which is the composer's song and the denominator of which are all songs in the folio, or all songs excluding public domain works. The composer may also get a reduced payment for any sequels or TV adaptations that make use of his music. In the event that someone else writes lyrics for the composer's music, his royalties for that composition are usually reduced by half, the other half going to the lyricist. As stated above, well-known writers may be able to bargain for a percentage of the publisher's customary one-half share.

The producer should try to include in the agreement a clause to the effect that if the score is assigned to a music publisher, the latter takes on full responsibility for payment of the writer's royalties. On the other hand, the agreement should also specify that the producer is in no way obligated to have the score published.

Recording Royalties

In addition to writer's royalties, composers who conduct may also receive the equivalent of a recording artist's or record producer's royalty for a sound track album and for single records derived from the sound track album. Whether or not the composer will receive such a royalty depends upon his bargaining power and, more particularly, on whether or not he is sufficiently known in the recording field to help sell records. The royalty here may range anywhere from 1 percent to 5 percent of either 100 percent or, more usually, 90 percent of the *retail* selling price of all albums manufactured, sold, and not returned, less excise taxes and cover and container charges, and reductions in the royalty rate for foreign sales, budget records, etc. The 90 percent figure, which originally took into account a 10 percent allowance for breakage of 78 rpm records (or tapes), is still used in deals with composers who have little bargaining power. In truth, there is no longer any practical basis for it, since today normally no breakage occurs and even if it does, broken records are accepted for return. Just as often the royalty is based upon the *wholesale* selling price, in which event the royalty rate is twice as high because the wholesale selling price is about one-half the retail selling price.

The royalty rate for compact discs may be based on an adjusted percentage (80 percent) of the wholesale selling price, or, if based on the retail selling price, that price will be a "deemed" amount which is less than actual retail. The reduced percentage here results from the increased cost of manufacturing CDs.

Sometimes the producer attempts to deduct from recording royalties the actual costs of producing and recording the score. This position is strongly resisted by composers, who consider it unfair. The most a composer will usually agree to is allowing the producer to deduct from royalties due some of the costs incurred in converting the score from the medium of film to the medium of sound track album and/or the union reuse payment to be discussed below.

Frequently, the composer's royalty accounting is based upon the accounting the producer receives from the record company. If the producer is dealing with a studio, the record company would normally be affiliated with the studio and the record royalty computation would be an exhibit to the P-D agreement.

If a producer knows that a sound track album is definitely going to be made, he should probably require the composer, when he scores the music for the film, to also do what is necessary to convert the score from film to sound track album. This may even mean rerecording and certain reediting of the score because the effects appropriate for the film may not work for the sound track album. The latter (which may be sold to a market different from that of the film) may require an updated form of scoring and, more important, may require fewer musicians and a higher technical quality of recording. For this reason, many composers will insist on producing the sound track album themselves. While the fee for such services is usually included in the composing fee, if the composer does produce the sound track album he will generally be able to negotiate an additional royalty equal to the royalty on album sales customary for a record producer (e.g., 3 percent).

Under the AFM Minimum Basic Agreement, when music recorded for use in one medium is then used in another medium, all of the musicians involved in the first recording session must receive a reuse payment. Thus, if thirty to forty musicians participated in the motion picture recording session, to pay all of them an additional fee would be much more expensive than rerecording the music for a sound track album with five or six musicians. Sometimes the two sessions are held at the same time; sometimes the sessions are arranged by the recording company after the album deal has been consummated.

If the producer owns his own record company, royalty payments for recording artists ordinarily become part of the hiring agreement. Of course, the royalty portion of the agreement is subject to negotiation in the same way that any other part of the agreement would be.

Again, it is sometimes cheaper to record music outside of the U.S., because of both the high cost of musicians here and the obligation to pay residuals in accordance with AFM requirements. For various production reasons, however, overseas recording may be impossible. In any event, the producer must always remain aware of the costs of recording sessions, studio charges and so on, as well as the total compensation due the composer.

Sound Track Royalties
From Outside Record Companies

If the composer receives recording artist royalties, and the producer, not affiliated with a record company, has licensed the album for a royalty, the producer will ordinarily agree that he and the composer are to get paid on the same basis by the outside company that makes the sound track album. In such a situation, the producer must make sure there is in the composer's agreement provision for reducing his royalties if royalties are also payable to other recording artists who perform in the recording. Otherwise, having to pay royalties to the composer as well as a large number of other recording artists may result in such a sum that the producer will no longer enjoy any profit from making a sound track album deal. Usually, therefore, recording royalties are prorated, and a fractional proportion paid to the artist featured on each track (or cut). If there are twelve tracks, each one would be worth one twelfth. If the composer records all twelve he would be entitled to one-half the total royalty, while a recording artist who performs on only one of the tracks is due one twenty-fourth of the total royalty, assuming they shared equally.

For a film producer, negotiations on a sound track album may differ significantly from the usual record negotiations. This is because he is likely to be more concerned about the distribution of the record than about his immediate remuneration. The album, after all, is a selling tool for the film, and he may exchange a cash advance for the guaranteed press of a minimum number of records, a guaranteed promotional budget, a record club deal, and so on. Moreover, he will be concerned about the date of the album's release, which should be coordinated with release of the film for maximum impact. See below: "Agreements with Recording Artist" and "The Sound Track Album Agreement."

Composer Billing

The form of the composer's billing will depend largely on what he does, and making provision for billing credit in the agreement is not always easy. For instance, a credit that says "Music by" the composer when the film uses some musical compositions written by other composers is, obviously, misleading. A credit that says "Music Scored and Conducted by" may be accurate but probably unsatisfactory to a composer who, having written the music, wants that fact explicitly mentioned. A common solution to such problems is to show on the screen one credit for the composer, another card for any composer and/or lyricist of songs not written specifically for the film, a third for any recording artists or recording groups, and so on. Sometimes music credits require several separate cards. The composer of the film's score will almost always receive a single card credit, sometimes in the main titles. The composer(s) and lyricist(s) of any songs used in the film, whether or not originally written for it, will receive credit in the end titles—indeed, usually as the last block of credits in the end titles. Some composers command credit in paid advertising. Usually the company releasing the film's sound track album also requires advertising billing since the ads help to sell the records.

Copublishing

If a copublishing agreement exists with any composer relating to any or all of the music in the film, then, in addition to the usual provisions of a copublishing agreement, the producer should try to gain the right to use the music in various ways free of charge. Just as he does not have to pay synchronization or publishing royalties for use of the music in the film, he does not want to pay for its use in sequels, television series, or perhaps other films in which he may have an interest. Since he is paying to have the music written, he will argue that he should not have to pay again if he wants to use the music in another context. This is, however, a negotiable point and one that is not always resolved in the producer's favor, particularly, if the other films are not derived from the original one.

Title Song

Once the film's score is written, or simultaneously with its writing, the producer may want another composer to write the title song. It is not unusual to hire one composer to do the underscoring and the background music, and a second to do the theme song of the photoplay, although an important composer will agree to this only under the most special circumstances. If the theme song writer (or writers should there be a separate lyricist) is well known and has written a number of hit songs, he (or they) can command a substantial fee—often a percentage of the publishing rights for the song, as well as main title and paid ad credit.

Agreements with Recording Artists

Sometimes, a producer may decide that having a well-known group or single artist ("the act") record the title song—and possibly the other songs—will add to the appeal of the film and will help sell a sound track album or singles. Dealing with the act can, however, create substantial problems. First, whether or not it has written the song, the act may attempt to obtain a percentage of the publishing rights. This is usually successfully resisted unless the act is very prominent. Second, the act will certainly demand, in addition to a fee that can range upwards from $5,000 (which may be an advance against a recording artist's royalty), a royalty of usually either 5 (or more) percent of the retail selling price prorated (subject to the various deductions as noted) or the standard royalty it receives from the company it records for. The act will also insist on billing credits, both on the screen and, sometimes, in advertising, but this should present no problem since one of the reasons to have the act in the picture is for its publicity value.

Most acts have exclusive recording contracts with a particular record company. Any such agreement may or may not contain a provision that allows the act to record for another medium such as film, and to participate financially in the sound track album of a picture. Sometimes the act may record for the film but be contractually barred from authorizing the release of the recording in audio-only form. Regardless of whether the relevant contract contains such a provision, the film producer will want the group to perform not only for the sound track album but also for any single records derived from it. Therefore, unless the act has obtained in its exclusive contract the right to do film albums with a record company to be selected by the producer (and many have done so), the group will ordinarily require a waiver from its regular record company. Generally, such a waiver can be had only under the most stringent terms. The record company may agree to permit the act to record the sound track but may demand that the album be released on its own label, and it will certainly want the right to release as a single any music the act may record. It will want the right to include tracks from the film as part of a compilation album of the act. Sometimes the record company will further require that it receive the royalty and advance that would otherwise be paid to the act or that it receive an additional royalty.

Such considerations aside, the fact is that the act and the company that holds its exclusive recording contract views a single in very different ways. For the act, recording one or more songs for the film offers a substantial fee—money in which the record company may not share—and a chance to enhance its reputation if the picture proves to be a success; income from the sound track album is incidental. For the recording company, a single from a film holds the threat of harming the act and reducing its future earning potential. Therefore, it is most concerned with the quality of the song, and if it decides the song is not good, it will not promote it and may not want it released at all. It certainly won't want to release the single without the follow-up album. Ordinarily, then, during negotiations the record company, which in most cases has the right to approve what it releases, will ask to hear the song and the recording before making a decision on whether or not to release it. Sometimes the approval is based on a demo record plus approval of the elements of the recording (e.g., the producer). The requirement that the record company pre-approve is vital because once the song has been recorded the act is automatically entitled to its compensation, and it is then often too late to get another act to record the song. Indeed, if an act has recorded the song but that act's own record company hesitates to release it, other acts usually learn about this and refuse to record the song.

If the record company does agree to release a single record, the company obligates itself to release the record as an "A" side. (Most single records have only one side that is heavily promoted, the "A" side. Record companies usually avoid releasing a single record with a strong song on each side on the theory that both songs will then receive air play and this division ends up hurting sales since the sides compete with each other, preventing the record from moving up on the charts. Moreover, two "A" sides on two records will obviously sell two records instead of one.) If the record company releases the song as the "B" or throwaway side of a record, the song may not get air play, and in that case cannot serve the purpose of free advertising for the film.

Since the record company is interested mainly in having the film advertise the record, it usually prefers to hold up release of the record until the film has come out. Then, if the film is a hit, the record company will promote the record; if it is not, the record company will do nothing.

Of course the producer wants the record company to do just the opposite: release the record in advance of the film so that promotion of the record will have the greatest impact. (It usually takes a record, at the very least, several weeks to start selling well.)

Another possible complication is that the record company may want to follow a pattern in releasing the act's singles. Ordinarily, if an act has a successful record in the shops the company will want to wait until it starts slipping off the charts before releasing follow-up records. This may be in direct conflict with the producer's plan to have the title song record released prior to the release of the film. Scheduling becomes even more difficult if the producer does not know far in advance when his picture will be released. Choice of that date is the province of the distributor and may depend on such unpredictables as whether a particular theater is available for the initial booking of the film.

For these reasons, it is usually extremely hard to coordinate the release of a single title song record, as performed by a top act, with the release of the film. And if more than one act does songs for the film, there is the further burdensome imperative of clearing all of them for a sound track album.

The Sound Track Album Agreement

In today's market, it is unusual for a sound track album of a film to sell well independently—that is, when the film does less than substantial business. Since for any film the chances of great commercial success are quite small, most record companies choose not to be bothered with the expense of pressing and promoting a sound track album—unless they are sure that the sound track is from an important picture that is likely to do well at the box office.

The situation differs, of course, when the motion picture is a musical and the sound track album has a chance for the same importance as the original cast album of a Broadway musical. Musical films are rare today and there is absolutely no rule of thumb covering deals that can be negotiated for their sound track albums.

With other kinds of albums, the royalty paid by the record company is usually somewhere between 7.5 and 15 percent of 85 percent to 100 percent of the album's retail selling price, which includes payments to the recording artists. The record company will pays as an advance the costs of rerecording the album or, if no rerecording is necessary, remastering to convert the sound on the film to a sound more suitable for discs, and any reuse fees involved; this advance is against the producer's future royalties. Sometimes an additional cash advance is paid. The producer is generally less concerned with advances and album sales than he is with seeing to it that as many sound track albums as possible are distributed, for he sees each album in the stores as point-of-sale advertising for his film, and to the extent that the record company can guarantee store window displays, ads in consumer publications, or other forms of promotion, it will obviously help the picture. The sound track album should be, and usually is, released a few weeks ahead of the film for point-of-sale advertising to have maximum effect.

It is for this reason that most producers (for our purposes here it should be borne in mind that record deals can be made either by the producer or the distributor, depending upon which has control of such rights) are less concerned about provisions in record company contracts relating to reduced royalties or "free" or "bonus" records than a recording artist would be. The producer is more interested in knowing that a minimum number of records will be pressed, that the records will be released in major foreign markets, that the record cover will contain a credit for the producer, the distributor, and the picture, and that the reverse side of the album cover will contain a synopsis of the plot, photographs, artwork, and usually credits for all those whose names are to appear in paid advertising.

The producer generally supplies the artwork to the record company; if he does not, he will want to approve the artwork that is used. He also wants to approve the description of the film that is contained in the album's liner notes. A component of the negotiation is the payment of royalties to the publisher of the music (a "mechanical royalty"). The publisher is entitled under the Copyright Act to a set payment per track or band of music per unit (i.e., disc or cassette sold). The statutory rate is currently 6.25 cents per side. If the publisher is affiliated with the producer or distributor, the record company may insist upon a lower rate, perhaps one half to two thirds of the statutory rate, but certainly three quarters of the statutory rate, with a cap on the rate, regardless of the number of tracks. Some record companies also have begun to agree to escalate the mechanical royalty rates based upon the sales achieved by the record. The rate is subject to reductions for budget records, record club sales, and the like.

Since the fate of the sound track album is so bound up with that of the film, a producer ordinarily has no difficulty in getting an interested record company to release the album in conjunction with the release of the picture. There may, however, be difficulty in getting a coordinated release of the album outside of the U.S., depending upon whether the record company has its own subsidiaries or sublicensees abroad.

PREEXISTING MUSIC

Rather than having music written specifically for a film, a producer may sometimes decide to use music that was written earlier because such music seems most fitting, given the picture's content or time period. For example, a particular era can be effectively recalled by using a standard hit song from that period. But there may be special problems involved in obtaining clearance for use of such music in a film.

A producer must first determine whether the music to be used remains in copyright; if it is, a license for it will have to be obtained; if it is now in the public domain, then it can be used without further concern. All this will require a search of the U.S.

Copyright Office records and an inquiry to the original publisher of the music and/or the Harry Fox Organization, a licensing agent that acts on behalf of its many publisher clients.

If it is found that the music is still protected by copyright, the producer must negotiate with the publisher for a "synchronization license," which is a license to synchronize the music with the visual portion of the film. This is also a theatrical performing license for the U.S., since in this country only the music publisher and not ASCAP or BMI grants the right to use the copyrighted music in movie theaters. The balance of the performing rights are cleared by the performing rights societies, which license television, other public venues exhibiting the film, and theatrical exhibitors overseas. If the music is to be arranged, the license should cover the right to arrange.

Clearance Problems

If the music was copyrighted prior to 1976, is in the original term of copyright when the synchronization license is granted, and the publisher of the first term of copyright does not control renewal rights in the U.S., the producer will face a problem: When the original U.S. copyright expires, the owners of the renewal copyright will be able to negotiate a deal for the 28-year renewal term, and, with the music already a part of the (presumably released) film, the producer will have no bargaining power. Therefore, at the start, one should acquire renewal rights from whomever controls them—the author, his wife and children, or the executor of his estate. Even then there is the risk that the author will not survive the original term or will have divorced the wife, have no children, or changed his executor. Of course, the problem does not arise if the music was copyrighted after 1976 or if the copyright is already in the renewal term when the film is being made. Present copyright law protects the work for a single and much longer period, with no renewal terms.

It is worth remembering that the renewal term of copyright only relates to the U.S. and the original grant of the synchronization license in the U.S. remains in effect in the rest of the world.

With some compositions it may be very hard to establish copyright status, and it may be worth dealing with a presumptive owner rather than risk a lawsuit to prove that the music is in fact in the public domain.

License Fee

The amount of the synchronization license fee depends upon the pricing policy of the publisher and, of course, the importance of the particular music or song. There are no rules of thumb, and a synchronization license may cost anywhere from $5,000 to $50,000 or even more, depending on the popularity of the work and the length and type of its use in the film. In negotiation the producer can argue that the publisher will greatly benefit from performing rights income to be earned if and when the picture is shown on television and in those movie houses abroad where exhibitors have to obtain licenses from local performing rights societies. (The television benefit is true mainly for network or cable telecasts since income derived from a film's exhibition on local television channels is not substantial.)

Rights Granted

The synchronization license will specify the name of the musical composition, the name of the motion picture, the use made of the musical composition, the number of uses, and the length and type of use. For instance, a song sung on screen by a performer is a visual vocal use, a composition played on screen by a pianist is a visual instrumental use, while music simply heard in the background—that is, with no one on screen performing it—would be a background use, either instrumental or vocal, as the case may be.

Granting performing rights for television and pay cable is conditioned on television stations obtaining licenses from ASCAP or BMI. This generally presents no problem since every television station will have a license from both. However, if the composition is controlled by SESAC (the Society of European Stage Artists and Composers), a third and much smaller performing rights society, there may be some difficulty since not all television stations license through SESAC.

No mention is usually made in the license of nontheatrical uses. Most of the places (college campuses, community auditoriums, etc.) where a film might be exhibited nontheatrically are also likely to have licenses from BMI and ASCAP that allows them to have music performed.

Music licenses will often contain a restriction on videocassette exhibition of the film and restrict new uses unless agreement is reached on compensation. While the producer may insist on the right to release the picture on videocassette, some music publishers are averse to granting it, claiming that they are entitled to a separate fee for such use based on a royalty per unit sold. Some analogize the fee to the statutory mechanical license royalty. The producer cannot be in a position of having his right to use music in the picture restricted in any way that could affect full distribution of the film. Sometimes, therefore, the producer will agree to a provision stating that if a fee is to be charged by the publisher and paid by the producer for such use as videocassette, then the producer may obtain the needed clearance upon payment of a fee equal to that generally charged by other music publishers. This at least permits videocassette use and sets some kind standard for the producer to pay for videocassette rights.

The synchronization license will generally provide that outside of the U.S. performing rights are to be cleared through the local performing rights societies; ordinarily this does not create any problems.

Lyrics

The music license usually provides that no change can be made in the lyrics of the composition, that the title of the musical composition cannot be used as the title of the motion picture, and that the "story" of the musical composition—if the lyrics tell a story, as they occasionally do—cannot be used as part of the story of the film. Obtaining clearance for such changes or use is analogous to the acquisition of motion picture rights to a literary property.

In distributing a motion picture abroad, it may be necessary to translate lyrics . If a song is to be translated, at the very least the music publisher wants to own all rights to the translation. In some cases, the music publisher wants to approve the translation as well. If the use of the music is a visual-vocal use and if there is dubbing rather than subtitling, then the translation must be written to reflect the lip movements of the singer. Since this can cause problems, in most films distributed abroad songs are sung on screen in English as written, and even if the film is otherwise dubbed, lyrics will be translated in subtitles. If this is not the case, the synchronization license may have to be modified to deal with the special necessity of a dubbed translation. Unfortunately, the producer does not generally know in advance whether dubbing will be required. In any case, the publisher will usually agree to permit dubbing on condition that all rights to the translation are assigned to it and on further condition that the writer of the translation be deemed an employee of the producer, or the producer's licensee and, therefore, not entitled to any songwriter royalties.

Limit on Liability

Most synchronization licenses will limit the music publisher's liability for infringement-type claims to the amount of the license fee. This limitation may prove woefully inadequate should the music publisher warrant that he owns the rights when in fact he does not. The clause is not usually negotiable and, in any event, such claims would be covered by the producer's errors-and-omissions insurance.

Pre-Existing Recordings

In using music already written, the producer may also want to use an existing recording of it rather than go to the expense of re-recording the music. Or it may be, as previously stated, that an old hit recording would be the best way to establish the mood and period flavor of the film. Sometimes the director may favor a particular recording of a symphonic composition as background music. Unfortunately, clearing such rights may be most difficult. In addition to securing a synchronization license, the producer must clear rights from the company that made the recording and the artists who performed the composition. There is no guide to how much these rights will cost, but whatever the price, if the recording was made in the U.S., it may be increased by the reuse fees required by the American Federation of Musicians (AFM). The necessity for and the amount of reuse payments will depend upon the terms of the guild agreement between the record company and the AFM when the recording was first made. If a reuse fee is imposed, it becomes necessary to determine how many musicians were involved in the original recording session and in fact who they were—information that is usually difficult for record companies (or the AFM) to reconstruct. If the music was originally recorded outside the U.S., where usually no reuse fees are required, the problem does not arise. But if the composition sought is a symphonic work, the record company involved, no matter where it is located, will probably want a good deal of money for the right to use it in a film.

PURCHASED MUSIC

If a producer does not have the money to undertake the expensive process of creating an original musical score, there are companies that will provide background music for relatively little or nothing. Such a company will provide the background music, as well as the synchronization and theatrical performing licenses but will retain all rights to publish and record the score. Ordinarily, the company will have the music composed at modest cost or may even use stock music that it already has, and it will have the music recorded out of the country so that no reuse or residual payments are necessary. Going this route will save the producer a good deal of money, obviously, but he will generally not get as good a score and will not have the benefit of whatever income can be derived from music recording and publishing rights, from which, of course, the company furnishing the music hopes to realize its profit.

13 CLEARANCE PROCEDURE FOR THE ACQUISITION OF RIGHTS IN A COMPLETED FILM

Rather than financing production to acquire distribution rights, a distributor may wish to purchase rights in a film that has already been made. There are no set financial terms to serve as a model in acquiring a completed film. It is simply a matter of bargaining. The various types of deals that can be negotiated were discussed in connection with P-Ds, with fractionalization of rights, with independent distributor arrangements, and, to some extent, with investor financing agreements.

No rule of thumb applies for the term of the license to distribute a film. The distributor ordinarily wants to cover theatrical release followed by videocassette, pay television, network television, a second round of pay television, and finally television syndication. Clearly, a motion picture can have a good deal of residual value over an extended period of time. Indeed, most purchasers acquire rights for at least ten or fifteen years, and all of them will try to get rights in perpetuity if possible.

Certain procedures should always be followed in determining the producer's rights in the photoplay. Ordinarily, a distributor who wants to acquire distribution rights in a completed film will take a number of preliminary steps. With a typical independent production, rights may be held by banks that lent money to the production, by subdistributors who have acquired distribution rights in certain territories in return for advances, and sometimes (although rarely) by talent who have profit participations and deferments. The first step for the distributor is to assure a proper chain of title. He should check the copyright notice on the film, as well as the U.S. Copyright Office to make sure that the photoplay has not been copyrighted here by somebody other than the person or entity granting the distribution license, and to see what licenses or liens have been recorded. (Most distributors record grants of exclusive licenses under copyright in the copyright office, and liens or mortgages should also be recorded in the copyright office.) Second, if the production company that is licensing the photoplay for distribution is a U.S. corporation, a lien search can and should be made in the state of its principal place of business and where the preprint materials are located, for tax liens and/or for financing statements that list the production company as debtor. This will determine whether the film being sold has already been mortgaged or licensed.

ACQUIRING DISTRIBUTION RIGHTS TO FILMS MADE ABROAD

As previously mentioned, films today are often produced outside the U.S. under co-production agreements, in order to take advantage of the subsidies or tax incentives some foreign countries offer. For a distributor that wishes to acquire rights to a picture made abroad, special considerations apply.

Both France and Italy maintain a central film registry, equivalent to our copyright office, in which all documents affecting the production of a motion picture are supposed to be recorded. If these documents are not recorded, a subsequent assignee who does record may prevail over a prior assignee who did not. Therefore, the distributor should ask the company licensing the film rights to furnish a certified copy of extracts from the motion picture film registry in order to learn exactly what rights are outstanding.

The purchaser should also examine such agreements as those under which rights in the literary property were acquired and those of the screenwriter, the director, and the principal cast members. In most foreign countries, matters covered by contract in the U.S. are covered by statute, and thus foreign agreements may to some extent seem incomplete.

In addition, the prospective distributor should remember that in some European countries there is a well-established tradition of *droit moral* (moral rights). Under this concept, the creator of an artistic work enjoys certain inalienable rights that he cannot contract away. For example, with a moral rights statute in effect, the director, regardless of contract, has the right to prevent anyone else, for any reason, from cutting and editing his film. Indeed, if a picture is based on another work, there may even be a question as to whether under his artistic license the director can in any way change the underlying work, other than to make it suitable for the film medium. In spite of the concept of *droit moral,* there does seem to be a generally accepted custom that permits a film to be cut and edited for television exhibition and for legal censorship. The case law on this subject is sketchy, however, even in those courts in which *droit moral* applies.

Under some foreign jurisdictions, there is further difficulty in that an author cannot create a work as an employee and can only convey rights in a literary property for a certain stated period. Obviously, this must be considered in acquiring distribution rights to a film produced abroad. Some countries also have certain statutes that entitle an author to a stated percentage of any resale or relicensing of rights. Ordinarily, producers who work in foreign jurisdictions cover such potential problems in their contracts with the authors. They may even circumvent the law by giving authors their compensation as an advance against a minuscule percentage of net profits, which assures that no portion of net profits will ever be payable. In any case, the prospective distributor should check all applicable statutes and contracts.

An additional problem with foreign-made motion pictures results from the complexity of the billing clauses. Quite frequently, even more so than in the U.S., producers trade billing credit for money—that is, rather than pay the talent large sums of money, they will offer them especially prominent billing. This may make it very difficult to design an effective ad. The problem will be compounded if different artists must get different billings in different countries: If a film stars both an Italian and a French actor, the former is likely to be billed in first position in Italy, the latter in first position in France.

DEALING WITH THIRD-PARTY INTERESTS, COPYRIGHT, AND BANKRUPTCY

To the extent that there are any liens or security interests in the film, or to the extent that any of the talent have bona fide net profit participations or deferments, it is usually wise for a distributor to get from such persons a "nondisturbance letter" (sometimes called an "estoppel certificate"). The letter will acknowledge that the film's producer has the right to enter into the agreement with the distributor, and that the person executing the nondisturbance letter will not interfere with the distributor's rights and for enforcement of his own rights will look only to the producer. In addition to securing nondisturbance letters, the distributor would do well to transfer to himself, with respect to all exclusive rights granted him, copyright of the motion picture in the territory in which he will be releasing it. In this way, as copyright proprietor and therefore legal owner of the film, he will be in a better legal position vis-a-vis his licensor should any disputes arise. Of course, the licensor may insist upon remaining the copyright proprietor. In such event, if the distributor is offering a cash advance or minimum guarantee or is incurring expenses for prints and advertising, the purchaser, to secure the rights he is to be granted, ought to have a security interest in the film throughout his distribution territory. Financing statements and an instrument of transfer in the U.S. Copyright Office should be appropriately filed to perfect that security interest.

The distributor should also request a laboratory access letter from the laboratory where preprint materials are stored, assuring him that his orders will at all times be honored even if the licensor owes money to the lab.

Finally, the distributor must be concerned about the possibility, however remote, that the licensor will file for bankruptcy. In that event, the bankruptcy law used to provide that the bankrupt's trustee appointed by the bankruptcy court could terminate "executory" contracts. An executory contract is one in which each party has continuing obligations to the other. Some courts have taken the position that only one party needs to have continuing obligations to the other. Since the distributor is obligated to distribute and account, among other things, and the licensor agrees not to convey to a third party the rights granted to the distributor, a typical distribution agreement may well be an executory contract. However, a recent amendment to the bankruptcy act provides that if the licensor files for bankruptcy, an executory copyright license entered into by the bankrupt party cannot be terminated by a bankruptcy trustee if the distributor wishes to keep the agreement in effect; this offers the distributor additional protection. That amendment also states that if the distributor has given the licensor an advance recoupable from royalties, the advance is treated in the bankruptcy as an unsecured claim payable to the extent all other claims of unsecured creditors are payable, and the distributor must pay royalties to the licensor even if the advance is unrecouped.

14 THEATRICAL EXHIBITION AGREEMENTS

A fter production of a film and a deal for its theatrical distribution have been completed, the motion picture is ready to be released to theaters throughout the U.S. Let us, then, examine in detail the agreement between a distributor and an exhibitor.

THE EXHIBITION AGREEMENT

Almost all exhibition agreements contain standard boilerplate provisions that exhibitors rarely negotiate. Distributors claim that these clauses are an integral part of the contract and enforceable by their terms. Exhibitors commonly say that the boilerplate means nothing at all, and the terms and conditions of the agreement are really governed by trade practices within the industry. Ordinarily, exhibitors execute exhibition agreements without change. In the event the distributor wants to vary the usual form of exhibition agreement in any material respect, the change is thoroughly publicized and discussed with the large exhibitor chains or through the exhibitors' trade associations. Quite frequently, exhibition agreements are either not executed at all or are incomplete in one or more respects. Since there are so many individual theater engagements, some branch personnel never bother getting signatures and some contracts are executed not by the exhibitors but by booking agents acting on the exhibitors' behalf.

EXHIBITING TERMS

Assuming that an exhibition agreement has been properly completed and executed, it will commonly specify the name of the theater, the corporate name and the address (city and state) of the exhibitor, title of the picture, and the extent of the engagement (i.e., whether for one or two weeks or longer).

Pictures are licensed in a number of ways: on the basis of the division of gross box office receipts, on the basis of a division of box office receipts after the exhibitor has recouped his house expenses (the cost of the operation of the theater) for the earliest playdates, and sometimes for a flat sum for the later playdates. When there is to be a division of box office receipts, there may or may not be a minimum guaranteed film rental paid by the exhibitor to the distributor. Since the "house expense figure" ordinarily includes a profit margin over and above the actual, direct out-of-pocket expense of operating the theater, the distributor sometimes demands to audit the figures. In any case, a fair amount of bargaining may go on in order to establish house expenses. Once the figure is established, however, the distributor generally continues to use it for engagements of all its films in that theater unless the exhibitor tries to increase it as a result of claimed higher operating expenses.

Occasionally, the division of box office receipts is based not on set percentages but on a sliding scale. That is, the distributor gets an increasing percentage of gross box office receipts as these receipts mount: the higher the box office receipts, the higher the distributor's share. An exhibition contract with a percentage of "25-50" means that the distributor receives a minimum of 25 percent of the box office receipts and that the number escalates until it reaches a ceiling of 50 percent. The distributor and exhibitor work out dollar amounts that trigger an escalation to each higher percentage; for instance, 25 percent commencing at $10,000, escalating to 26 percent at $11,000, escalating to 27 percent at $12,000, and so on.

Supposedly the 25 percent figure (or whatever the lowest percentage is) is equal to the theater's operating expense. In other words, if the gross box office receipts for a particular week do not exceed the point at which the division takes place, the exhibitor keeps all of the receipts. After that point is reached, the distributor gets 25 percent or more, the exhibitor 75 percent or less, depending upon how high receipts climb.

Many important pictures play on the basis of a 90-10 division over the house floor. In such situations the exhibitor and distributor agree on a figure that presumably covers the exhibitor's overhead but actually leaves him a profit margin. Any gross box office receipts in excess of that figure are divided 90 percent to the distributor and 10 percent to the exhibitor. The advantage of this agreement to the distributor is that even with a high house floor if the theater has large grossing potential and the picture is an extremely popular one, the distributor can make more money than if he were to receive merely 50 or 60 percent of the total box office receipts. On the other hand, if the picture proves unsuccessful, the distributor may end up losing money because he is almost always responsible for the entire cooperative advertising costs. Sometimes, for very successful films, the distributor is able to command the better of the two alternatives: a 90-10 division over house expenses or 50 or 60 percent of box office receipts.

"FOUR WALL" DEALS

Rarely, distributors will either lease theaters and operate them themselves or license theaters from exhibitor-owners. In the lease, or "four wall" concept, the distributor takes over the theater and runs it—that is, the distributor hires and pays the management and staff and acts just as a regular lessee would act. Under a license arrangement, the distributor pays a weekly sum to the theater owner to cover his overhead plus an agreed upon profit.

From that sum the owner meets all his regular expenses, while the distributor enjoys the right to decide what pictures will play in the theater, for how long a period and under what terms. The distributor is booking the theater and making most of the decisions of an exhibitor, and if he is successful, he can make a substantial profit. But, in any event, even if the distributor sustains a loss, the exhibitor-owner has a guaranteed profit. The advantage to a distributor of either the lease or the license arrangement is that the theater is always available to play pictures he distributes and thus guarantees him an outlet for his product. Another obvious way to assure this is for the distributor to own his own theater(s). But, under the Paramount Consent Decree, which compelled the large studios to divest themselves of theaters to settle antitrust claims, distributor-theater owners, to the extent they are permitted to own theaters, when booking films cannot discriminate against the films of other distributors.

Vis-a-vis profit participants, the distributor either agrees to book the picture into a distributor-owned or leased theater on an arms-length basis, or provides that the box office receipts become film rentals and the leasing or operating costs of the theater become a distribution expense. This latter approach increases the amount of the distribution fee, since the box office receipts, and not the distributor's share of box office receipts, are treated as film rental.

Still another arrangement for exhibiting films is to license them on a flat sale basis. Here the distributor receives a fixed sum for the engagement from the exhibitor, who then keeps all of the box office receipts and ordinarily pays for all of the advertising.

PATTERNS OF THEATRICAL EXHIBITION

All contractual dealings between exhibitors and distributors are subject to the peculiar patterns of motion picture distribution. Let us consider in detail these patterns that sometimes lead to charges of violation of antitrust laws.

The underlying concept of motion picture distribution is that it proceeds in waves emanating from the first release in a major city. Sometimes a picture will open in one or two theaters in a downtown area, then be exhibited at neighborhood showcase theaters, and finally brought to local neighborhood theaters for subsequent runs. Sometimes the film will open in many theaters in the city and the surrounding suburbs. No distributor manufactures enough prints of a picture to play every theater in a city at the same time. By opening a picture in several theaters in a few key cities around the country and then playing it in selected neighborhood engagements, saturating one or two markets at a time, a distributor can get by with fewer prints than he would need to play a huge number of theaters simultaneously. Sometimes a picture will open in every major city simultaneously in a number of downtown theaters and in theaters in the suburbs to take advantage of national advertising. Sometimes the release is regional and the film is exhibited in one region at a time.

Obviously, then, in determining whether or not to enter into a licensing agreement for various theater engagements, the distributor must make sure that there will be prints available to service these engagements. One of the prime functions of the distributor's print department is to keep track of where the prints are and which prints will be available on specific dates, so that the sales department does not book the film into too many theaters. If more prints are ordered than are absolutely necessary, wasteful distribution expenses are incurred.

RUNS, HOLDOVERS, CLEARANCES, AND AVAILABILTY

A number of terms are commonly used in connection with motion picture exhibition and licensing arrangements between distributor and exhibitor. A "run" is a period of time during which a theater plays a picture. The length of the run may be stipulated in the licensing agreement, thus requiring the theater to play a particular picture for a given number of weeks. A "holdover" is the right of a distributor or an exhibitor to insist that a theater exhibit a picture for additional weeks if the box office receipts equal a minimum weekly figure specified in the contract. "Clearance" is the fixed amount of time a theater can prohibit the exhibition of the film in competing theaters. "Availability" is the date by which the distributor makes a given motion picture available to an exhibitor. Generally, the distributor has an exclusive right to set this date.

BIDDING

Ordinarily, each distributor, by survey, makes an initial determination as to which theaters are competitive with one another. In a survey, a sales representative of the distributor will visit theaters in a particular area or zone and make note of the distance between them, the population from which each draws its patrons, their respective parking facilities and seating capacities, the availability of public transportation between one theater and another, and various other factors. After a judgment based on this information has been made, the distributor will negotiate with the theaters in the competitive zone for the right to exhibit a particular picture. If one of the theaters in the zone believes that it is not getting a fair opportunity to acquire a film, that theater can request competitive bidding. Usually the distributor will then allow all the theaters in that zone to bid for the run of the picture as of a designated availability date.

The bidding procedure is quite simple. The distributor will send a notice to all of the theater owners specifying the number of theaters within the particular zone to which he wishes to license the film, the availability date, and various minimum terms he intends to impose. Most distributors try to make an invitation to bid as vague as possible in order to give themselves flexibility in determining which bid to accept. Bidders can either offer a cash advance against the distributor's share of box office receipts or any other terms the exhibitor believes will get him the picture. The distributor's invitation to bid generally provides that any bids not received by a specified date will not be considered. After all the bids are in, the distributor opens them and decides which, if any, he wants to accept. While the distributor exercises his own discretion and reasonable business judgment in deciding which bids to accept and which to reject, the fact is his choices may sometimes lead to litigation.

If one theater has a superior grossing capacity, that theater will normally get the picture, unless a smaller theater, with less grossing capacity, is willing to pay a substantial cash advance or agree to some other provisions that make the engagement at the smaller theater more attractive. The distributor can also decide to reject all of the bids received, in which case he can then negotiate separately with each theater in order to make the best possible deal.

Although competitive bidding may be attractive from the distributor's point of view, it is not from the exhibitor's. In the customary agreement between distributor and exhibitor, there is an implied understanding that if a picture does disappointing business, the exhibitor will be able to get some relief from the contractual terms. In a bidding situation, however, there can be no such adjustments, because any adjustment could give rise to a claim that the bidding was rigged and that the successful bidder had a side deal whereby some of the distributor's demands would later be reduced or relaxed. For this reason, exhibitors prefer not to bid against one another.

Any renegotiation that follows an unsuccessful engagement is called an "adjustment." The amount of the adjustment or whether there will even be one is solely dependent upon bargaining. If the distributor refuses to make a requested adjustment, there is always the chance that the exhibitor will refuse to play the distributor's future films or that he will insist on different contractual terms for exhibiting them. In bidding situations, an adjustment for a successful bidder can lead to bid-rigging claims from unsuccessful bidders.

ANTITRUST ISSUES

One way for an exhibitor to avoid bidding is to claim that his theater is not competitive with another theater and that, rather than bidding against it, he should be permitted to play "day and date" with that theater. This means simply that the two theaters may play the same picture as of the same opening date. Although it is possible that two theaters may not, strictly speaking, be competitive with each other, a distributor may nevertheless institute bidding because he has only a limited number of prints for the particular run.

To illustrate, if a distributor wants to play a picture in Milwaukee but with only one print available can open the picture in only one theater there, he may invite competitive bids from all the first-run theaters in the city. Two theaters at opposite ends of town could argue that, since they are not competitive, both should have the right to play the picture. While they may have a valid point, if the distributor has the right to determine the number of prints to be made available for a particular engagement—in this case, one—how can he decide which Milwaukee theater should play the picture except by bidding all of them? Still, one theater owner may argue that he should not be forced to bid against the others and that, in violation of the antitrust laws, the distributor and the other theater owners are conspiring to drive him out of business. This is the stuff of which motion picture exhibition lawsuits are made.

In addition to disputes that arise when theaters are forced to bid against each other, problems may stem from distinctions based on the distributor's assessment of various theaters' grossing power. A theater that is small and not as well maintained as larger ones may protest when it is automatically relegated to a subsequent run and not invited to engage in competitive bidding at all. Contrariwise, a theater that is invited to bid for a first run may decline and instead choose to accept competitive bidding for a second or even a third run.

A question that has long plagued the film industry is what happens when two cities are fairly close to each other and theaters in one start playing a picture before theaters in the other. Imagine, for instance, a situation in which one city is located fifty miles north of another and there are movie theaters directly in between the two. Theaters considered to be in the zone encompassing city A exhibit a picture earlier than theaters considered to be in the zone encompassing city B, and the peripheries of the two zones are, obviously, very close to each other. In such a case, should the zones be modified in order to "move" some theaters from one to the other, or should the zones remain the way they are? Zones are usually based upon historical factors, but as populations shift and new theaters are built, the zones are subject to change. Contributing to the problem is the fact that some theater owners deliberately build their theaters so that while they fall within the zone they consider most beneficial, they may at the same time draw patronage from the population of another zone.

When a theater is built on the border between zones, the theater owner can insist that it be included in zone A as opposed to zone B. This poses a problem for film distributors. Owners of theaters located at the periphery of zone B, very near the new theater that claims to be in zone A, will argue that they are competitive with that theater and should be able to bid against it. If, on the other hand, the new theater is placed in zone B, its owner will argue that it is competitive with the periphery theaters in zone A and therefore should be permitted to bid against those theaters and not forced to show films subsequent to them. Again, there is no simple solution to problems of this kind, and each case turns on its own facts. Unfortunately, disputes with exhibitors often do lead to antitrust litigation, the costs of which are substantial and add to the woes of the distributor.

But, then, distributors may bring charges of their own. They will, for example, claim that in some cities the theater owners have gotten together to divide up the available product, to indulge in what is called a "split of product." Some theater owners will play only the pictures of certain distributors and the others will play only the pictures of the balance of the distributors. Such a pattern tends to defeat competitive bidding. The Justice Department has brought lawsuits to eliminate product splits, claiming them to be a horizontal conspiracy in violation of the antitrust laws.

"BLIND BIDDING"

Exhibitors resent the fact that they are sometimes forced to engage in what is known as "blind bidding." This happens when, for various reasons, a distributor with a new picture cannot or will not show it to the exhibitors prior to the time they are invited to bid for it. Exhibitors claim that blind bidding defeats competitive bidding. Sometimes exhibitors are forced to blind bid because a picture is not ready for release early enough to have advance screenings. In such an event, the winning exhibitor has the right to terminate his license agreement prior to the opening of the picture if, after he has seen it, he decides he does not wish to play it. Some smaller independent exhibitors feel that the large chains of theaters sometimes use their circuit buying power to coerce distributors into giving them preferential treatment in blind bidding. Many states have outlawed the practice and have placed other restrictions on the kinds of arrangements distributors can make with exhibitors.

THEATER ADVERTISING

Advertising for each theater engagement is covered by the agreement between distributor and exhibitor. It provides that the exhibitor be furnished with a press book that contains sample advertising, along with whatever publicity and promotional materials are available. The agreement also includes cooperative advertising terms for the particular engagement, indicating the amount of money to be spent on advertising and the media in which the advertising will be run. Ordinarily, the exhibitor will have the right to select the particular newspaper(s), radio station(s), and/or television channels that will carry the advertising and also the right to select from the press book the type of advertising that he considers most effective for his marketing area. Sometimes the exhibitor will prepare his own advertising, even though this may be a violation of his contract with the distributor. The distributor and the exhibitor share advertising costs, usually in proportion to the division of box office receipts. In the case of the 90-10 deal over the house floor, the distributor ordinarily pays for all of the advertising.

MECHANICS OF THEATRICAL DISTRIBUTION

Each distributor has sales offices in many of the larger cities of the U.S. The major motion picture distributors used to maintain as many as thirty such offices, but in recent years the number has been cut to somewhere between ten and twenty. The offices are called "film exchanges," with the word "exchange" referring to the movement of a print from one theater to another. An exchange's staff usually consists of one or more salespersons, bookkeepers, and secretaries. The salespeople report to a general sales manager or possibly to a division head who is responsible for running a number of exchanges. Each exchange serves not only a particular city but an entire geographical area. Each salesperson has a detailed knowledge of every theater in the exchange area—its location, how many seats it holds and its grossing capacity, the film it is playing and how well that film is doing, what it will be playing next, and so on.

The general sales manager or the division manager will instruct salespeople about the distributor's general policies with respect to a particular theater and about the kind of terms that are to be sought for a particular picture, including perhaps the preferred theaters for that picture and whom to call on. If there is to be bidding for a particular engagement, the head of the exchange will prepare and send out the necessary forms and receive the bids. Depending on the distributor's established practice, bids will then be handled at the local level or forwarded to the main office of the organization. A large part of the exchange function is calling on the various exhibitors in the area to tell them what films are or will soon be available and to find out what deals can be made. Major decisions are usually made by the division head or by the general sales manager.

When an agreement has been reached between the distributor and an exhibitor with respect to a particular picture, the exchange will fill in on the distributor's printed form whatever information is required to set forth the terms—the run, the clearance, and so on—and send the form to the exhibitor.

After the exhibitor has signed the contract, it is forwarded to (or accepted at) the distributor's headquarters, usually in Los Angeles. This is done for a number of reasons. First, it helps to erase any suggestion that a distributor is doing business in various states where it does not have an exchange but where its salesmen solicit engagements for pictures. Second, it gives the general sales manager in the home office a chance to review all contracts and make sure they are in order. The general sales manager countersigns the contract and sends one copy back to the exchange for forwarding to the exhibitor, another copy to the exchange for filing, and remaining copies to various concerned departments in the distribution organization.

A week or two prior to the engagement, the respective parties will itemize the terms of the cooperative advertising agreement that has been entered into and the exchange will arrange for a print of the film to be delivered to the theater and picked up at the end of the engagement. If you multiply all these functions by the five thousand or more separate exhibitions a film may have during its theatrical release, you can begin to understand the complexity of the distribution business.

15 CONCLUSION

Putting a film together is an extremely complex process. We hope that the reader has gained from this book at the very least an awareness of the interdependence of all the parts necessary to form the totality that becomes the motion picture. The reader should also have learned that in this industry the unexpected is to be anticipated.

The business operates on the "chicken and egg" principle, and it is difficult to assemble all the elements necessary to create and finance a film under circumstances in which all agreements are consistent with each other, and all parties are satisfied with the arrangements.

What so often happens in this business is that the parties agree in principle to an arrangement that is vague, ambiguous, and omits many of the most crucial terms. When it comes time to put that arrangement into writing, it is the lawyers who must attempt to draft the contract. By its very nature the contract must be thorough and must contain many items not originally discussed or even contemplated. As a result, disputes arise, negotiations become bogged down, and the lawyers are faulted for their thoroughness.

Lawyers in their capacity as lawyers don't make deals—they prepare contracts for a client that set forth the deals the client at least thinks he has made. It is true that constructive lawyers can help to make deals just as unimaginative lawyers can help to ruin them. But some deals as initially worked out are not really deals at all, and when the respective parties examine all of the undecided or previously ignored issues, they find that they have more disagreement than agreement.

The most important thing to learn in negotiating contracts is where to compromise. There are some artistic compromises that destroy the value of a film, and there are some business compromises that make a venture foolhardy. Which compromises should be made, and which should not?

It is to be hoped that this book has contributed to the process of negotiating film contracts by presenting certain parameters and describing the consequences of agreeing or disagreeing to certain requests. To the extent that customs exist we have tried to explain what those customs are. We think this book should make negotiating easier if only by pointing out extreme positions—so that if in any instance you choose to take one you at least know that it *is* an extreme position.

We hope this book makes producing, financing, and distributing a film easier. While the motion picture industry keeps changing and there are few certainties, we have tried to provide insight into typical problems and have tried to suggest some possible solutions. If we have been successful in doing so, we have accomplished our purpose.

ABOUT THE AUTHORS

Paul A. Baumgarten is a partner in the New York law firm of Rosenman & Colin, specializing in entertainment law with an emphasis on corporate finance. He represents distributors, lenders, producers, investors, and financiers in the entertainment industry. Prior to joining his present firm, he was a partner at Krause, Hirsch & Gross, general counsel of AVCO Embassy Pictures Corp., and counsel to Hill & Range Songs, Inc. He has served as a trustee of the Copyright Society of the United States of America, a designated arbitrator for the American Film Marketing Association, and as chairman of the Practicing Law Institute's Seminar on Financing and Distributing Motion Pictures. He is a graduate of Swarthmore College and Harvard Law School.

Donald C. Farber is one of the foremost theatre, film, and entertainment attorneys in New York. He has written four other books on the business of show business: *Producing on Broadway, Actor's Guide: What You Should Know About the Contracts You Sign, Producing Theatre: A Comprehensive Legal and Business Guide,* and *From Option to Opening: A Guide to Producing Plays Off-Broadway.* He is the general editor of four volumes of *Entertainment Industry Contracts,* published by Matthew Bender, and the author of the theater volume. He served as business consultant and adviser as well as attorney for the original production of *The Fantasticks,* the subject of his most recent book, *The Amazing Story of* The Fantasticks—*America's Longest Running Play,* of which he is the co-author. A partner in the law firm of Tanner Propp Fersko & Sterner, he continues to teach a course on Producing Theatre at the New School for Social Research in New York City, which he has taught twice a year for twenty years.

Mark Fleischer graduated from the University of Southern California Law Center and is a partner in the Los Angeles law firm of Manatt, Phelps, Phillips & Kantor in the motion picture and television department. He has been an associate film producer, president of Global Television, Inc., and general manager of the L.A.-area TV station KSCI. A member of ASCAP, he has also composed music for film and television.